The Essence of the Covenant
Features, History, and Implications

Shahin Vafai

Books in the Essential Teachings Training Program

The Essence of the Covenant: Features, History, and Implications

The Path Toward Spirituality: Sacred Duties and Practices of the Bahá'í Life

Raising the Call: The Individual and Effective Teaching

ISBN 1-890101-27-3
Copyright Shahin Vafai 2005
All Rights Reserved.
Published August 2005

Palabra Publications
7369 Westport Place
West Palm Beach, Florida 33413
U.S.A.
561-697-9823 (voice)
561-697-9815 (fax)
Palabrapub@aol.com
http://www.palabrapublications.com

Acknowledgments
The valuable assistance of Victor Ahdieh, Eugene Andrews, Susan Aude, Fares Behmardi, Leah Black, Jo Ann Borovicka, Zach Brown, Charles Cornwell, Abdu'l-Missagh Ghadirian, Sherlock Graham-Haynes, Elizabeth Hartman, Paul Lample, Kathy Lee, John Lowry, Jack McCants, Nathan Miller, Malik Nash, Brent Poirier, Mark Reddy, Jason Ritchie, Barbara Sheridan, David Smith, Melissa Smith-Venters, Nancy Songer, Radiance Vafai, Frances Worthington, and Ebbie Yazdani is gratefully acknowledged.

Permission
All previously unpublished letters by, or on behalf of, the Universal House of Justice are quoted with permission. Extracts from lectures by Peter Khan and Ian Semple are quoted with permission. Extracts from the following works are quoted with the permission of George Ronald, Publisher: Youness Afroukhteh, *Memories of Nine Years in 'Akká* (2003); H.M. Balyuzi, *'Abdu'l-Bahá: The Centre of the Covenant of Bahá'u'lláh* (1987); Anita Ioas Chapman, *Leroy Ioas: Hand of the Cause of God* (1998); Adib Taherzadeh, *The Child of the Covenant* (2000); Adib Taherzadeh, *The Covenant of Bahá'u'lláh* (1992). Cover photo: Lacey J. Crawford (1920-2002).

Dedicated to
the Universal House of Justice,
"which God hath ordained
as the source of all good
and freed from all error"

SUMMARY OF CONTENTS

CONTENTS

PREFACE

The theme of the Covenant of Bahá'u'lláh is explored in the current text through various approaches. Each chapter is divided into the following sections:

1. **Overview**
2. **Study Questions**
3. **Quotations for Reflection**
4. **Illustrations**
5. **Analysis Questions**
6. **Memorization and Presentation Exercises**

Quoting extensively from the authoritative Writings of the Bahá'í Faith, the **Overview** offers a general explanation of the chapter's theme. The **Study Questions** that immediately follow present content and application/discussion questions related to key ideas in the **Overview**. **Quotations for Reflection** present additional authoritative texts reinforcing concepts previously discussed; after each set of quotations appear two types of questions—queries derived from the text and others probing the implications of the text. Drawn from secondary sources, **Illustrations** offer examples and stories that may inspire further insights. Next, the **Analysis Questions** provide a vehicle for testing one's learning. Finally, **Memorization and Presentation Exercises** identify important quotations that the reader is encouraged to memorize and suggest topics for a brief presentation on the theme of the chapter. The book's format is designed for individual or group study.

INTRODUCTION

A. The Importance of the Covenant

For Bahá'ís, "the most important principle of faith is firmness in the Covenant . . . ."[1] Bahá'u'lláh's Covenant is central to "all aspects of the religion He has established."[2] The power of the Covenant "quickens every distinguishing element of Bahá'í life."[3] Its light "is the educator of the minds, the spirits, the hearts and souls of men."[4]

The Covenant has direct bearing on the spiritual life of the individual. Steadfastness in the Covenant is "the foundation of true spirituality,"[5] and knowledge and appreciation of the Covenant is "the stronghold of the faith of every Bahá'í, and that which enables him to withstand every test."[6] Moreover, the Covenant is intimately linked to the development of society. Its "purpose" is "to unite the races and nations of the earth,"[7] for "the pivot of the oneness of mankind is nothing else but the power of the Covenant."[8] Described in the Bahá'í Writings as "divine,"[9] "explicit,"[10] and "indestructible,"[11] the Covenant of Bahá'u'lláh is "unique in the spiritual annals of mankind."[12] It is "a Covenant so firm and mighty that from the beginning of time until the present day no religious Dispensation hath produced its like."[13]

Because of its significance, the Covenant of Bahá'u'lláh must be clearly and comprehensively understood by believers. Shoghi Effendi encouraged Bahá'ís to gain a "thorough understanding" of Bahá'u'lláh's Covenant.[14] In a letter written on his behalf, he emphasized that "particular attention" should be devoted to "deepening the friends in the Covenant, which is the ark of safety for every believer."[15] A deep understanding of the Covenant "is the rock-foundation without which no sound super-structure can be built. Neither the administration, nor the general teaching work of the Cause . . . will progress, or be able to accomplish anything, unless the believers are truly firm, deep, spiritually convinced Bahá'ís."[16]

The Universal House of Justice has underscored the continuing importance of the study of the Covenant. It has stated that concentration on the theme of the Covenant of Bahá'u'lláh enables Bahá'ís "to obtain a deeper appreciation of the meaning and purpose of His Revelation."[17]

The House of Justice has further commented that in light of the accelerating disintegration of society and the disunity afflicting the planet, "the requirements of the Covenant assume even more critical importance than before."[18] In recent years, the House of Justice has specially urged the Bahá'ís of North America to "manifest unwavering adherence to the provisions of the Covenant, while ever striving for a deeper understanding of its challenging features and of its implications, which far transcend the familiar arrangements of present society."[19]

B. Approaching the Study of the Covenant

The Covenant of Bahá'u'lláh is simple and "clearly defined."[20] At the same time, it is complex and mysterious, being likened by 'Abdu'l-Bahá to "a vast and fathomless ocean."[21] Thus, one may be able to easily grasp the basic truths of the Covenant, but must ever strive to discover its deeper ramifications. The purpose of the current book is not to provide an exhaustive treatment of the Covenant, a task that may well be impossible. Rather, its aim is to review certain fundamentals. The Universal House of Justice has explained that "[t]he essence of the Covenant is the continuation of divine guidance after the Ascension of the Prophet through the presence in this world of an institution to which all the friends turn and which can indisputably state what is the Will of God. After 'Abdu'l-Bahá the Guardianship and the Universal House of Justice are such institutions."[22] The present work principally focuses on the features, history, and implications of this basic aspect of the Covenant—the continuity of divine guidance through the Faith's authorized institutions. It seeks to explore such questions as: What is the purpose of the Covenant? How, and for what purposes, did Bahá'u'lláh appoint 'Abdu'l-Bahá as the Center of the Covenant? What is the scriptural foundation for the institutions of the Guardianship and the Universal House of Justice? What are the objectives and powers of these twin successors of Bahá'u'lláh and 'Abdu'l-Bahá? Why did Shoghi Effendi not appoint a successor Guardian? How can the Universal House of Justice function in the absence of a living Guardian? What is the basis for the infallibility of the Universal House of Justice? How does the Covenant protect the Faith? And what is the individual's relationship to the Covenant?

2

In exploring these and related questions, the text begins with the assumption that the reader has already recognized Bahá'u'lláh's divine and unerring authority; the object here is not to prove that Bahá'u'lláh is a Manifestation of God.[23] The "whole theory of Divine Revelation rests on the infallibility of the Prophet, be He Christ, Muḥammad, Bahá'u'lláh, or one of the Others. If they are not infallible, then they are not divine, and thus lose that essential link with God which, we believe, is the bond that educates men and causes all human progress."[24] "Once the mind and heart have grasped the fact that God guides men through a Mouthpiece, a human being, a Prophet, infallible and unerring, it is only a logical projection of this acceptance to also accept the station of 'Abdu'l-Bahá," as well as those of the Guardian and the Universal House of Justice.[25] The current work examines this "logical projection."

C. Documents Establishing and Elucidating the Covenant

The Covenant has been established through the written Word of Bahá'u'lláh; it has been extended by the pen of 'Abdu'l-Bahá; and its characteristics have been elucidated in the writings of the Guardian and the communications of the Universal House of Justice. Any study of the Covenant must find its starting point and its constant terms of reference in these authoritative texts. Such texts include:

> (1) The Kitáb-i-'Ahd (The Book of the Covenant), by Bahá'u'lláh[26]
> (2) The Will and Testament of 'Abdu'l-Bahá
> (3) "The Dispensation of Bahá'u'lláh," by Shoghi Effendi[27]
> (4) "The Constitution of the Universal House of Justice"
> (5) Letters dated March 9, 1965, May 27, 1966, and December 7, 1969, by the Universal House of Justice.[28]

Described by Bahá'u'lláh as His "Most Great Tablet,"[29] the Kitáb-i-'Ahd establishes His Covenant.[30] The Will and Testament of 'Abdu'l-Bahá, "His greatest legacy to posterity" and "the brightest emanation of His mind,"[31] is "the Charter of the New World Order."[32] The Kitáb-i-'Ahd and the Will and Testament of 'Abdu'l-Bahá "constitute the very bedrock upon which the entire administrative system of the Faith has been raised and established."[33] As to "The Dispensation of Bahá'u'lláh," it constitutes "an invaluable supplement" to the Kitáb-i-'Ahd and the Will and Testament of 'Abdu'l-Bahá.[34] Shoghi Effendi is reported to have remarked that "he had said all he had to say, in many ways, in the *Dispensation*."[35] Characterized by the Guardian as the Most Great Law of the Faith of Bahá'u'lláh,[36] "The Constitution of the Universal House of Justice" is yet another document critical to the study of the Covenant. Finally, three seminal letters written by the Universal House of Justice in the 1960's clarify such vital covenantal issues as the Faith's successorship following Shoghi Effendi's passing, the basis for the election of the Universal House of Justice, and the relationship of the institutions of the Guardianship and the Universal House of Justice.[37]

The current work draws heavily upon these foundational documents. In seeking a deeper understanding of the Covenant, the reader is encouraged to continually refer back to these primary sources.

D. Spiritual Qualities Essential for the Study of the Covenant

Increasing one's understanding of the Covenant is not only dependent upon gaining knowledge of the relevant Bahá'í Writings, but is also conditional upon acquiring certain spiritual qualities. Among these are faith and humility. The Universal House of Justice has explained: "Every true believer, if he is to deepen in his understanding of the Cause of Bahá'u'lláh, must needs combine profound faith in the unfailing efficacy of His Message and His Covenant, with the humility of recognizing that no one of this generation can claim to have embraced the vastness of His Cause nor to have comprehended the manifold mysteries and potentialities it contains."[38] Many features of the Covenant may be immediately clear. Other aspects may become evident through further study of the Bahá'í Writings, through prayer, meditation, or consultation. Still other facets of the Covenant may be understood only with the passage of time or through the additional guidance of the Universal House of Justice.[39]

There are mysteries in the Faith, "but they are not of a kind to shake one's faith once the essential tenets of the Cause and the indisputable facts of any situation are clearly understood."[40] When "issues are approached with an understanding of the unity underlying all the Teachings, clarification results."[41] However, if one is "influenced by a spirit of mistrust and conflict, then unending problems appear."[42] The history of religion teaches the importance of faith and humility:

> In past dispensations many errors arose because the believers in God's Revelation were overanxious to encompass the Divine Message within the framework of their limited understanding, to define doctrines where definition was beyond their power, to explain mysteries which only the wisdom and experience of a later age would make comprehensible, to argue that something was true because it appeared desirable and necessary. Such compromises with essential truth, such intellectual pride, we must scrupulously avoid.[43]

When the Covenant is approached with the requisite spiritual qualities, it evokes feelings of wonder and thanksgiving at the inestimable gift Bahá'u'lláh has conferred upon humanity.

The Universal House of Justice has described the Covenant as "the instrument designed by the Lord of the Age for the unification and pacification of the nations and peoples of the earth."[44] Bahá'ís have been called to gain a deeper understanding of the features, history, and implications of this "instrument." It is hoped that the current text will contribute, in some small way, toward that objective.

CHAPTER 1

The Covenant of Bahá'u'lláh: Significance, Meaning, and Purposes

. . . in the beginning the believers must make their steps firm in the Covenant . . . .
— 'Abdu'l-Bahá

Overview

A. Firmness in the Covenant

For Bahá'ís, firmness in the Covenant is "their Fortress, their greatest protection."[1] 'Abdu'l-Bahá declared that "steadfastness and firmness in this new and wonderful Covenant is indeed the spirit that quickeneth the hearts which are overflowing with the love of the Glorious Lord; verily, it is the power which penetrates into the hearts of the people of the world!"[2] He expressed the hope that believers would "daily increase in their firmness and steadfastness"[3] and promised that "God will help those who are firm in His Covenant in every matter . . . ."[4]

Exhorting North American believers "to strive to attain the exalted station of Apostles of Bahá'u'lláh," 'Abdu'l-Bahá specified "firmness in the Covenant to be a prerequisite for this achievement."[5] He wrote:

> The first condition is firmness in the Covenant of God. For the power of the Covenant will protect the Cause of Bahá'u'lláh from the doubts of the people of error. It is the fortified fortress of the Cause of God and the firm pillar of the religion of God. Today no power can conserve the oneness of the Bahá'í world save the Covenant of God; otherwise differences like unto a most great tempest will encompass the Bahá'í world. It is evident that the axis of the oneness of the world of humanity is the power of the Covenant and nothing else.

... [I]n the beginning the believers must make their steps firm in the Covenant so that the confirmations of Bahá'u'lláh may encircle them from all sides, the cohorts of the Supreme Concourse may become their supporters and helpers, and the exhortations and advices of 'Abdu'l-Bahá, like unto the pictures engraved on stone, may remain permanent and ineffaceable in the tablets of all hearts.[6]

B. The Meaning of the Covenant and Its Forms

To strive for firmness in the Covenant, it is necessary to understand its meaning and implications. "A Covenant in the religious sense is a binding agreement between God and man, whereby God requires of man certain behaviour in return for which He guarantees certain blessings, or whereby He gives man certain bounties in return for which He takes from those who accept them an undertaking to behave in a certain way."[7] The Bahá'í Writings identify various Covenants,[8] including the Greater Covenant and the Lesser Covenant.

The Greater Covenant is the agreement "every Manifestation of God makes with His followers, promising that in the fullness of time a new Manifestation will be sent, and taking from them the undertaking to accept Him when this occurs."[9] The Báb explained: "The Lord of the universe hath never raised up a prophet nor hath He sent down a Book unless He hath established His covenant with all men, calling for their acceptance of the next Revelation and of the next Book; inasmuch as the outpourings of His bounty are ceaseless and without limit."[10] 'Abdu'l-Bahá illustrated the existence of the Greater Covenant:

> His Holiness Abraham . . . made a covenant concerning His Holiness Moses and gave the glad-tidings of His coming. His Holiness Moses made a covenant concerning the Promised One, i.e. His Holiness Christ, and announced the good news of His Manifestation to the world. His Holiness Christ made a covenant concerning the Paraclete* and gave the tidings of His

---

*Cf. on behalf of Shoghi Effendi, *Letters from the Guardian to Australia and New Zealand: 1923-1957*, p. 41 ("References in the Bible to . . . 'Paraclete' refer to Muḥammad's Revelation.").

coming. His Holiness the Prophet Muḥammad made a covenant concerning His Holiness the Báb and the Báb was the One promised by Muḥammad, for Muḥammad gave the tidings of His coming. The Báb made a Covenant concerning the Blessed Beauty of Bahá'u'lláh and gave the glad-tidings of His coming for the Blessed Beauty was the One promised by His Holiness the Báb. Bahá'u'lláh made a covenant concerning a promised One who will become manifest after one thousand or thousands of years.[11]

As to the Greater Covenant, Bahá'u'lláh confirmed that the next Manifestation of God would not appear before the passing of at least a thousand years: "Whoso layeth claim to a Revelation direct from God ere the expiration of a full thousand years, such a man is assuredly a lying impostor."[12] In October 1852, Bahá'u'lláh "received, in the Síyáh-Chál of Ṭihrán, the intimation of His Revelation."[13] This point "marks the birth of His Prophetic Mission and hence the commencement of the one thousand years or more that must elapse before the appearance of the next Manifestation of God."[14]

In addition to the Greater Covenant, there exists the Lesser Covenant. The Manifestation of God makes the Lesser Covenant with His followers "that they will accept His appointed successor after Him."[15] "It is a Covenant of this kind that Bahá'u'lláh made with His followers regarding 'Abdu'l-Bahá, and that 'Abdu'l-Bahá perpetuated through the Administrative Order that Bahá'u'lláh had already created."[16]

Although the Lesser Covenant has "invariably been the feature of every previous religion,"[17] it has, in the past, been "shrouded in mystery."[18] For instance, in Christianity, "the primacy of Peter and his right to succession after Jesus" were "established by the latter, though only orally and not in explicit and definite language."[19] The utterances of Jesus in the Gospel did not offer specific guidance "regarding the future administration of His Church, or the nature of the authority of His Successors."[20] The "fundamental reason why the unity of the Church of Christ was irretrievably shattered, and its influence was in the course of time undermined, was that the Edifice which the Fathers of the Church reared" after the passing of Peter "rested in nowise upon the explicit directions of Christ Himself."[21] Likewise, in the religion of Muḥammad, the absence of definite, written guidance on the issue of successorship became "the source of all the dissensions, the controversies, and schisms which have dismembered and discredited Islám."[22] Muḥammad is reported to have orally appointed the Imám 'Alí as His successor,[23] but "the text of the Qur'án . . . gives no definite guidance regarding the Law of Succession . . . ."[24] Because the Lesser Covenant has not in past ages been clear, definite, and in writing,[25] the religion of God has become divided and its force dissipated.[26]

"The Covenant of Bahá'u'lláh" is, however, "unique in religious history because it was made clearly and explicitly in writing."[27] Bahá'u'lláh's Covenant was "established firmly by His clear and manifest words" and "writ and revealed by His All-Glorious Pen."[28] 'Abdu'l-Bahá explained that from "the early days of creation down to the present time, throughout all the divine dispensations, such a firm and explicit Covenant hath not been entered upon."[29] Further:

> Unlike the Dispensation of Christ, unlike the Dispensation of Muḥammad, unlike all the Dispensations of the past, the apostles of Bahá'u'lláh in every land . . . have before them in clear, in unequivocal and emphatic language, all the laws, the regulations, the principles, the institutions, the guidance, they require for the prosecution and consummation of their task. Both in the administrative provisions of the Bahá'í Dispensation, and in the matter of succession, as embodied in the twin institutions of the House of Justice and of the Guardianship, the followers of Bahá'u'lláh can summon to their aid such irrefutable evidences of Divine Guidance that none can resist, that none can belittle or ignore. Therein lies the distinguishing feature of the Bahá'í Revelation.[30]

C. The Overall Purposes of the Covenant of Bahá'u'lláh

While the Covenant of Bahá'u'lláh addresses issues of succession within the Bahá'í Faith, its import and implications are, as the Universal House of Justice has made clear, far broader:

> The foundation of our belief rests on our recognition of the sovereignty of God, the Unknowable Essence, the Supreme Creator, and on our submission to His will as revealed for this age by Bahá'u'lláh. To accept the Messenger of God in His Day and to abide by His bidding are the two essential, inseparable duties which each soul was created to fulfill. . . . The vehicle in this resplendent age for the practical fulfillment of these duties is the Covenant of Bahá'u'lláh. It is the instrument by which belief in Him is translated into constructive deeds.[31]

Thus, the Covenant is the means for practically fulfilling life's purpose—recognizing God's Manifestation and carrying out His will. As revealed by Bahá'u'lláh, God's will in this age is "to establish the unity of all mankind."[32] Through the Covenant, Bahá'u'lláh's mission of unifying humanity will be accomplished:[33]

> The oneness of humankind is the pivotal principle and ultimate goal of His mission. This principle means far more than the reawakening of the spirit of brotherhood and goodwill among people: "It implies an organic change in the structure of present-day society, a change such as the world has not yet experienced." The Covenant of Bahá'u'lláh embodies the spirit, instrumentality and method to attain this essential goal. In addition to laying down, in His Book of Laws, the fundamentals for a new World Order, Bahá'u'lláh, in the Book of His Covenant, confirmed the appointment of His Son 'Abdu'l-Bahá as the interpreter of His Word and the Center of His Covenant. As the interpreter,

11

'Abdu'l-Bahá became the living mouth of the Book, the expounder of the Word; as the Center of the Covenant, He became the incorruptible medium for applying the Word to practical measures for the raising up of a new civilization.[34]

Through His Word, Bahá'u'lláh set forth the pattern for a unified world; through His Son, Bahá'u'lláh provided humanity the means for better understanding that Word and offered a model for "applying the Word to practical measures for the raising up of a new civilization."[35] 'Abdu'l-Bahá "perpetuated" the Covenant "through the Administrative Order"[36]—"the nucleus" and "the very pattern of the New World Order destined to embrace in the fullness of time the whole of mankind."[37]

Accordingly, "[t]he essence of the Covenant is the continuation of divine guidance after the Ascension of the Prophet through the presence in this world of an institution to which all the friends turn and which can indisputably state what is the Will of God."[38] By turning toward "the continuing centre of divine guidance in the world"[39]—"'Abdu'l-Bahá the Centre of the Covenant and His designated successors, the Guardian and the Universal House of Justice"[40]—believers can come to know and apply God's will in striving toward the goal of the unity of humankind.

D. The Specific Purposes of the Covenant of Bahá'u'lláh

In order to realize Bahá'u'lláh's objective of "the unification and pacification of the nations and peoples of the earth,"[41] His Faith must maintain its unity, preserve its integrity, and experience world-wide expansion.[42] Through the Covenant of Bahá'u'lláh, all of these specific purposes are fulfilled.

Bahá'u'lláh's Covenant maintains the unity of His Faith. "As the central teaching of the Bahá'í Faith is the unity of mankind, it is essential that the Faith itself remain one and undivided if it is to achieve its purpose."[43] "The central, unifying element of the Faith is the Covenant."[44] 'Abdu'l-Bahá explained that "[w]ere it not for the protecting power of the Covenant to guard the impregnable fort of the Cause of God, there would arise among the Bahá'ís, in one day, a thousand different sects as was the case in former

12

ages."[45] Therefore, the "Covenant is the guarantee against schism; that is why those who occasionally attempt to create a cleavage in the community utterly fail in the long run."[46] The strength of the Covenant in maintaining unity is indisputably demonstrated by the fact that for more than a century and half, every attempt to create division within the Bahá'í Faith has failed.[47]

To ensure the integrity of the Faith is yet another fundamental purpose of the Covenant. Ensuring the Faith's integrity is a purpose distinct from preserving its unity. A group of people could, in theory, remain unified but deviate from the group's original purposes or beliefs. The Covenant of Bahá'u'lláh prevents such deviation. The Covenant "is the institution which guarantees that the Faith and its teachings will remain true to the Revelation brought by Bahá'u'lláh and expounded by His divinely guided Interpreters. It is the one agency which can protect the Faith against the distortion and disruption to which all previous Revelations have been subjected by the efforts—whether well-intentioned or not—of the self-opinionated and ambitious among their followers to force the Cause of God into patterns which they personally favoured."[48] As such, the Covenant is "the ultimate guarantee that the Faith will remain true to its divine origin throughout the centuries."[49]

The Covenant also serves to stimulate the Faith's world-wide expansion. Almost immediately after the ascension of Bahá'u'lláh, "through the impelling influence of the newly proclaimed Covenant," the Faith spread "as far West as the North American continent" and from there diffused itself "to the countries of Europe, and subsequently shed its radiance over both the Far East and Australasia."[50] Since 'Abdu'l-Bahá's passing, the "Administrative Order to which the Covenant has given birth,"[51] has stimulated the Faith's expansion. During the course of Shoghi Effendi's ministry, the Faith spread to scores of countries and thousands of localities around the world.[52] That expansion has continued under the guidance of the Universal House of Justice. By 1988, the Bahá'í Faith was recognized as "the most widely spread religion after Christianity."[53] Just over a century after Bahá'u'lláh's passing, because of "the phenomenal effects of His Covenant, a world community has been raised up on an 'unassailable foundation.'"[54]

In sum, the Covenant instituted by Bahá'u'lláh has canalized "the forces released by His Revelation."[55] It has "preserved the integrity of His Faith, maintained its unity and stimulated its world-wide expansion."[56] "The glorious, ultimate effect" of the Covenant "will be to ensure the establishment of the Kingdom of God on earth, as promised in the Holy Books of old and as proclaimed by Bahá'u'lláh Himself."[57]

Study Questions

Answer the following questions based on the above Overview:

CONTENT QUESTIONS

1. "The first condition is _____ in the _____ of God. . . . It is the fortified _____ of the Cause of God and the firm _____ of the religion of God."

2. What is the definition of "Covenant" in the religious sense? What is the Greater Covenant? What is the Lesser Covenant?

3. How is the Covenant of Bahá'u'lláh "unique in religious history"? How does it compare with those of Christianity and Islám?

4. The Covenant of Bahá'u'lláh is the vehicle for the practical fulfillment of what two duties?

5. "[A]s the Center of the Covenant, He ['Abdu'l-Bahá] became the incorruptible _____ for applying the _____ to practical measures for the raising up of a new _____."

6. "The essence of the Covenant is the continuation of _____ _____ after the Ascension of the Prophet through the presence in this world of an _____ to which all the friends turn and which can indisputably state what is the _____ ___ _____."

7. List at least three specific purposes of the Covenant.

8. "Were it not for the _____ power of the _____ to guard the impregnable fort of the Cause of God, there would arise among

the Bahá'ís, in one _____, a _____ different sects as was the case in former ages."

9. The Covenant is "the ultimate guarantee that the Faith will remain true to its divine _____ throughout the _____."

APPLICATION/DISCUSSION QUESTIONS

1. "The foundation of our belief rests on our recognition of the sovereignty of God, the Unknowable Essence, the Supreme Creator, and on our submission to His will as revealed for this age by Bahá'u'lláh." Why is this the "foundation" of Bahá'í belief? What attitudes and actions reflect that a believer's "foundation" is strong?

2. What is most reassuring about the Covenant of Bahá'u'lláh?

3. How does the Covenant of Bahá'u'lláh embody "the spirit, instrumentality and method to attain" the goal of the oneness of humankind?

4. "The essence of the Covenant is the continuation of divine guidance after the Ascension of the Prophet through the presence in this world of an institution to which all the friends turn and which can indisputably state what is the Will of God." How does a believer's understanding of the "essence of the Covenant" impact his or her service to the Faith?

Quotations for Reflection

Answer the questions following the quotations below:

1. "O ye beloved of God, know that steadfastness and firmness in this new and wonderful Covenant is indeed the spirit that quickeneth the hearts which are overflowing with the love of the Glorious Lord; verily, it is the power which penetrates into the hearts of the people of the world! Your Lord hath assuredly promised His servants who are firm and steadfast to render them victorious at all times, to exalt their word, propagate their power, diffuse their lights, strengthen their hearts, elevate

15

their banners, assist their hosts, brighten their stars, increase the abundance of the showers of mercy upon them, and enable the brave lions to conquer."
('Abdu'l-Bahá, *Bahá'í World Faith*, p. 357)

"The Youth must ponder deeply over the significance and implications of the Covenants of Bahá'u'lláh and 'Abdu'l-Bahá, for these form the hub of the Bahá'í wheel, so to speak, the point of unity and strength for all the believers all over the world. Without these Covenants the Divine Protection of God over this new world Faith would not exist. Obedience to these Covenants is the stronghold of all the Bahá'ís, everywhere."
(On behalf of Shoghi Effendi, *The Light of Divine Guidance*, vol. 2, p. 89)

What promises are given to those who are firm and steadfast in the Covenant?

Why is the Covenant so important in the Faith?

2. "As regards the meaning of the Bahá'í Covenant: The Guardian considers the existence of two forms of covenant both of which are explicitly mentioned in the literature of the Cause. First is the covenant that every Prophet makes with humanity or, more definitely, with His people that they will accept and follow the coming Manifestation Who will be the reappearance of His reality. The second form of covenant is such as the one Bahá'u'lláh made with His people that they should accept the Master ['Abdu'l-Bahá]. This is merely to establish and strengthen the succession of the series of Lights that appear after every Manifestation. Under the same category falls the covenant the Master made with the Bahá'ís that they should accept His administration after Him."
(On behalf of Shoghi Effendi, *Lights of Guidance*, p. 181)

"The Greater Covenant into which . . . God had, from time immemorial, entered, through the Prophets of all ages, with the whole of mankind, regarding the newborn Revelation, had already been fulfilled. It had now to be supplemented by a Lesser Covenant . . . . Such a Covenant had invariably been the feature of every previous religion. It had existed, under various forms, with varying degrees of emphasis, had always been

16

couched in veiled language, and had been alluded to in cryptic prophecies, in abstruse allegories, in unauthenticated traditions, and in the fragmentary and obscure passages of the sacred Scriptures."

(Shoghi Effendi, *God Passes By*, p. 27)

What are two forms of Covenant, and what is the nature of each?

What were characteristics of the Lesser Covenants of previous religions?

3. "This Covenant [inaugurated by Bahá'u'lláh] is unique in the entire span of religious history by virtue of its provision of institutions which preserve the unity of the Faith and maintain the purity and integrity of the Bahá'í teachings . . . ."

(On behalf of the Universal House of Justice, to an individual believer, June 23, 1987)

What is unique about the Covenant inaugurated by Bahá'u'lláh?

How do Bahá'í institutions preserve the unity of the Faith and maintain the purity and integrity of the Bahá'í teachings?

4. "The vantage point that gives us perspective and is the foundation of our belief and actions rests on our recognition of the sovereignty of God and our submission to His will as revealed by Bahá'u'lláh, His supreme Manifestation for this promised Day. To accept the Prophet of God in His time and to abide by His bidding are the two essential, inseparable duties which each soul was created to fulfill. One exercises these twin duties by one's own choice, an act constituting the highest expression of the free will with which every human being has been endowed by an all-loving Creator.

"The vehicle in this resplendent Age for the practical fulfillment of these duties is the Covenant of Bahá'u'lláh; it is, indeed, the potent instrument by which individual belief in Him is translated into constructive deeds. The Covenant comprises divinely conceived arrangements necessary to preserve the organic unity of the Cause. It therefore engenders a motivating power which, as the beloved Master tells us, 'like unto the artery, beats and pulsates in the body of the world'. 'It is indubitably clear,' He asserts, 'that the pivot of the oneness of mankind is nothing else but the power of the Covenant.' Through it the meaning of the Word, both in theory and practice, is made evident in the life and work of 'Abdu'l-Bahá, the appointed Interpreter, the perfect Exemplar, the Center of the Covenant. Through it the processes of the Administrative Order—'this unique, this wondrous System'—are made to operate."

(The Universal House of Justice, *Individual Rights and Freedoms in the World Order of Bahá'u'lláh,* pp. 4-5)

"The Covenant comprises _____ *conceived* _____ *necessary to preserve the* _____ _____ *of the Cause."*

In what ways is the Covenant of Bahá'u'lláh the vehicle for "the practical fulfillment" of the duties of accepting the Prophet of God and abiding by His bidding?

In what ways is the Covenant of Bahá'u'lláh "the potent instrument by which individual belief in Him is translated into constructive deeds"?

5. "The Covenant is the 'axis of the oneness of the world of humanity' because it preserves the unity and integrity of the Faith itself and protects it from being disrupted by individuals who are convinced that only their understanding of the Teachings is the right one—a fate that has overcome all past Revelations. The Covenant is, moreover, embedded in the Writings of Bahá'u'lláh Himself. Thus, . . . to accept Bahá'u'lláh is to accept His Covenant; to reject His Covenant is to reject Him."

(On behalf of the Universal House of Justice, *Messages from the Universal House of Justice: 1963-1986*, p. 519)

"It was to preserve the unity of the Faith and the purity of His Message that Bahá'u'lláh instituted His Covenant, an institution which protects the Cause from individuals who, through the assertion of their own wills, would try to force God's Cause into the paths of their own preference and thus divide the faithful and subvert the world-wide establishment of divine justice."

(The Universal House of Justice, quoted in *The Covenant: Its Meaning and Origin and Our Attitude Toward It*, p. 52)

What does rejection of the Covenant imply?

How does the Covenant protect the Cause "from individuals who, through the assertion of their own wills, would try to force God's Cause into the paths of their own preference"?

6. "Bahá'u'lláh . . . has proclaimed the advent of God's Kingdom on earth, has formulated its laws and ordinances, enunciated its principles, and ordained its institutions. To direct and canalize the forces released by His Revelation He instituted His Covenant, whose power has preserved the integrity of His Faith, maintained its unity and stimulated its world-wide expansion throughout the successive ministries of 'Abdu'l-Bahá and Shoghi Effendi. It continues to fulfil its life-giving purpose through the agency of the Universal House of Justice whose fundamental object, as one of the twin successors of Bahá'u'lláh and 'Abdu'l-Bahá, is to ensure the continuity of that divinely-appointed authority which flows from the Source of the Faith, to safeguard the unity of its followers, and to maintain the integrity and flexibility of its teachings."

(*The Constitution of the Universal House of Justice*, pp. 3-4)

What has the power of the Covenant of Bahá'u'lláh achieved?

Why is the purpose of the Covenant described as "life-giving"?

Illustrations

What is the most striking aspect of the following illustration for you? Why?

"Tuesday evening, October 24 [1912], the friends all gathered at the home of Helen Goodall. It was to be our farewell meeting with 'Abdu'l-Bahá, and our hearts were heavy at the thought of the separation. When we entered the room, the Master was seated. There was a reverent silence as He started speaking in soft tones. Again, He seemed enveloped in a golden light, and His face reflected love and sweetness. He repeated how happy He was to be with the friends of California and that our love had drawn Him to us. He praised the friends for spreading and establishing the Faith. He said He had done what He could to spread His Father's Revelation. He offered us good cheer and hope, and assured us of His prayers at the Holy Shrines.

"One felt His great humility as He told of Bahá'u'lláh's life and suffering, His banishment with His Family from Irán, their native land. Tears filled His eyes and ran down His cheeks, and with a catch in His voice He told of the deprivations and hardships endured by His beloved Father and Family and the little band of followers who had accompanied them. He said that during their exile from Constantinople to Adrianople, they had to walk in the snow. His delicate Mother, Navváb, was forced to melt ice to get water for drinking and for washing clothes. He reminded us of the two years of lonely solitude Bahá'u'lláh had spent in Sulaymáníyyih, and He said that Bahá'u'lláh's only aim was to unite mankind. The Master seemed to be reliving those days of heartbreak. Sadness filled our hearts; tears streamed down our faces while He told us of the cruelties and great injustices inflicted upon His Father. In that quiet room one felt the love and deep sympathy pouring from our souls to our blessed 'Abdu'l-Bahá.

"All at once His voice became strong and firm, His eyes luminous, and with great authority He told of the Declaration of Bahá'u'lláh in the Garden of Riḍván—that He was the Promised One for this day! He told how later, in 'Akká, Bahá'u'lláh gave the Principles of His Revelation and explained that the establishment of His Covenant would forever safeguard His Cause. 'Abdu'l-Bahá said that His Father had written: "'. . . I have appointed one who is the Center of my Covenant. All must obey him; all must turn to him; he is the expounder of my book. . . .'"

"Suddenly the atmosphere in the room became electrified.

'Abdu'l-Bahá rose majestically from His chair and in a powerful voice declared: 'I am the Center of that Covenant! I am the Center of that Covenant!' The friends stood up. They seemed stunned by this great announcement and filled with indescribable emotion. Wonder, joy, and happiness showed in their faces. Gradually we became aware in Whose presence we stood: 'The Mystery of God,' God's special gift to all mankind. Several moments passed before 'Abdu'l-Bahá spoke again. Then, looking at each one, almost pleading, He asked those who believed to spread the Teachings, to be firm and steadfast, to teach not by words alone but by deeds. He said, 'These wonderful days are passing swiftly; and, once gone, they will never come again.'"

(Ramona Allen Brown, *Memories of 'Abdu'l-Bahá*, pp. 83-85)

Analysis Questions

Answer the following questions. Suggested answers appear in Appendix A.

1. Which one of the following choices best describes the Covenant of Bahá'u'lláh in comparison with the Covenants of previous Manifestations?

   A. Bahá'u'lláh revealed a Lesser Covenant, but previous Manifestations never revealed Lesser Covenants.

   B. Bahá'u'lláh's Lesser Covenant is explicit, just like the Lesser Covenants of previous Manifestations.

   C. Bahá'u'lláh's Lesser Covenant was made clearly and explicitly in writing, whereas the Lesser Covenants of previous Manifestations were shrouded in mystery.

   D. Bahá'u'lláh's Lesser Covenant, like those of previous Manifestations, is shrouded in mystery.

2. Which of the following statements about the relationship of the Covenant to the oneness of humanity are correct? Circle all correct answers.

   A. The Covenant embodies the spirit to attain the goal of the oneness of humanity.

B. The Covenant embodies the instrumentality and method to attain the goal of the oneness of humanity.

C. 'Abdu'l-Bahá was the medium for applying the Word to practical measures for the raising up of a new civilization.

D. The Covenant does not have a relationship to the oneness of humanity.

3. Hypothetical: A few believers insist that the Bahá'í Administrative Order, with its two branches of the institutions of the Counsellors and of Spiritual Assemblies, is incomplete and that it is in need of a "third branch." This "third branch," it is urged, would consist of individuals with academic expertise whose advice Spiritual Assemblies would be obligated to follow. Which one of the following choices best describes how the Covenant is relevant to such a situation?

A. The Covenant discourages believers from making creative suggestions.

B. The Covenant does not allow believers to freely express their opinions.

C. The Covenant safeguards the unity of the Faith.

D. The Covenant ensures the integrity of the Faith, so that it may remain true to its divine origin.

Memorization and Presentation Exercises

A. Memorizing the Sacred and Authoritative Writings

Commit to memory the following quotations (or two of your choosing from this chapter):

". . . in the beginning the believers must make their steps firm in the Covenant so that the confirmations of Bahá'u'lláh may encircle them from all sides, the cohorts of the Supreme Concourse may become their supporters and helpers, and the exhortations and advices of 'Abdu'l-Bahá, like unto the pictures engraved on stone, may remain permanent and ineffaceable in the tablets of all hearts."

('Abdu'l-Bahá, *Tablets of the Divine Plan*, p. 52)

"The essence of the Covenant is the continuation of divine guidance after the Ascension of the Prophet through the presence in this world of an institution to which all the friends turn and which can indisputably state what is the Will of God. After 'Abdu'l-Bahá the Guardianship and the Universal House of Justice are such institutions."

(The Universal House of Justice, quoted in *The Covenant: Its Meaning and Origin and Our Attitude Toward It*, p. 39)

B. Presenting the Themes of the Covenant

Prepare a brief presentation on the theme of the significance, meaning, and purposes of Bahá'u'lláh's Covenant.

In your explanation, include discussion of:

1. the meaning of "Covenant," including the Greater and Lesser Covenants;
2. the overall purposes of Bahá'u'lláh's Covenant; and
3. the specific purposes of Bahá'u'lláh's Covenant.

Share your presentation with a partner or group.

CHAPTER 2
'Abdu'l-Bahá:
The Center of the Covenant

. . . turn your faces toward Him Whom God hath purposed,
Who hath branched from this Ancient Root.
— Bahá'u'lláh

Overview

A. Documents Disclosing 'Abdu'l-Bahá's Rank and Station

Bahá'u'lláh's Covenant, "unique in religious history because it was made clearly and explicitly in writing,"[1] was "firmly established prior to His ascension."[2] Bahá'u'lláh "incorporated" the Covenant in a special document He designated the Kitáb-i-'Ahd (The Book of the Covenant).[3] In the Kitáb-i-'Ahd, Bahá'u'lláh appointed 'Abdu'l-Bahá as the Center of the Covenant and the Head of the Faith.[4] However, even prior to the revelation of the Kitáb-i-'Ahd, Bahá'u'lláh had "unequivocally disclosed" the "rank and station of 'Abdu'l-Bahá."[5]

During the period of His exile in Adrianople in the 1860's, Bahá'u'lláh revealed the Tablet of the Branch, which foreshadowed 'Abdu'l-Bahá's future station.[6] In that Tablet, Bahá'u'lláh referred to 'Abdu'l-Bahá in these exalted terms:

> There hath branched from the Sadratu'l-Muntahá* this sacred
> and glorious Being, this Branch of Holiness; well is it with
> him that hath sought His shelter and abideth beneath His
> shadow. Verily the Limb of the Law of God hath sprung
> forth from this Root which God hath firmly implanted in
> the Ground of His Will, and Whose Branch hath been so

---

* The term "Sadratu'l-Muntahá" means "the Tree beyond which there is no passing" and is often used in the Bahá'i Writings to symbolize the Manifestation of God. *See The Kitáb-i-Aqdas*, Note #128.

uplifted as to encompass the whole of creation . . . Render thanks unto God, O people, for His appearance; for verily He is the most great Favor unto you, the most perfect bounty upon you; and through Him every mouldering bone is quickened. Whoso turneth towards Him hath turned towards God, and whoso turneth away from Him hath turned away from My Beauty, hath repudiated My Proof, and transgressed against Me. He is the Trust of God amongst you, His charge within you, His manifestation unto you and His appearance among His favored servants . . .We have sent Him down in the form of a human temple . . .They who deprive themselves of the shadow of the Branch, are lost in the wilderness of error, are consumed by the heat of worldly desires, and are of those who will assuredly perish.[7]

In another Tablet revealed in Adrianople, Bahá'u'lláh alluded to 'Abdu'l-Bahá as "the one amongst His sons 'from Whose tongue God will cause the signs of His power to stream forth,' and as the one Whom 'God hath specially chosen for His Cause.'"[8]

After His banishment to 'Akká, Bahá'u'lláh revealed the Kitáb-i-Aqdas, which "anticipated" the Covenant.[9] In the Kitáb-i-Aqdas, Bahá'u'lláh alluded "to the future Center of His Covenant" and invested Him with "the right of interpreting" Bahá'u'lláh's "holy Writ."[10] The appointment of 'Abdu'l-Bahá to the positions of Center of the Covenant and of Interpreter was evidenced in two separate passages of the Kitáb-i-Aqdas:

When the ocean of My presence hath ebbed and the Book of My Revelation is ended, turn your faces toward Him Whom God hath purposed, Who hath branched from this Ancient Root.[11]

O people of the world! When the Mystic Dove will have winged its flight from its Sanctuary of Praise

26

and sought its far-off goal, its hidden habitation, refer ye whatsoever ye understand not in the Book to Him Who hath branched from this mighty Stock.[12]

In the first passage quoted above, Bahá'u'lláh "alludes to 'Abdu'l-Bahá as His Successor and calls upon the believers to turn towards Him."[13] Bahá'u'lláh "subsequently elucidated" the intent of this passage in the Kitáb-i-'Ahd.[14] In the second passage, Bahá'u'lláh "invests 'Abdu'l-Bahá with the right of interpreting His holy Writ."[15] 'Abdu'l-Bahá, "writing in confirmation of the authority conferred upon Him by Bahá'u'lláh," stated: "'In accordance with the explicit text of the Kitáb-i-Aqdas Bahá'u'lláh hath made the Center of the Covenant the Interpreter of His Word . . . .'"[16] "In the Book of Aqdas, He [Bahá'u'lláh] has given positive command in two clear instances and has explicitly appointed the Interpreter of the Book."[17]

B. The Kitáb-i-'Ahd (The Book of the Covenant)

The rank bestowed upon 'Abdu'l-Bahá in the Kitáb-i-Aqdas was "elucidated and confirmed"[18] by the Kitáb-i-'Ahd—Bahá'u'lláh's "Will and Testament."[19] In the Kitáb-i-'Ahd, Bahá'u'lláh expressly appointed 'Abdu'l-Bahá as "His Successor and the Center of the Covenant."[20] In *God Passes By*, Shoghi Effendi described the history and significance of the Kitáb-i-'Ahd:

Written entirely in His [Bahá'u'lláh's] own hand; unsealed, on the ninth day after His ascension in the presence of nine witnesses chosen from amongst His companions and members of His Family; read subsequently, on the afternoon of that same day, before a large company assembled in His Most Holy Tomb, including His sons, some of the Báb's kinsmen, pilgrims and resident believers, this unique and epoch-making Document, designated by Bahá'u'lláh as His "Most Great Tablet," and alluded to by Him as the "Crimson Book" in His "Epistle to the Son of the Wolf," can find no parallel

27

in the Scriptures of any previous Dispensation, not excluding that of the Báb Himself.[21]

"[N]owhere in the books pertaining to any of the world's religious systems . . . do we find any single document establishing a Covenant endowed with an authority comparable to the Covenant which Bahá'u'lláh had Himself instituted."[22]

Bahá'u'lláh disclosed critical features of the Covenant in the Kitáb-i-'Ahd:

> The Will of the divine Testator is this: It is incumbent upon the Aghsán, the Afnán and My Kindred to turn, one and all, their faces towards the Most Mighty Branch. Consider that which We have revealed in Our Most Holy Book: 'When the ocean of My presence hath ebbed and the Book of My Revelation is ended, turn your faces toward Him Whom God hath purposed, Who hath branched from this Ancient Root.' The object of this sacred verse is none other except the Most Mighty Branch ['Abdu'l-Bahá]. . . . Verily God hath ordained the station of the Greater Branch [Muḥammad 'Alí] to be beneath that of the Most Great Branch ['Abdu'l-Bahá]. . . . We have chosen 'the Greater' after 'the Most Great', as decreed by Him Who is the All-Knowing, the All-Informed.[23]

In this passage, Bahá'u'lláh commanded all of His male descendents ("the Aghsán"[24]), His relatives ("My Kindred"), and the Báb's relatives ("the Afnán"[25]) to turn toward 'Abdu'l-Bahá ("the Most Mighty Branch"). The Arabic word "Aghsán" (plural of "Ghusn") literally means "branches."[26] This term was used by Bahá'u'lláh to designate His male descendents, each of whom was a "Branch." For example, Mírzá Mihdí, one of Bahá'u'lláh's sons, was known as the "Purest Branch."[27] Mírzá Muḥammad-'Alí, another son, was the "Greater Branch."[28] Bahá'u'lláh reserved the titles of the "Most Mighty Branch" or the "Most Great Branch" for His eldest Son, 'Abdu'l-Bahá. In His Writings and oral statements, Bahá'u'lláh referred to 'Abdu'l-Bahá by these designations.[29] Moreover, prior to Bahá'u'lláh's ascension, believers knew 'Abdu'l-Bahá by these titles.[30] It was only after Bahá'u'lláh's passing that 'Abdu'l-Bahá chose for Himself the name "'Abdu'l-Bahá."[31]

In addition to commanding all to turn to 'Abdu'l-Bahá, the above-cited excerpt from the Kitáb-i-'Ahd is also important because of the reference it made to the Kitáb-i-Aqdas. As discussed earlier, in the Kitáb-i-Aqdas, Bahá'u'lláh had instructed believers to turn their faces toward "Him Whom God hath purposed, Who hath branched from this Ancient Root." The Kitáb-i-'Ahd quoted this verse from the Kitáb-i-Aqdas and confirmed that the "object of this sacred verse is none other except the Most Mighty Branch ['Abdu'l-Bahá]." The Kitáb-i-'Ahd thus "makes it clear that this reference is to 'Abdu'l-Bahá,"[32] confirming His appointment as the Center of the Covenant.[33]

The portion of the Kitáb-i-'Ahd referenced above is also significant because of the relative positions it assigned to 'Abdu'l-Bahá and His younger half-brother Mírzá Muhammad-'Alí: "Verily God hath ordained the station of the Greater Branch [Muhammad-'Alí] to be beneath that of the Most Great Branch ['Abdu'l-Bahá]. . . . We have chosen 'the Greater' after 'the Most Great'. . . ." In this verse, Bahá'u'lláh assigned Muhammad-'Alí a "rank second" to none except 'Abdu'l-Bahá.[34]

C. 'Abdu'l-Bahá: The Center of the Covenant, Interpreter, and Exemplar

'Abdu'l-Bahá, "by virtue of the rank bestowed upon Him by His Father," incarnates "an institution that has no parallel in the entire field of religious history."[35] "This unique figure is" at once "the Centre and Pivot of the Covenant which the Author of the Bahá'í Revelation made with all who recognize Him," "the divinely inspired authoritative Interpreter of His Teachings," and "the Exemplar of the pattern of life taught by His Father."[36] Through each of these three roles—as Center of the Covenant, as Interpreter, and as Exemplar—'Abdu'l-Bahá served the purposes of the Covenant.

Bahá'u'lláh appointed 'Abdu'l-Bahá as "the Center of His Covenant, an office without parallel in all religious history."[37] "By this appointment and provision," Bahá'u'lláh "safeguarded and protected the religion of God against differences and schisms, making it impossible for anyone to create a new sect or faction of belief."[38] As confirmed in 'Abdu'l-Bahá's own writings, Bahá'u'lláh "explicitly declared that whatever misunderstanding may arise should be referred to the Center of the Covenant" for "[n]o power can eliminate misunderstandings except that of the Covenant."[39] Further, Bahá'u'lláh commanded that "the One Whom He has appointed the Center of the Covenant shall be turned to and obeyed by all. . . . Any opinion expressed by the Center of the Covenant is correct, and there is no reason for disobedience by anyone."[40] "Therefore, whosoever obeys the Center of the Covenant appointed by Bahá'u'lláh has obeyed Bahá'u'lláh, and whosoever disobeys Him has disobeyed Bahá'u'lláh."[41] As such, through "the dynamic person and peerless office of the Center of the Covenant," the will of Bahá'u'lláh and His Herald, the Báb, "has been translated into viable means for actualizing the unity of mankind and building a world civilization."[42] In His capacity as the Center of the Covenant, 'Abdu'l-Bahá became "the incorruptible medium for applying the Word to practical measures for the raising up of a new civilization."[43]

'Abdu'l-Bahá was also "the appointed interpreter of the utterances of both Bahá'u'lláh and the Báb."[44] Commenting on this function, 'Abdu'l-Bahá wrote: "I am . . . according to the explicit texts of the Kitáb-i-Aqdas and the Kitáb-i-'Ahd the manifest Interpreter of the Word of God . . ."[45] 'Abdu'l-Bahá explained that to "ward off . . . dissensions . . . and prevent any person from creating a division or sect the Blessed Perfection, Bahá'u'lláh, appointed a central authoritative Personage, declaring Him to be the expounder of the Book. This implies that the people in general do not understand the meanings of the Book, but this appointed One does understand."[46] The authoritative interpretation of 'Abdu'l-Bahá "is a divinely guided statement of what the Word of God means."[47] 'Abdu'l-Bahá's writings "throw a clear light upon passages which may have been considered obscure, they point up the intimate interrelationship between various teachings, they expound the implications of scriptural allusions, and they educate the Bahá'ís in the tremendous significances of the Words of Bahá'u'lláh. Rather than in any way supplanting the Words of the Manifestation, they lead us back to them time and again."[48]

'Abdu'l-Bahá was likewise the "perfect Exemplar"[49] of Bahá'u'lláh's teachings—Bahá'u'lláh's purpose having been "thoroughly infused into the conduct of 'Abdu'l-Bahá."[50] "The Covenant is, therefore, unique as a divine phenomenon, in that Bahá'u'lláh, further to conferring upon 'Abdu'l-Bahá the necessary authority to fulfill the requirements of His singular office, vested in Him the virtues of perfection in personal and social behavior, that humanity may have an enduring model to emulate. In no annals of the past is there recorded such an arrangement for ensuring the realization of the purpose of the Manifestation of God."[51] 'Abdu'l-Bahá called on believers to emulate His example: "Follow in the footsteps of 'Abdu'l-Bahá . . . ."[52] Similarly, He is reported to have said, "look at Me, follow Me, be as I am . . . ."[53] In particular, He called upon believers to follow His example in the fields of service and teaching.[54] He directed that His example be inculcated: "guide ye the people and educate them in the ways of 'Abdu'l-Bahá."[55] His "luminous examples" of the application of the teachings to "personal conduct shed light on a way of life we must strive diligently to follow."[56] Accordingly, "as Bahá'ís we should think of 'Abdu'l-Bahá and study His life and ask ourselves what would He have done, for He is our perfect example in every way."[57]

D. The Infallibility of 'Abdu'l-Bahá

Through 'Abdu'l-Bahá's appointment as the Center of the Covenant, the "continuity of that unerring guidance," vouchsafed to the Faith since its birth, was "assured."[58] Referring to 'Abdu'l-Bahá, Bahá'u'lláh emphasized: "Whoso turneth towards Him hath turned towards God, and whoso turneth away from Him hath turned away from My Beauty, hath repudiated My Proof, and transgressed against Me."[59] Moreover, Bahá'u'lláh addressed 'Abdu'l-Bahá with these words: "We pray God to illumine the world through Thy knowledge and wisdom . . . ."[60] And further: "The glory of God rest upon Thee . . . and upon whosoever serveth Thee and circleth around Thee. Woe, great woe, betide him that opposeth and injureth Thee."[61]

As the authorized Interpreter of Bahá'u'lláh's Word, 'Abdu'l-Bahá confirmed that infallible guidance had been conferred upon Him:

... the Blessed Beauty [Bahá'u'lláh] ... has through the Supreme Pen written the Covenant and the Testament; He appointed a Center, the Exponent of the Book and the annuller of disputes. Whatever is written or said by Him is conformable to the truth and under the protection of the Blessed Beauty. He is infallible.[62]

He [Bahá'u'lláh] hath ... commanded that whatever emanateth from the Centre of the Covenant is right and is under His protection and favour, while all else is error.[63]

I am ... according to the explicit texts of the Kitáb-i-Aqdas and the Kitáb-i-'Ahd the manifest Interpreter of the Word of God ... Whoso deviates from my interpretation is a victim of his own fancy.[64]

Addressing all the people of the world He [Bahá'u'lláh] saith: When the Mystic Dove flieth away from the orchard of praise to the Most Supreme and Invisible Station—that is, when the Blessed Beauty turneth away from the contingent world towards the invisible realm—refer whatever ye do not understand in the Book to Him Who hath branched from the Ancient Root. That is, whatever He saith is the very truth.[65]

In the *Tablet of The Branch* He [Bahá'u'lláh] explicitly states: "Whatsoever the Branch says is right, or correct . . . .' Whatsoever his ('Abdu'l-Bahá's) tongue utters, whatsoever his pen records, that is correct; according to the explicit text of Bahá'u'lláh in the *Tablet of The Branch*.[66]

'Abdu'l-Bahá was, as repeatedly affirmed by Shoghi Effendi, the focal point of Bahá'u'lláh's "unerring" guidance.[67] Thus, 'Abdu'l-Bahá's "interpretation of the Holy Texts" was "unerring."[68] Because the "interpretations of 'Abdu'l-Bahá . . . are divinely guided statements of what the Word of God means," these interpretations are "binding on the friends":[69]

> Any opinion expressed by the Center of the Covenant is correct, and there is no reason for disobedience by anyone. . . . Read the Book of the Covenant. All have been commanded to obey the Covenant, and the first admonition is addressed to the sons of Bahá'u'lláh, the Branches: "You must turn to the appointed Center; He is the expounder of the Book."
> Should any soul so clearly violate and disobey this command, can he even say he is a Bahá'í? If anyone disobeys the explicit command of Christ, can he truthfully say he is a Christian?[70]

> He [Bahá'u'lláh] . . ., with His Supreme Pen, entered into a great Covenant and Testament with all the Bahá'ís whereby they were all commanded to follow the Center of the Covenant after His departure, and turn not away even to a hair's breadth from obeying Him.[71]

E. The Station of 'Abdu'l-Bahá

Although infallibly guided, "'Abdu'l-Bahá is not a Manifestation of God . . . ."[72] Nevertheless, "He reflects even as a clear and perfect Mirror the rays of Bahá'u'lláh's glory . . . ."[73] 'Abdu'l-Bahá "reflects the qualities of the Manifestations as if He were a mirror. He reflects not only those of Bahá'u'lláh but also of Christ as He is the exemplar of the spirit of the Prophet. . . ."[74] Bahá'u'lláh conferred on 'Abdu'l-Bahá the title "the Mystery of God," a "designation so appropriate to One Who, though essentially human and holding a station radically and fundamentally different from that occupied by Bahá'u'lláh and His Forerunner, could still claim to be the perfect Exemplar of His Faith, to be endowed with super-human knowledge, and to be regarded as the stainless mirror reflecting His light."[75] Though 'Abdu'l-Bahá's "words are not equal in rank, . . . they possess an equal validity with the utterances of Bahá'u'lláh . . . ."[76]

By virtue of His station, 'Abdu'l-Bahá forms together with Bahá'u'lláh and the Báb what may be called the "Three Central Figures" of the Bahá'í Faith.[77] 'Abdu'l-Bahá "towers," in conjunction with Bahá'u'lláh and the Báb, "above the destinies of this infant Faith of God."[78] 'Abdu'l-Bahá's station is at "a level to which no individual or body ministering" to the Faith's "needs after Him, and for no less a period than a full thousand years, can ever hope to rise."[79]

In describing His own station, 'Abdu'l-Bahá declared: "My station is the station of servitude—a servitude which is complete, pure and real, firmly established, enduring, obvious, explicitly revealed and subject to no interpretation whatever . . . I am the Interpreter of the Word of God; such is my interpretation."[80] From such a statement, however, we should not "infer that 'Abdu'l-Bahá is merely one of the servants of the Blessed Beauty, or at best one whose function is to be confined to that of an authorized interpreter of His Father's teachings."[81] To "regard Him in such a light is a manifest betrayal of the priceless heritage bequeathed by Bahá'u'lláh to mankind."[82] Rather, 'Abdu'l-Bahá

> is, and should for all time be regarded, first and foremost, as the Center and Pivot of Bahá'u'lláh's peerless and all-enfolding Covenant, His most exalted handiwork, the stainless Mirror of His light, the perfect Exemplar of His teachings, the unerring Interpreter of His Word, the embodiment of every Bahá'í ideal, the incarnation of every Bahá'í virtue, the Most Mighty Branch sprung from the Ancient Root, the Limb of the Law of God, the Being "round Whom all names revolve," the Mainspring of the Oneness of Humanity, the Ensign of the Most Great Peace, the Moon of the Central Orb of this most holy Dispensation—styles and titles that are implicit and find their truest, their highest and fairest expression in the magic name 'Abdu'l-Bahá. He is, above and beyond these appellations, the "Mystery of God"—an expression by which Bahá'u'lláh Himself has chosen to designate Him, and which, while it does not by any means justify us to assign to Him the station of Prophethood, indicates how

34

in the person of 'Abdu'l-Bahá the incompatible characteristics of a human nature and superhuman knowledge and perfection have been blended and are completely harmonized.[83]

Study Questions

Answer the following questions based on the above Overview:

CONTENT QUESTIONS

1. The Covenant was "incorporated" in what document? Which of Bahá'u'lláh's Writings alluded to 'Abdu'l-Bahá's future station?

2. The Kitáb-i-Aqdas conferred what two functions upon 'Abdu'l-Bahá?

3. Does the Kitáb-i-'Ahd have a parallel in the Scriptures of the past? If not, why not?

4. What does the term "Aghsán" mean? What does the term "Afnán" mean?

5. Who is the "Most Great Branch" (or "Most Mighty Branch")? Who is the "Greater Branch"?

6. What verse from the Kitáb-i-Aqdas did Bahá'u'lláh quote in the Kitáb-i-'Ahd? Why is this reference to the Kitáb-i-Aqdas significant?

7. What three roles did 'Abdu'l-Bahá fulfill?

8. "Whatever is written or said by Him ['Abdu'l-Bahá] is conformable to the _____ and under the protection of the _____ _____. He is _____."

9. What does the expression "the Mystery of God" indicate about 'Abdu'l-Bahá?

APPLICATION/DISCUSSION QUESTIONS

1. What do you personally find most striking about Bahá'u'lláh's description of 'Abdu'l-Bahá in the Tablet of the Branch (a portion of which is quoted above in section A of the Overview)?

2. How are 'Abdu'l-Bahá's three roles as Center of the Covenant, as Interpreter, and as Exemplar distinct? How do these roles serve the purposes of the Covenant?

3. How is our attitude and obedience to God expressed in our attitude and obedience to 'Abdu'l-Bahá's teachings?

4. What does it mean that 'Abdu'l-Bahá "is our perfect example in every way"? What practical steps can each believer take to follow 'Abdu'l-Bahá's example?

Quotations for Reflection

Answer the questions following the quotations below:

1. "As to the most great characteristic of the revelation of Bahá'u'lláh, a specific teaching not given by any of the Prophets of the past: It is the ordination and appointment of the Center of the Covenant. By this appointment and provision He has safeguarded and protected the religion of God against differences and schisms, making it impossible for anyone to create a new sect or faction of belief. To ensure unity and agreement He has entered into a Covenant with all the people of the world, including the interpreter and explainer of His teachings, so that no one may interpret or explain the religion of God according to his own view or opinion and thus create a sect founded upon his individual understanding of the divine Words."

('Abdu'l-Bahá, *The Promulgation of Universal Peace*, pp. 455-56)

What is the most great characteristic of the revelation of Bahá'u'lláh? What does the Covenant ensure?

'Abdu'l-Bahá passed away in 1921. Is His position as the Center of the Covenant still relevant today? Explain.

2. "The point at issue is clear, direct and of utmost brevity. Either Bahá'u'lláh was wise, omniscient and aware of what would ensue, or was ignorant and in error. He entered, by His supreme pen, into such a firm Covenant and Testament with all the Bahá'ís, first with the Aghsán, the Afnán and His kindred, and commanded them to obey and turn toward Him. By His supreme pen He hath explicitly declared that the object of the following verse of the *Kitáb-i-Aqdas* is the Most Great Branch:

"'When the ocean of My presence hath ebbed and the Book of My Revelation is ended, turn your faces toward Him Whom God hath purposed, Who hath branched from this Ancient Root.' Its meaning briefly is this: that after My ascension it is incumbent upon the Aghsán, the Afnán and the kindred, and all the friends of God, to turn their faces to Him Who hath branched from the Ancient Root.

"He also plainly saith in the *Kitáb-i-Aqdas*: 'O ye people of the world! When the Mystic Dove will have winged its flight from its Sanctuary of Praise and sought its far-off goal, its hidden habitation, refer ye whatsoever ye understand not in the Book to Him Who hath branched from this mighty Stock.' Addressing all the people of the world He saith: When the Mystic Dove flieth away from the orchard of praise to the Most Supreme and Invisible Station—that is, when the Blessed Beauty turneth away from the contingent world towards the invisible realm—refer whatever ye do not understand in the Book to Him Who hath branched from the Ancient Root. That is, whatever He saith is the very truth.

"And in the Book of the Covenant He explicitly saith that the object of this verse 'Who hath branched from this Ancient Root' is the Most Mighty Branch. And He commandeth all the Aghsán, the Afnán, the kindred and the Bahá'ís to turn toward Him."

(*Selections from the Writings of 'Abdu'l-Bahá*, pp. 213-14)

What are the two verses from the Kitáb-i-Aqdas that refer to 'Abdu'l-Bahá?

Do these two verses serve different functions? If so, what?

3. "Inasmuch as great differences and divergences of denominational belief had arisen throughout the past, every man with a new idea attributing it to God, Bahá'u'lláh desired that there should not be any ground or reason for disagreement among the Bahá'ís. Therefore, with His own pen He wrote the Book of His Covenant, addressing His relations and all people of the world, saying, 'Verily, I have appointed One Who is the Center of My Covenant. All must obey Him; all must turn to Him; He is the Expounder of My Book, and He is informed of My purpose. All must turn to Him. Whatsoever He says is correct, for, verily, He knoweth the texts of My Book. Other than He, no one doth know My Book.' The purpose of this statement is that there should never be discord and divergence among the Bahá'ís but that they should always be unified and agreed."

('Abdu'l-Bahá, *The Promulgation of Universal Peace*, pp. 322-23)

What was Bahá'u'lláh's purpose in appointing 'Abdu'l-Bahá as the Center of the Covenant?

What does it mean to "turn to" 'Abdu'l-Bahá?

4. "Through it [the Covenant of Bahá'u'lláh] the meaning of the Word, both in theory and practice, is made evident in the life and work of 'Abdu'l-Bahá, the appointed Interpreter, the perfect Exemplar, the Center of the Covenant."

(The Universal House of Justice, *Individual Rights and Freedoms in the World Order of Bahá'u'lláh*, p. 5)

"In contemplating the Master's divine example we may well reflect that His life and deeds were not acted to a pattern of expediency, but were the inevitable and spontaneous expression of His inner self. We, likewise, shall act according to His example only as our inward spirits, growing and maturing through the disciplines of prayer and practice of the Teachings, become the wellsprings of all our attitudes and actions."

> (The Universal House of Justice, *Messages from the Universal House of Justice: 1963-1986*, p. 147)

What roles did 'Abdu'l-Bahá serve?

What insights does the passage immediately above offer as to how practically we may act according to 'Abdu'l-Bahá's example?

5. "He [Bahá'u'lláh] said, 'Verily, He is the appointed one; other than He, there is none,' intending that no sects or prejudices should be formed, and preventing every man here and there with a new thought from creating dissension and variance. It is as though a king should appoint a governor-general. Whosoever obeys him, obeys the king. Whosoever violates and disobeys him, violates the king. Therefore, whosoever obeys the Center of the Covenant appointed by Bahá'u'lláh has obeyed Bahá'u'lláh, and whosoever disobeys Him has disobeyed Bahá'u'lláh. It has nothing to do with Him ('Abdu'l-Bahá) at all—precisely as the governor-general appointed by the king—whosoever obeys the governor-general obeys the king; whosoever disobeys the governor-general disobeys the king."

> ('Abdu'l-Bahá, *The Promulgation of Universal Peace*, p. 323)

What analogy does 'Abdu'l-Bahá use to convey His role as the Center of the Covenant?

How can obedience to 'Abdu'l-Bahá be manifested today by believers?

6. "That such a unique and sublime station should have been conferred upon 'Abdu'l-Bahá did not, and indeed could not, surprise those exiled companions who had for so long been privileged to observe His life and conduct, nor the pilgrims who had been brought, however fleetingly, into personal contact with Him, nor indeed the vast concourse of the faithful who, in distant lands, had grown to revere His name and to appreciate His labors, nor even the wide circle of His friends and acquaintances who, in the Holy Land and the adjoining countries, were already well familiar with

the position He had occupied during the lifetime of His Father.

". . . He alone had been accorded the privilege of being called 'the Master,' an honor from which His Father had strictly excluded all His other sons. Upon Him that loving and unerring Father had chosen to confer the unique title of 'Sirru'lláh' (the Mystery of God), a designation so appropriate to One Who, though essentially human and holding a station radically and fundamentally different from that occupied by Bahá'u'lláh and His Forerunner, could still claim to be the perfect Exemplar of His Faith, to be endowed with super-human knowledge, and to be regarded as the stainless mirror reflecting His light."

(Shoghi Effendi, *God Passes By*, pp. 240, 242)

Was the station conferred upon 'Abdu'l-Bahá a surprise to those familiar with Him?

Why is the title "the Mystery of God" so appropriate a description of 'Abdu'l-Bahá?

Illustrations

Reflect on how the following excerpts illustrate the significance of 'Abdu'l-Bahá's station:

"The word Áqá (The Master) was a designation given to 'Abdu'l-Bahá. I recall that one day when Bahá'u'lláh was in the Garden of Vashshásh which was a delightful place situated outside Baghdád, which He occasionally used to visit, someone referred to certain individuals as the Áqá. On hearing this Bahá'u'lláh was heard to say with a commanding voice: 'Who is the Áqá? There is only one Áqá, and He is the Most Great Branch.'

"Bahá'u'lláh said the same thing again in the Garden of Riḍván in 'Akká . . . On that occasion, someone addressed Mírzá Muḥammad-'Alí as Áqá, whereupon Bahá'u'lláh admonished him saying: 'There is one and only one Áqá and He is the Most Great Branch, others should be addressed by their names.'

"Many a time I was in the presence of Bahá'u'lláh when the Master was also present. Because of His presence Bahá'u'lláh would be filled with the utmost joy and gladness. One could see His blessed countenance beaming with delight and exultation so lovingly that no words can adequately describe it. Repeatedly He would laud and glorify the Master, and the mere mention of His name would suffice to evoke an indescribable feeling of ecstasy in the Person of the Blessed Beauty. No pen is capable of fully describing this."

(Summary translation of the notes of Mírzá Maḥmúd-i-Káshání, quoted in Adib Taherzadeh, *The Covenant of Bahá'u'lláh*, pp. 138-39)

"Bahá'u'lláh had entrusted His Will and Testament to the care of 'Abdu'l-Bahá. On the ninth day after His ascension its contents became known. Earlier in the day nine of the Bahá'ís, including members of Bahá'u'lláh's family who were chosen by 'Abdu'l-Bahá, gathered to witness the breaking of the seal and to learn the counsel of the Testament. Later, the same day, within the walls of the Shrine of Bahá'u'lláh, Mírzá Majdi'd-Dín—the son of Mírzá Músá, Bahá'u'lláh's faithful brother and valiant supporter throughout forty years, then alas deceased—stood up to read the Will. No doubt could be entertained. It was evident to Whom the Bahá'ís had to turn, and Whom they had to obey, on Whose shoulders the mantle of total authority now rested. No one expressed dissent. Everyone who was there, and heard that 'Abdu'l-Bahá was the successor to Bahá'u'lláh, submitted to what He had ordained. Ṭarázu'lláh Samandarí vividly recalled that felicitous day, and the obedience that was unquestionably rendered to 'Abdu'l-Baha."

(H.M. Balyuzi, *'Abdu'l-Bahá: The Centre of the Covenant of Bahá'u'lláh*, pp. 51-52)

Analysis Questions

Answer the following questions. Suggested answers appear in Appendix A.

1. Which one of the following choices best describes how Bahá'u'lláh established the Covenant?

> A. Bahá'u'lláh incorporated the Covenant in the Kitáb-i-Aqdas.
>
> B. Bahá'u'lláh anticipated the Covenant in the Kitáb-i-'Ahd.
>
> C. Bahá'u'lláh incorporated the Covenant in both the Kitáb-i-Aqdas and the Kitáb-i-'Ahd.
>
> D. Bahá'u'lláh anticipated the Covenant in the Kitáb-i-Aqdas and incorporated it in the Kitáb-i-'Ahd.

2. A believer claims that he has been inspired by Bahá'u'lláh in interpreting a particular verse of the Kitáb-i-Aqdas. This believer is now insisting that the rest of the community follow his interpretation. How is the Covenant relevant to this situation? Circle all correct answers.

> A. Because Bahá'u'lláh inspired the believer, the community should follow the believer's interpretation.
>
> B. 'Abdu'l-Bahá is the authorized Interpreter of Bahá'u'lláh's Word; the interpretation of this believer is not authorized or binding upon others.
>
> C. In order to maintain unity, the community should follow the believer's interpretation.
>
> D. The Covenant ensures the unity of the Faith because the community must turn toward the authorized Interpreter, not to individual believers.

3. A believer says that he accepts Bahá'u'lláh, but does not believe in 'Abdu'l-Bahá's interpretations that appear to the believer to contradict Bahá'u'lláh's Writings. How is the Covenant relevant to this situation? Circle all correct answers.

> A. By rejecting 'Abdu'l-Bahá, this believer is, in effect, rejecting Bahá'u'lláh.
>
> B. This believer is not rejecting Bahá'u'lláh because Bahá'u'lláh

is the Manifestation of God, whereas 'Abdu'l-Bahá is the Servant of God.

C. Because 'Abdu'l-Bahá was the unerring Interpreter, His interpretations are consistent with Bahá'u'lláh's Writings.

D. A believer can reject 'Abdu'l-Bahá's interpretations if he feels that they are inconsistent with Bahá'u'lláh's Writings.

Memorization and Presentation Exercises

A. Memorizing the Sacred and Authoritative Writings

Commit to memory the following quotations (or two of your choosing from this chapter):

"O people of the world! When the Mystic Dove will have winged its flight from its Sanctuary of Praise and sought its far-off goal, its hidden habitation, refer ye whatsoever ye understand not in the Book to Him Who hath branched from this mighty Stock."

(Bahá'u'lláh, *The Kitáb-i-Aqdas*, parag. 174)

"The Will of the divine Testator is this: It is incumbent upon the Aghsán, the Afnán and My Kindred to turn, one and all, their faces towards the Most Mighty Branch. Consider that which We have revealed in Our Most Holy Book: 'When the ocean of My presence hath ebbed and the Book of My Revelation is ended, turn your faces toward Him Whom God hath purposed, Who hath branched from this Ancient Root.' The object of this sacred verse is none other except the Most Mighty Branch ['Abdu'l-Bahá]."

(*Tablets of Bahá'u'lláh*, p. 221)

B. Presenting the Themes of the Covenant

Prepare a brief presentation on the theme of 'Abdu'l-Bahá as the Center of the Covenant.

In your explanation, include discussion of:

1. the documents alluding to and establishing the Covenant;
2. the major roles and functions of 'Abdu'l-Bahá; and
3. the infallibility and station of 'Abdu'l-Bahá.

Share your presentation with a partner or group.

CHAPTER 3
The Rebellion and Excommunication of Mírzá Muḥammad-'Alí

*Should he for a moment pass out from under
the shadow of the Cause, he surely shall be brought to naught.*
— Bahá'u'lláh

Overview

A. The Rebellion of Mírzá Muḥammad-'Alí

After Bahá'u'lláh's passing, the community of believers turned toward 'Abdu'l-Bahá as Bahá'u'lláh's Successor. Through the influence of the Covenant, 'Abdu'l-Bahá would in succeeding years spread the light of the Faith to the North American continent, and from there to the countries of Europe and subsequently to the Far East and Australasia.[1] However, before the Faith could spread its radiance over vast portions of the Western world, "the newly born Covenant of Bahá'u'lláh had . . . to be baptized with a fire which was to demonstrate its solidity and proclaim its indestructibility to an unbelieving world."[2] At "the very moment" of the Covenant's "inception," Mírzá Muḥammad-'Alí—Bahá'u'lláh's son and 'Abdu'l-Bahá's younger half-brother—brought about a crisis that was to "shake that Covenant to its foundations."[3] Mírzá Muḥammad-'Alí and others whom he persuaded turned away from 'Abdu'l-Bahá and launched an attack on the Covenant Bahá'u'lláh had established.

In *God Passes By*, Shoghi Effendi described the origin and effects of the crisis precipitated by Mírzá Muḥammad-'Alí:

> This crisis, misconceived as a schism, . . . was precipitated at the very heart and center of His [Bahá'u'lláh's] Faith, and was provoked by no one less than a member of His own family, a half-brother of 'Abdu'l-Bahá, specifically named in the book of the

Covenant, and holding a rank second to none except Him Who had been appointed as the Center of that Covenant. For no less than four years that emergency fiercely agitated the minds and hearts of a vast proportion of the faithful throughout the East, eclipsed, for a time, the Orb of the Covenant, created an irreparable breach within the ranks of Bahá'u'lláh's own kindred, sealed ultimately the fate of the great majority of the members of His family, and gravely damaged the prestige, though it never succeeded in causing a permanent cleavage in the structure, of the Faith itself.[4]

The "true ground" of this crisis was "the burning, the uncontrollable, the soul-festering jealousy" of Mírzá Muḥammad-'Alí toward 'Abdu'l-Bahá.[5] This jealousy had been aroused by "the admitted preeminence of 'Abdu'l-Bahá in rank, power, ability, knowledge and virtue" above all the other members of Bahá'u'lláh's family.[6] For several years prior to Bahá'u'lláh's ascension, Mírzá Muḥammad-'Alí's envy had been inflamed as he witnessed the "unnumbered marks of distinction, of admiration and favor accorded to 'Abdu'l-Bahá not only by Bahá'u'lláh Himself, His companions and His followers, but by the vast number of unbelievers who had come to recognize that innate greatness which 'Abdu'l-Bahá had manifested from childhood."[7]

Mírzá Muḥammad-'Alí's envy did not abate following Bahá'u'lláh's passing:

Far from being allayed by the provisions of a Will [the Kitáb-i-'Ahd] which had elevated him to the second-highest position within the ranks of the faithful, the fire of unquenchable animosity that glowed in the breast of Mírzá Muḥammad-'Alí burned even more fiercely as soon as he came to realize the full implications of that Document. All that 'Abdu'l-Bahá could do, during a period of four distressful years, His incessant exhortations, His earnest pleadings, the favors and kindnesses He showered upon him, the admonitions and warnings He uttered, even His voluntary withdrawal in the hope of averting the threatening storm, proved to be of no avail. Gradually and with unyielding persistence, through lies, half-truths, calumnies and gross exaggerations, this "Prime Mover of sedition" succeeded in ranging on his side almost the entire family of Bahá'u'lláh, as well as a considerable number of those who had formed his immediate entourage.[8]

Thus, 'Abdu'l-Bahá was betrayed by nearly all of His relatives as He faced the assault of Mírzá Muḥammad-'Alí and the other repudiators of the Covenant.

B. Misrepresentations and Other Misdeeds of Mírzá Muḥammad-'Alí

Mírzá Muḥammad-'Alí and his supporters launched a campaign of abuse and defamation against 'Abdu'l-Bahá. To "friend and stranger, believer and unbeliever alike, to officials both high and low, openly and by insinuation, verbally as well as in writing," they falsely represented 'Abdu'l-Bahá as an ambitious and unprincipled person—Who had disregarded the instructions of His Father; assumed a rank co-equal with the Manifestation Himself; was beginning to claim to be the return of Jesus Christ; caused discord and fostered enmity for His private ends; perverted the purpose of the Kitáb-i-'Ahd; deprived His siblings of their lawful allowance and spent it on officials for His personal gain; declined all the invitations extended to Him to discuss and resolve the problems that had arisen; and corrupted the Holy Text.[9] Mírzá Muḥammad-'Alí claimed that, as a result, "the standard of rebellion had . . . been raised by the Oriental believers, that the community of the faithful had been rent asunder, was rapidly declining and was doomed to extinction."[10]

Yet, it was Mírzá Muḥammad-'Alí,

who . . . had, in the lifetime of Bahá'u'lláh, so openly and shamelessly advanced in a written statement, signed and sealed by him, the very claim now falsely imputed

47

by him to 'Abdu'l-Bahá, that his Father had, with His own hand, chastised him. He it was who, when sent on a mission to India, had tampered with the text of the holy writings entrusted to his care for publication. He it was who had the impudence and temerity to tell 'Abdu'l-Bahá to His face that just as 'Umar had succeeded in usurping the successorship of the Prophet Muḥammad, he, too, felt himself able to do the same. He it was who, obsessed by the fear that he might not survive 'Abdu'l-Bahá, had, the moment he had been assured by Him that all the honor he coveted would, in the course of time, be his, swiftly rejoined that he had no guarantee that he would outlive Him. He it was who, as testified by Mírzá Badí''ulláh* in his confession, written and published on the occasion of his repentance and his short-lived reconciliation with 'Abdu'l-Bahá, had, while Bahá'u'lláh's body was still awaiting interment, carried off, by a ruse, the two satchels containing his Father's most precious documents, entrusted by Him, prior to His ascension, to 'Abdu'l-Bahá. He it was who, by an exceedingly adroit and simple forgery of a word recurring in some of the denunciatory passages addressed by the Supreme Pen to Mírzá Yaḥyá, and by other devices such as mutilation and interpolation, had succeeded in making them directly applicable to a Brother Whom he hated with such consuming passion. And lastly, it was this same Mírzá Muḥammad-'Alí who, as attested by 'Abdu'l-Bahá in His Will, had . . . conspired to take His life . . . .[11]

C. The Excommunication of Mírzá Muḥammad-'Alí

In the Kitáb-i-'Ahd, Bahá'u'lláh had conferred on Mírzá Muḥammad-'Alí a rank second only to 'Abdu'l-Bahá: "Verily God hath ordained the station of the Greater Branch [Muḥammad 'Alí] to be beneath that of the Most Great Branch ['Abdu'l-Bahá]. . . . We have chosen 'the

---

*Brother of Mírzá Muḥammad-'Alí. A portion of Mírzá Badí'u'lláh's confession appears as the second excerpt in the Illustrations section of this chapter.

Greater' after 'the Most Great', as decreed by Him Who is the All-Knowing, the All-Informed."[12] However, Mírzá Muḥammad-'Alí's position was dependent upon his firmness in the Covenant.

Mírzá Muḥammad-'Alí was a person of great capacity in utterance and in calligraphy. But from his early days, he had entertained an ambition to assume a position of prominence in the Faith. During Bahá'u'lláh's lifetime, Mírzá Muḥammad-'Alí had made the preposterous claim in his writings that he was a partner with Bahá'u'lláh in divine Revelation. Mírzá Muḥammad-'Alí had also claimed that he was the revealer of the verses of God.[13] Such assertions had evoked Bahá'u'lláh's condemnation and wrath. Bahá'u'lláh had rebuked and warned him about the consequences of deviating from God's law.[14] In referring to Mírzá Muḥammad-'Alí, Bahá'u'lláh had written: "He, verily, is but one of My servants . . . Should he for a moment pass out from under the shadow of the Cause, he surely shall be brought to naught."[15] Moreover, in no less emphatic language, Bahá'u'lláh warned in relation to Mírzá Muḥammad-'Alí: "By God, the True One! Were We, for a single instant, to withhold from him the outpourings of Our Cause, he would wither, and would fall upon the dust."[16] Unfortunately, because of his unfaithfulness, Mírzá Muḥammad-'Alí came to realize what Bahá'u'lláh had promised.

In His Will and Testament, 'Abdu'l-Bahá confirmed that Mírzá Muḥammad-'Alí had broken Bahá'u'lláh's Covenant:

> The Center of Sedition, the Prime Mover of mischief, Mírzá Muḥammad 'Alí, hath passed out from under the shadow of the Cause, hath broken the Covenant, hath falsified the Holy Text, hath inflicted a grievous loss upon the true Faith of God, hath scattered His people, hath with bitter rancor endeavored to hurt 'Abdu'l-Bahá and hath assailed with the utmost enmity this servant of the Sacred Threshold.[17]

'Abdu'l-Bahá's Will and Testament presented unmistakable proofs of Mírzá Muḥammad-'Alí's deviation from the Cause:

> . . . He [Bahá'u'lláh] said:—"Should he for a moment

49

pass out from under the shadow of the Cause, he surely shall be brought to naught." Reflect! What stress He layeth upon one moment's deviation: that is, were he to incline a hair's breadth to the right or to the left, his deviation would be clearly established and his utter nothingness made manifest. . . .

What deviation can be greater than breaking the Covenant of God! What deviation can be greater than interpolating and falsifying the words and verses of the Sacred Text, even as testified and declared by Mírzá Badí'u'lláh! What deviation can be greater than calumniating the Center of the Covenant himself! What deviation can be more glaring than spreading broadcast false and foolish reports touching the Temple of God's Testament! What deviation can be more grievous than decreeing the death of the Center of the Covenant, supported by the holy verse:—"He that layeth a claim ere the passing of a thousand years . . .," whilst he (Muḥammad 'Alí) without shame in the days of the Blessed Beauty had advanced such a claim as this and been confuted by Him in the aforementioned manner, the text of his claim being still extant in his own handwriting and bearing his own seal. What deviation can be more complete than falsely accusing the loved ones of God! What deviation can be more evil than causing their imprisonment and incarceration! What deviation can be more severe than delivering into the hands of the government the Holy Writings and Epistles, that haply they (the government) might arise intent upon the death of this wronged one! What deviation can be more violent than threatening the ruin of the Cause of God, forging and slanderously falsifying letters and documents so that this might perturb and alarm the government and lead to the shedding of the blood of this wronged one,—such letters and documents being now in the possession of the government! What deviation can be more odious than his iniquity and rebellion! What deviation can be more shameful than dispersing the gathering of the people of salvation! What deviation can be more infamous than the vain and feeble interpretations of the people of doubt! What deviation can be more wicked than joining hands with strangers and with the enemies of God!¹⁸

Thus, the Will and Testament of 'Abdu'l-Bahá declared: "In short, O ye beloved of the Lord! The Center of Sedition, Mírzá Muḥammad 'Alí, in accordance with the decisive words of God and by reason of his boundless transgression, hath grievously fallen and been cut off from the Holy Tree."¹⁹ Thus, this "arch-breaker of Bahá'u'lláh's Covenant"²⁰ forfeited the position that had been intended for him and was excommunicated from the Cause of God.

'Abdu'l-Bahá explained that had Bahá'u'lláh not "graciously vouchsafed" His "promised aid" to 'Abdu'l-Bahá, Mírzá Muḥammad-'Alí "surely would have destroyed, nay exterminated the Cause of God and utterly subverted the Divine Edifice."²¹ In a similar vein, 'Abdu'l-Bahá wrote that should Covenant-breakers (such as Mírzá Muḥammad-'Alí) be allowed to continue, "they would, in but a few days' time, exterminate the Cause of God, His Word, and themselves."²²

Mírzá Muḥammad-'Alí outlived 'Abdu'l-Bahá by nearly twenty years, but in the end, his designs were frustrated, and he failed to bring about a schism in the Faith. He was "stricken with paralysis which crippled half his body; lay bedridden in pain for months before he died; and was buried according to Muslim rites."²³ Upon Mírzá Muḥammad-'Alí's death in 1937, Shoghi Effendi issued a cable announcing that the Hand of Omnipotence had removed the archbreaker of Bahá'u'lláh's Covenant.²⁴ Shoghi Effendi explained that whereas the hopes of Mírzá Muḥammad-'Alí had been shattered, his plottings frustrated, and the society of his fellow-conspirators extinguished, by contrast, God's triumphant Faith was forging on, its unity unimpaired, its purpose unsullied, and its stability unshaken.²⁵ Finally, he observed that Mírzá Muḥammad-'Alí's death called for neither exultation nor recrimination, but evoked overwhelming pity at so tragic a downfall unparalleled in religious history.²⁶ Because

Mírzá Muḥammad-'Alí deviated "from under the shadow of the Cause," he was, as had been foretold by Bahá'u'lláh, "brought to naught"[27] and defeated in his attempts to undermine "the indestructible Covenant"[28] of the Cause of God.

Study Questions

Answer the following questions based on the above Overview:

CONTENT QUESTIONS

1. In terms of familial relations, Mírzá Muḥammad-'Alí was Bahá'u'lláh's _____ and 'Abdu'l-Bahá's _____.

2. Bahá'u'lláh had conferred upon Mírzá Muḥammad-'Alí "a rank _____ to none except Him Who had been appointed as the Center of that Covenant."

3. What were the effects of the crisis precipitated by Mírzá Muḥammad-'Alí?

4. What was the true ground of the crisis precipitated by Mírzá Muḥammad-'Alí?

5. How did 'Abdu'l-Bahá respond to Mírzá Muḥammad-'Alí during the "four distressful years" of the latter's rebellion?

6. What were some of Mírzá Muḥammad-'Alí's misdeeds during Bahá'u'lláh's lifetime? After Bahá'u'lláh's passing?

7. In reference to Mírzá Muḥammad-'Alí, Bahá'u'lláh declared: "He, verily, is but one of My servants . . . Should he for a _____ pass out from under the shadow of the Cause, he surely shall be brought to _____."

8. What "deviations" of Mírzá Muḥammad-'Alí did 'Abdu'l-Bahá recount

in His Will and Testament, justifying Mírzá Muḥammad-'Alí's excommunication?

9. What was the ultimate fate of Mírzá Muḥammad-'Alí?

APPLICATION/DISCUSSION QUESTIONS

1. What is the difference between a crisis and a schism? Why was Mírzá Muḥammad-'Alí's rebellion a crisis in the Faith, but not a schism?

2. Why would Bahá'u'lláh have appointed Mírzá Muḥammad-'Alí to succeed 'Abdu'l-Bahá if Bahá'u'lláh could foresee that Mírzá Muḥammad-'Alí might break the Covenant?

3. Why have those closest to the Manifestation of God often broken His Covenant?

4. What implications does the example and fate of Mírzá Muḥammad-'Alí have for every Bahá'í, particularly those serving in special capacities in the Faith?

Quotations for Reflection

Answer the questions following the quotations below:

1. "The Centre of Sedition [Mírzá Muḥammad-'Alí] had imagined that it needed but his arrogant rebellion to bring down the Covenant and Testament in ruins; it needed but this, so he thought, to turn the righteous away from the Holy Will. Wherefore he sent out far and wide his leaflets of doubt, devising many a secret scheme. Now he would cry out that God's edifice had been subverted and His divine commands annulled, and that accordingly, the Covenant and Testament was abolished. Again he would set himself to sighing and groaning that he was being held a prisoner and was kept hungry and thirsty day and night. Another day he would raise an uproar, saying that the oneness of God had been denied, since another Manifestation had been proclaimed, prior to the expiration of a thousand years.

"When he saw that his calumnies had no effect, he gradually formed a plan to incite a disturbance. He began stirring up mischief, and went knocking at every door. He started making false accusations to the officials of the Government. He approached some of the foreigners, made himself their intimate, and together with them prepared a document and presented it to the Seat of the Sultanate, bringing consternation to the authorities. Among the many slanderous charges was this, that this hapless one had raised up a standard of revolt, a flag bearing the words *Yá Bahá'u'l-Abhá*; that I had paraded this throughout the countryside, to every city, town and village, and even among the desert tribes, and had summoned all the inhabitants to unite under this flag. . . .

"Another of his slanders was that the Shrine on Mount Carmel was a fortress that I had built strong and impregnable—this when the building under construction compriseth six rooms—and that I had named it Medina the Resplendent, while I had named the Holy Tomb* Mecca the Glorified. Yet another of his calumnies was that I had established an independent sovereignty, and that—God forbid! God forbid! God forbid!—I had summoned all the believers to join me in this massive wrongdoing. How dire, O my Lord, is his slander!"

(*Selections from the Writings of 'Abdu'l-Bahá*, pp. 216-18)

What were some of the misrepresentations Mírzá Muhammad-'Alí spread about 'Abdu'l-Bahá?

What motivated Mírzá Muhammad-'Alí's actions?

2. ". . . their chief [Mírzá Muhammad-'Alí], O my God, hath dared to interpolate Thy Book, to fraudulently alter Thy decisive Holy Text and falsify that which hath been revealed by Thy All-Glorious Pen."
(*Will and Testament of 'Abdu'l-Bahá*, p. 17)

"Ye know well what the hands of the Center of Sedition, Mírzá Muhammad-'Alí, and his associates have wrought. Among his doings, one of them is the corruption of the Sacred Text whereof ye are all aware, the Lord be praised, and know that it is evident, proven and confirmed by the testimony of his brother, Mírzá Badí'u'lláh, whose confession is

---

*at Bahjí.

54

written in his own handwriting, beareth his seal, is printed and spread abroad. This is but one of his misdeeds. Can a transgression be imagined more glaring than this, the interpolation of the Holy Text? Nay, by the righteousness of the Lord! His transgressions are writ and recorded in a leaflet by itself."

(*Will and Testament of 'Abdu'l-Bahá*, pp. 20-21)

What did Mírzá Muḥammad-'Alí corrupt?

What did Mírzá Muḥammad-'Alí's actions reveal about his attitude toward Bahá'u'lláh?

3. "A few months ago, in concert with others, he that hath broken the Covenant, hath prepared a document teeming with calumny and slander wherein, the Lord forbid, among many similar slanderous charges, 'Abdu'l-Bahá is deemed a deadly enemy, the ill-wisher of the Crown. They so perturbed the minds of the members of the Imperial Government that at last a Committee of Investigation was sent from the seat of His Majesty's Government which, violating every rule of justice and equity that befit His Imperial Majesty, nay, with the most glaring injustice, proceeded with its investigations. The ill-wishers of the One True God surrounded them on every side and explained and excessively enlarged upon the text of the document whilst they (the members of the Committee) in their turn blindly acquiesced. One of their many calumnies was that this servant had raised aloft a banner in this city, had summoned the people together under it, had established a new sovereignty for himself, had erected upon Mount Carmel a mighty stronghold, had rallied around him all the peoples of the land and made them obedient to him, had caused disruption in the Faith of Islám, had covenanted with the following of Christ and, God forbid, had purposed to cause the gravest breach in the mighty power of the Crown. May the Lord protect us from such atrocious falsehoods! . . .

". . . What transgression can be more abominable, more odious, more wicked than this!

"In like manner, the focal Center of Hate, hath purposed to put 'Abdu'l-Bahá to death . . . . It is evident and indisputable that they are

privily and with the utmost subtlety engaged in conspiring against me."
(*Will and Testament of 'Abdu'l-Bahá*, pp. 7-8)

What were some of the transgressions of Mírzá Muḥammad-'Alí recounted by 'Abdu'l-Bahá in His Will and Testament?

Why was it necessary for 'Abdu'l-Bahá to highlight, in His Will and Testament, Mírzá Muḥammad-'Alí's transgressions?

4. "In short, according to the explicit Divine Text the least transgression shall make of this man [Mírzá Muḥammad-'Alí] a fallen creature, and what transgression is more grievous than attempting to destroy the Divine Edifice, breaking the Covenant, erring from the Testament, falsifying the Holy Text, sowing the seeds of doubt, calumniating 'Abdu'l-Bahá, advancing claims for which God hath sent down no warrant, kindling mischief and striving to shed the very blood of 'Abdu'l-Bahá, and many other things whereof ye are all aware! It is thus evident that should this man succeed in bringing disruption into the Cause of God, he will utterly destroy and exterminate it."
(*Will and Testament of 'Abdu'l-Bahá*, p. 21)

According to the explicit Divine Text, what would be the result of the least transgression by Mírzá Muḥammad-'Alí?

What does Mírzá Muḥammad-'Alí's life teach about free will?

5. "And finally, he [Mírzá Muḥammad-'Alí] who, from the moment the Divine Covenant was born until the end of his life, showed a hatred more unrelenting than that which animated the afore-mentioned adversaries of 'Abdu'l-Bahá, who plotted more energetically than any one of them against Him, and afflicted his Father's Faith with a shame more grievous than any which its external enemies had inflicted upon it—such a man, together with the infamous crew of Covenant-breakers whom he had misled and instigated, was condemned to witness, in a growing measure . . . the frustration of his evil designs, the evaporation of all his hopes, the exposition of his true motives and the complete extinction of his erstwhile honor and glory. . . .

". . . Surviving 'Abdu'l-Bahá by almost twenty years, he who had so audaciously affirmed to His face that he had no assurance he might outlive Him, lived long enough to witness the utter bankruptcy of his cause, leading meanwhile a wretched existence within the walls of a Mansion that had once housed a crowd of his supporters; was denied by the civil authorities, as a result of the crisis he had after 'Abdu'l-Bahá's passing foolishly precipitated, the official custody of his Father's Tomb; was compelled, a few years later, to vacate that same Mansion, which, through his flagrant neglect, had fallen into a dilapidated condition; was stricken with paralysis which crippled half his body; lay bedridden in pain for months before he died; and was buried according to Muslim rites, in the immediate vicinity of a local Muslim shrine, his grave remaining until the present day devoid of even a tombstone—a pitiful reminder of the hollowness of the claims he had advanced, of the depths of infamy to which he had sunk, and of the severity of the retribution his acts had so richly merited."

(Shoghi Effendi, *God Passes By*, pp. 319-20)

What was the fate of Mírzá Muḥammad-'Alí?

What does the rebellion of Mírzá Muḥammad-'Alí teach about the greatness of Bahá'u'lláh's Covenant?

Illustrations

What do the following excerpts reveal about Mírzá Muḥammad-'Alí? What do the excerpts suggest about the suffering that 'Abdu'l-Bahá underwent as a result of Mírzá Muḥammad-'Alí's actions?

"In a celebrated Tablet, the *Lawḥ-i-Hizár Baytí* (Tablet of One Thousand Verses) 'Abdu'l-Bahá describes the grievous events which occurred immediately before and just after the ascension of Bahá'u'lláh. He states that during the days of Bahá'u'lláh's illness, He, 'Abdu'l-Bahá, was in attendance on His blessed Person by day and by night, most of the time in a state of deep sorrow and depression. One day as He lay in His sick-bed, Bahá'u'lláh ordered 'Abdu'l-Bahá to gather all those of His

57

papers which were in the room and place them in two special cases. It was Bahá'u'lláh's practice that whenever He left the Mansion for 'Akká or elsewhere, He used to put all His papers in these large cases. Aware of the implications of this command, 'Abdu'l-Bahá was shaken to the very depths of his being. . . .

". . . When all the papers, the seals and other items had been locked into the cases, Bahá'u'lláh said to 'Abdu'l-Bahá, 'These two now belong to you.' These words, implying the approach of the final hours of Bahá'u'lláh's earthly life, pierced 'Abdu'l-Bahá's heart like an arrow.

"When the ascension took place, 'Abdu'l-Bahá's grief knew no bounds. The shock He sustained as a result of this calamitous event was so intense that He found it difficult to describe it. He says that in the morning, along with His brother, He began the task of preparing the remains for burial. When they were about to wash Bahá'u'lláh's blessed body, Mírzá Muḥammad-'Alí suggested to 'Abdu'l-Bahá that since the floor would become wet, it would be better to take the two cases out of the room into Badí'u'lláh's room. 'Abdu'l-Bahá was at that point in such a state of shock and grief that He was almost unconscious of His surroundings. He never thought that behind this suggestion could be a treacherous plot designed to rob Him of that precious trust.

"He agreed, and the two cases were taken out and that was the last He saw of them.

". . . The *Kitáb-i-'Ahd* was read by Áqá Riḍáy-i-Qannád on the ninth day after the ascension of Bahá'u'lláh in the presence of nine witnesses chosen from among Bahá'u'lláh's companions and members of Bahá'u'lláh's family, including Mírzá Muḥammad-'Alí. . . .

"Soon after that historic day when the *Kitáb-i-'Ahd* was read, one of the Afnán asked 'Abdu'l-Bahá to use one of Bahá'u'lláh's blessed seals to seal a Tablet which had been revealed by Bahá'u'lláh in his honour. When 'Abdu'l-Bahá asked His brothers to give Him the seals of Bahá'u'lláh which had been placed in the cases, they pleaded ignorance, saying they did not know anything about the two cases! Bewildered and perplexed by such a remark, 'Abdu'l-Bahá was plunged further into sorrow and grief. He describes how His whole being began to tremble when He heard such a response from His brothers, and knew that great tests and trials lay ahead. . . ."

(Adib Taherzadeh, *The Covenant of Bahá'u'lláh*, pp. 148-150)

"When the time came to wash the sacred body of Bahá'u'lláh, they brought water into the room. Mírzá Muḥammad-'Alí said to 'Abdu'l-Bahá that since water would be poured around the room, it would be better to remove the two cases to another room so that they would not get wet. 'Abdu'l-Bahá assented and Mírzá Muḥammad-'Alí asked Majdu'd-Dín to move them to my room. This was done and the cases were placed in a special cabinet and locked.

"Three days after the ascension of Bahá'u'lláh, Mírzá Muḥammad-'Alí asked me to give him the keys so that he might open the cases. He said: 'Bahá'u'lláh has placed a certain document in these cases which needs to be studied.' He took the keys from me. The next thing I noticed was that with the help of Majdu'd-Dín, 'Alí Riḍá, his sister, and the mother of Shu'á'u'lláh the cases were taken out of the window onto the balcony of the mansion and from there into the room of Mírzá Muḥammad-'Alí. He took out all the Tablets of Bahá'u'lláh which were addressed to individual believers. When I protested at his action, he explained, among other things, that the responsibility of the protection of the holy writings had been given to him by Bahá'u'lláh and that he had a Tablet to this effect. However, he did not show me any such Tablet. . . . He also indicated to me in a subtle way that the Most Great Branch was against the Cause of Bahá'u'lláh and if these holy writings were to fall into His hands He would destroy them and would obliterate the name and every trace of the Blessed Beauty from this world!

"Another violation by Mírzá Muḥammad-'Alí was the interpolation of the holy writings. For a long time . . . he used to say that he possessed a Tablet from the Supreme Pen concerning the person of 'Abdu'l-Bahá and that if he were to publish it, the credibility of 'Abdu'l-Bahá would be finished and His name effaced forever. He spoke of this on numerous occasions to members of the family. Some time elapsed, during which a few individuals questioned me concerning the Tablet in question. I, therefore, asked Mírzá Muḥammad-'Alí to show it to us but every time I mentioned it to him, he offered me an excuse and sought a pretext to avoid it. Then one day he took out of the case a blessed Tablet which was revealed before Bahá'u'lláh's imprisonment in the Most Great Prison and gave it to me to read. In it Bahá'u'lláh condemns the iniquities and wicked deeds perpetrated by His brother Mírzá Yaḥyá, whom He

59

addresses as 'My brother'. I said to Mírzá Muḥammad-'Alí that this Tablet had no relevance to the present situation. He said: 'I have permission from Bahá'u'lláh to use my pen and interpolate His writings for the protection of the Cause. Now since some individuals have exaggerated the station of 'Abdu'l-Bahá and the Master claims to be the embodiment of divinity, I will erase the words "My brother" and insert in its place "My Greatest Branch". This I will show to some people in order to check His influence.'

"...After a few minutes, he carried out this interpolation in front of my eyes. Successfully, he changed the words 'My brother' to 'My Greatest Branch'. I pointed out to him that this action amounted to the betrayal of God's trust and constituted a sin. I warned him that if he showed the Tablet in this form to anyone, I would divulge the whole event and report the act of interpolation . . . On hearing these words he became disturbed and promised that he would not show the Tablet to anyone. He also requested me not to reveal the matter."

(Summary translation of the confession of Mírzá Badí'u'lláh, quoted in Adib Taherzadeh, *The Child of the Covenant*, pp. 174-75)

Analysis Questions

Answer the following questions. Suggested answers appear in Appendix A.

1. In His Will and Testament, 'Abdu'l-Bahá recounted in detail the evil doings of Mírzá Muḥammad-'Alí. What may have been the reasons for 'Abdu'l-Bahá's emphasis on Mírzá Muḥammad-'Alí's misdeeds? Circle all correct answers.

A. 'Abdu'l-Bahá was seeking revenge for all that Mírzá Muḥammad-'Alí had done to Him.

B. 'Abdu'l-Bahá was establishing why Mírzá Muḥammad-'Alí had deviated from the Covenant and had forfeited the station conferred upon him by Bahá'u'lláh.

C. 'Abdu'l-Bahá was seeking to protect the Faith from Mírzá Muḥammad-'Alí.

D. 'Abdu'l-Bahá was attempting to secure His place in history by showing that He was superior to His half-brother.

2. Even though Bahá'u'lláh had appointed Mírzá Muhammad-'Alí to a rank second only to 'Abdu'l-Bahá, Mírzá Muhammad-'Alí broke the Covenant. Which of the following explanations related to this fact are true? Circle all correct answers.

A. Although he was the son of the Manifestation of God, Mírzá Muhammad-'Alí still possessed free will and could decide whether to be faithful to the Covenant.

B. Bahá'u'lláh could not foresee that Mírzá Muhammad-'Alí would deviate from the Faith.

C. Oftentimes, it is those closest to the Manifestation of God who are least faithful to Him.

D. Even though Bahá'u'lláh may have desired that Mírzá Muhammad-'Alí be faithful, his rebellion demonstrates the power of the Covenant—that not even Bahá'u'lláh's own son could create a schism within the Faith.

3. Which of the following reasons accurately explain why Mírzá Muhammad-'Alí's actions constituted a rebellion but not a schism? Circle all correct answers.

A. Bahá'u'lláh had clearly appointed 'Abdu'l-Bahá as His successor; therefore, any person who deviated was rebelling against the explicit, written authority of Bahá'u'lláh.

B. Although Mírzá Muhammad-'Alí initially attracted a few followers, the verdict of history has been the utter failure of his attempt to create a schism within the Faith.

C. Mírzá Muhammad-'Alí was not attempting to create a schism, but was attempting to bring about minor reforms in the Faith.

D. Because the Covenant of Bahá'u'lláh is so clear, any person who deviates from it has removed himself from the circle of the Faith, not created a division within the circle.

Memorization and Presentation Exercises

A. Memorizing the Sacred and Authoritative Writings

Commit to memory the following quotations (or two of your choosing from this chapter):

"He, verily, is but one of My servants . . . Should he for a moment pass out from under the shadow of the Cause, he surely shall be brought to naught."

> (Bahá'u'lláh, quoted in Shoghi Effendi, *God Passes By*, p. 251)
> (referring to Mírzá Muḥammad-ʿAlí)

"In short, O ye beloved of the Lord! The Center of Sedition, Mírzá Muḥammad'Alí, in accordance with the decisive words of God and by reason of his boundless transgression, hath grievously fallen and been cut off from the Holy Tree."

> (*Will and Testament of ʿAbdu'l-Bahá*, p. 9)

B. Presenting the Themes of the Covenant

Prepare a brief presentation on the theme of the rebellion and excommunication of Mírzá Muḥammad-ʿAlí.

In your explanation, include discussion of:

1. how Mírzá Muḥammad-ʿAlí rebelled against ʿAbdu'l-Bahá;
2. what were the misrepresentations and other misdeeds of Mírzá Muḥammad-ʿAlí; and
3. how and why ʿAbdu'l-Bahá excommunicated Mírzá Muḥammad-ʿAlí.

Share your presentation with a partner or group.

CHAPTER 4
Shoghi Effendi:
The Guardian of the Cause of God

. . . turn unto Shoghi Effendi . . . as he is the sign of God,
the chosen branch, the Guardian of the Cause of God . . . .
— 'Abdu'l-Bahá

Overview

A. The Administrative Order: Establishment,
Uniqueness, and Pillars

'Abdu'l-Bahá's Will and Testament, the first section of which was "composed during one of the darkest periods of His incarceration in the prison-fortress of 'Akká,"[1] exposed the rebellion of Mírzá Muhammad-'Alí and confirmed his excommunication.[2] However, the greater significance of this Document—'Abdu'l-Bahá's "greatest legacy to posterity" and "the brightest emanation of His mind"[3]—was its proclamation and formal establishment of the Administrative Order of the Faith of Bahá'u'lláh.[4] The Will and Testament of 'Abdu'l-Bahá unveiled the character of the Administrative Order, the "precursor, the nucleus and pattern" of the future World Order of Bahá'u'lláh.[5]

In their Writings, the Báb and Bahá'u'lláh had anticipated this World Order. In the Persian Bayán, the Báb had announced the advent of the World Order and explicitly associated it with the name of Bahá'u'lláh: "Well is it with him who fixeth his gaze upon the Order of Bahá'u'lláh, and rendereth thanks unto his Lord! For He will assuredly be made manifest . . ."[6] Bahá'u'lláh had referred to this same Order in the Kitáb-i-Aqdas: "The world's equilibrium hath been upset through the vibrating influence of this most great, this new World Order. Mankind's ordered life hath been revolutionized through the agency of this unique, this wondrous System—the like of which mortal eyes have never witnessed."[7] Confirming, supplementing, and correlating the provisions of the Kitáb-i-Aqdas,[8] the Will and Testament of 'Abdu'l-Bahá "called into being, outlined the features and set in motion the processes"[9] of the Administrative Order, which "would herald the establishment of that World Order."[10] As such, the Will and Testament is the "Charter of Bahá'u'lláh's New World Order."[11]

Because of its "origin and character," the Administrative Order is unique in the world's religious history.[12] The "Administrative Order is fundamentally different from anything that any Prophet has previously established"[13] inasmuch as

> Bahá'u'lláh has Himself revealed its principles, established its institutions, appointed the person to interpret His Word and conferred the necessary authority on the body designed to supplement and apply His legislative ordinances. Therein lies the secret of its strength, its fundamental distinction, and the guarantee against disintegration and schism. Nowhere in the sacred scriptures of any of the world's religious systems . . . do we find any provisions establishing a covenant or providing for an administrative order that can compare in scope and authority with those that lie at the very basis of the Bahá'í Dispensation. Has either Christianity or Islám . . . anything to offer that can measure with, or be regarded as equivalent to, either the Book of Bahá'u'lláh's Covenant or to the Will and Testament of 'Abdu'l-Bahá?[14]. . .
>
> Alone of all the Revelations gone before it this Faith has, through the explicit directions, the repeated warnings, the authenticated safeguards incorporated and elaborated in its teachings, succeeded in raising a structure which the bewildered followers of bankrupt and broken creeds might well approach and critically examine, and seek, ere it is too late, the invulnerable security of its world-embracing shelter.
>
> No wonder that He Who through the operation of His Will has inaugurated so vast and unique an Order

and Who is the Center of so mighty a Covenant should have written these words: "So firm and mighty is this Covenant that from the beginning of time until the present day no religious Dispensation hath produced its like."[15]

Through this Administrative Order to which the Covenant has given birth, Bahá'u'lláh and 'Abdu'l-Bahá have provided "an unfailing source of divine guidance that will endure throughout the Dispensation."[16]

The "twin pillars" of this divinely guided Administrative Order are the institutions of the Guardianship and the Universal House of Justice.[17] In His lifetime, Bahá'u'lláh "instituted the House of Justice and anticipated the Guardianship."[18] Bahá'u'lláh explicitly referred to the institution of the House of Justice in the Kitáb-i-Aqdas and in His other Writings.[19] Moreover, His Most Holy Book contained verses "the implications of which clearly anticipate the institution of the Guardianship."[20]

In His Will and Testament, 'Abdu'l-Bahá unequivocally instituted the Guardianship and outlined its essential functions.[21] In the same Document, He also reaffirmed and elucidated the authority of the Universal House of Justice,[22] described the method for its election, and explained its relationship to the Guardianship.[23] Bahá'u'lláh and 'Abdu'l-Bahá have, therefore, appointed the "twin institutions of the House of Justice and of the Guardianship as their chosen Successors."[24] Upon 'Abdu'l-Bahá's passing in 1921, He was immediately succeeded by the Guardian; however, in principle, the succession passed "not just to the Guardian, but to the Administration, of which the Guardianship and the Universal House of Justice are the crowning institutions."[25]

B. The Appointment and Functions of Shoghi Effendi as Guardian of the Cause of God

In addition to establishing the institution of the Guardianship (and further elucidating the role of the Universal House of Justice), "'Abdu'l-Bahá, in His Will and Testament, appointed Shoghi Effendi .. . as the Guardian and Head of the Faith."[26] The appointment of Shoghi Effendi as "the point of authority in the Faith to which all were to turn"[27] is clear in the Will and Testament. 'Abdu'l-Bahá wrote:

After the passing away of this wronged one, it is incumbent upon the Aghṣán (Branches), the Afnán (Twigs) of the Sacred Lote-Tree, the Hands (pillars) of the Cause of God and the loved ones of the Abhá Beauty to turn unto Shoghi Effendi—the youthful branch branched from the two hallowed and sacred Lote-Trees and the fruit grown from the union of the two offshoots of the Tree of Holiness,—as he is the sign of God, the chosen branch, the Guardian of the Cause of God, he unto whom all the Aghṣán, the Afnán, the Hands of the Cause of God and His loved ones must turn. He is the Interpreter of the Word of God and after him will succeed the first-born of his lineal descendents.[28]

In this passage of His Will, 'Abdu'l-Bahá commanded that after His own death, the male descendents of Bahá'u'lláh ("the Aghṣán"), the relatives of the Báb ("the Afnán"), as well as believers appointed to a special rank ("the Hands of the Cause of God") and other followers of Bahá'u'lláh ("His loved ones") turn to Shoghi Effendi as "the Guardian of the Cause of God." Related to both Bahá'u'lláh and the Báb,[29] Shoghi Effendi was described in the Will and Testament of 'Abdu'l-Bahá as "the youthful branch branched from the two hallowed and sacred Lote-Trees."[30] The term "Lote-Tree" is often used in the Bahá'í Writings "to designate the Manifestation of God."[31]

'Abdu'l-Bahá conferred upon Shoghi Effendi, in his capacity as Guardian, the function of authoritative interpretation of the Word of God: "He is the Interpreter of the Word of God . . . ."[32] As the Guardian would later explain, he was "specifically endowed with such power . . . to reveal the purport and disclose the implications of the utterances of Bahá'u'lláh and of 'Abdu'l-Bahá."[33] "[T]he interpretations of the Guardian represent the true intent inherent in the Sacred Texts."[34] Accordingly, "the Guardian's interpretation is a statement of truth which cannot be varied."[35] "His words are not the Word of God itself. But his interpretation is as binding as the Word."[36] Although the Guardian was the "interpreter of the teachings," he could not "reveal anything apart from the given teachings."[37]

Further to conferring the interpretive function on the Guardian, the Will and Testament of 'Abdu'l-Bahá confirmed the legislative authority of the Universal House of Justice: "It enacteth all ordinances and regulations that are not to be found in the explicit Holy Text."[38] "The interpretation of the Guardian, functioning within his own sphere, is as authoritative and binding as the enactments of the International House of Justice, whose exclusive right and prerogative is to pronounce upon and deliver the final judgment on such laws and ordinances as Bahá'u'lláh has not expressly revealed. Neither can, nor will ever, infringe upon the sacred and prescribed domain of the other."[39] Thus, "the function of making authoritative interpretations of the Teachings is confined solely and exclusively to the Guardian. Neither the Universal House of Justice, nor any other institution, person or group of persons can assume that function."[40]

The Guardian's fundamental object was "to insure the continuity of that divinely-appointed authority which flows from the Source of our Faith, to safeguard the unity of its followers and to maintain the integrity and flexibility of its teachings."[41] He also possessed the authority to "administer" the Faith's "affairs, coordinate its activities, promote its interests, execute its laws and defend its subsidiary institutions."[42]

C. The Infallibility and Station of the Guardian of the Cause of God

An "essential element of the Covenant of Bahá'u'lláh is the acceptance of the infallibility of the Guardian."[43] 'Abdu'l-Bahá declared in His Will and Testament that the Guardian would be divinely and unerringly guided:

> The sacred and youthful branch, the Guardian
> of the Cause of God, as well as the Universal House of
> Justice to be universally elected and established, are both
> under the care and protection of the Abhá Beauty, under
> the shelter and unerring guidance of the Exalted One . . .
> . Whatsoever they decide is of God.[44]

Whatever the Guardian decided was "of God," and he, like the Universal House of Justice, was protected and unerringly guided by Bahá'u'lláh ("the Abhá Beauty") and the Báb ("the Exalted One"): "He is assured the guidance of both Bahá'u'lláh and the Báb, as the Will and Testament of 'Abdu'l-Bahá clearly reveals."[45] Thus, the Guardian's interpretations were "divinely guided."[46]

What was the sphere of the Guardian's unerring guidance? During his ministry, Shoghi Effendi was several times asked to define the sphere of his infallibility. Through his secretary, he provided the following responses:

> The Guardian's infallibility covers interpretation of the revealed word and its application. Likewise any instructions he may issue having to do with the protection of the Faith, or its well being must be closely obeyed, as he is infallible in the protection of the Faith.[47]

> The infallibility of the Guardian is confined to matters which are related strictly to the Cause and interpretation of the teachings . . . .[48]

In sum, as the above passages make clear, the Guardian was infallible in "interpretation of the revealed word," "its application," "protection of the Faith," and "matters . . . related strictly to the Cause." The overwhelming majority of the Guardian's writings fall into these areas.

The Guardian's infallibility was not, however, unlimited. As the Guardian explained, he was "not an infallible authority on subjects such as economics and science, nor does he go into technical matters since his infallibility is confined to 'matters which are related strictly to the Cause.'"[49] Some have suggested that a few factual errors, such as incorrect dates or names, may appear in the Guardian's historical writings. The Universal House of Justice has explained that "in the matter of accuracy of historical fact, Shoghi Effendi had to rely on available information."[50] Further elucidating this point, the House of Justice has stated:

The faith of the believers should not be disturbed, nor their adherence to the provisions of the Covenant diminished, by the occasional discovery of factual inaccuracies in the Guardian's writings such as *God Passes By* or his translation of *Nabil's Narrative*. It is useful to recall the following description penned by Amatu'l-Bahá Rúḥíyyih Khánum of Shoghi Effendi's preparation for writing *God Passes By*, taken from her book *The Priceless Pearl*:

> The method of Shoghi Effendi in writing *God Passes By* was to sit down for a year and read every book of the Bahá'í Writings in Persian and English, and every book written about the Faith by Bahá'ís, whether in manuscript form or published, and everything written by non-Bahá'ís that contained significant references to it. I think, in all, this must have covered the equivalent of at least two hundred books. As he read he made notes and compiled and marshalled his facts. Anyone who has ever tackled a work of an historical nature knows how much research is involved, how often one has to decide, in the light of relevant material, between this date given in one place and that date given in another, how back-breaking the whole work is. How much more so then was such a work for the Guardian who had, at the same time, to prepare for the forthcoming Centenary of the Faith and make decisions regarding the design of the superstructure of the Báb's Shrine. When all the ingredients of his book had been assembled Shoghi Effendi commenced weaving them into the fabric of his picture of the significance of the first century of the Bahá'í Dispensation.

That some of the historical reference material he consulted may have contained inaccuracies, which inadvertently found their way into his book, should not be surprising. Such factual discrepancies do not result in any blemish on the infallible insight with which the Guardian treats such subjects as the development of the Cause of Bahá'u'lláh, the significance and import of the turbulent events in its history, and the interpretation of its Teachings.[51]

The Guardian's decisions were "guided by God," but he was not "like the Prophet, omniscient at will, in spite of the fact that he often senses a situation or condition without having any detailed knowledge of it."[52] As has been further explained on Shoghi Effendi's behalf:

The Guardian's personal powers are not unlimited and are different from those possessed by the Master. But the degree of guidance which God may choose to vouchsafe him is unlimited, as it comes from Bahá'u'lláh and not himself. Any extraordinary manifestation of knowledge or intuition he might on some occasions demonstrate must not be attributed to his possession of powers akin to the Master's, but rather to a manifestation of the will of Bahá'u'lláh guiding him for His own reasons on that occasion.[53]

The Guardian shared with 'Abdu'l-Bahá "the right and obligation to interpret the Bahá'í teachings"[54] and was infallibly guided like 'Abdu'l-Bahá in discharging this function—"overshadowed by the unfailing, the unerring protection of Bahá'u'lláh and of the Báb."[55] Yet, Shoghi Effendi did not have the same station as 'Abdu'l-Bahá. Shoghi Effendi was "essentially human" and could never claim to be "the perfect exemplar of the teachings of Bahá'u'lláh or the stainless mirror that reflects His light."[56] The distance separating the Guardian from 'Abdu'l-Bahá was "far, far greater" than the distance separating 'Abdu'l-Bahá from Bahá'u'lláh.[57] Because the Guardian was essentially human, to pray to him or to celebrate or commemorate any act associated with his life would not be appropriate.[58] Nevertheless, his interpretations are as binding on believers as the Word of God itself.[59]

D. Obedience to the Guardian of the Cause of God

'Abdu'l-Bahá commanded obedience to the Guardian of the Faith:

> The mighty stronghold shall remain impregnable and safe through obedience to him who is the Guardian of the Cause of God. It is incumbent upon the members of the House of Justice, upon all the Aghsán, the Afnán, the Hands of the Cause of God to show their obedience, submissiveness and subordination unto the Guardian of the Cause of God, to turn unto him and be lowly before him. He that opposeth him hath opposed the True One, will make a breach in the Cause of God, will subvert His Word and will become a manifestation of the Center of Sedition.[60]

Further, in reference to both Shoghi Effendi (as Guardian) and the Universal House of Justice, 'Abdu'l-Bahá wrote:

> Whoso obeyeth him not, neither obeyeth them, hath not obeyed God; whoso rebelleth against him and against them hath rebelled against God; whoso opposeth him hath opposed God; whoso contendeth with them hath contended with God; whoso disputeth with him hath disputed with God; whoso denieth him hath denied God; whoso disbelieveth in him hath disbelieved in God; whoso deviateth, separateth himself and turneth aside from him hath in truth deviated, separated himself and turned aside from God. May the wrath, the fierce indignation, the vengeance of God rest upon him![61]

In this passage, 'Abdu'l-Bahá equated disobedience to the Guardian as disobedience to God Himself. Today, obedience to the

Guardian requires adherence to his interpretations: "The interpretations written by the beloved Guardian . . . are equally binding" as the Sacred Text itself.[62] In a letter on his behalf, the Guardian explained: "It is not for individual believers to limit the sphere of the Guardian's authority, or to judge when they have to obey the Guardian and when they are free to reject his judgement. Such an attitude would evidently lead to confusion and to schism. The Guardian being the appointed interpreter of the Teachings, it is his responsibility to state what matters which, affecting the interests of the Faith, demand on the part of the believers complete and unqualified obedience to his instructions."[63]

Study Questions

Answer the following questions based on the above Overview:

CONTENT QUESTIONS

1. What Document proclaimed and formally established the Administrative Order?

2. The "Administrative Order is fundamentally different from anything that any _____ has previously established, inasmuch as _____ has Himself revealed its _____, established its _____, appointed the person to _____ His Word and conferred the necessary authority on the body designed to _____ and _____ His legislative ordinances."

3. What institutions were the "chosen Successors" of Bahá'u'lláh and 'Abdu'l-Bahá?

4. 'Abdu'l-Bahá's Will and Testament conferred what major function upon the Guardian?

5. List at least four general responsibilities of the Guardian.

6. "The sacred and youthful branch, the Guardian of the Cause of God, as well as the Universal House of Justice . . ., are both under the care and

_____ of the _____ _____, under the shelter and _____ guidance of the _____ _____ .... Whatsoever they decide is of _____."

7. What was the sphere of the infallibility of the Guardian?

8. How did Shoghi Effendi's station compare with 'Abdu'l-Bahá's?

9. "The mighty stronghold shall remain impregnable and _____ through _____ to him who is the Guardian of the Cause of God."

APPLICATION/DISCUSSION QUESTIONS
1. Shoghi Effendi wrote: "They [Bahá'u'lláh and 'Abdu'l-Bahá] have . . ., in unequivocal and emphatic language, appointed those twin institutions of the House of Justice and of the Guardianship as their chosen Successors . . . ." Based on this passage, draw a diagram of the succession of authority in the Bahá'í Faith. Next, draw a diagram illustrating the chronological succession of authority in the Bahá'í Faith.

2. Were the interpretations of the Guardian just for the period in which he lived, or are they relevant today? If the latter, explain how the Guardian's interpretations continue to guide Bahá'ís and Bahá'í institutions.

3. What are examples of actions of the Guardian that would have been unerringly guided?

4. Today, what does it mean to show "obedience" to the Guardian? How can such obedience be "complete and unqualified"?

Quotations for Reflection
Answer the questions following the quotations below:

1. "The Will and Testament of 'Abdu'l-Bahá is one of the instrumentalities through which the divinely ordained Administrative Order of Bahá'u'lláh is perpetuated and the essential unity of His Cause maintained. Thus

acceptance of the Master's Will and Testament is basic in the faith of every Bahá'í and is an integral part of the Covenant which the believer undertakes to uphold when he becomes a Bahá'í."
    (The Universal House of Justice, to an individual, March 23, 1975)

What is an integral part of the Covenant?

Why is acceptance of the Will and Testament of 'Abdu'l-Bahá essential in the faith of every Bahá'í?

2. "No Prophet before Bahá'u'lláh . . . has established, authoritatively and in writing, anything comparable to the Administrative Order which the authorized Interpreter of Bahá'u'lláh's teachings has instituted, an Order which, by virtue of the administrative principles which its Author has formulated, the institutions He has established, and the right of interpretation with which He has invested its Guardian, must and will, in a manner unparalleled in any previous religion, safeguard from schism the Faith from which it has sprung."
    (Shoghi Effendi, *God Passes By*, p. 326)

What features of the Administrative Order will safeguard the Faith from schism?

How does the right of interpretation invested in the Guardian continue to safeguard the Faith from schism?

3. "They [Bahá'u'lláh and 'Abdu'l-Bahá] have . . ., in unequivocal and emphatic language, appointed those twin institutions of the House of Justice and of the Guardianship as their chosen Successors, destined to apply the principles, promulgate the laws, protect the institutions, adapt loyally and intelligently the Faith to the requirements of progressive society, and consummate the incorruptible inheritance which the Founders of the Faith have bequeathed to the world."
    (Shoghi Effendi, *The World Order of Bahá'u'lláh*, pp. 19-20)

Who are the "chosen Successors" of Bahá'u'lláh and 'Abdu'l-Bahá, and what are the roles they are destined to play?

Why is it significant that Bahá'u'lláh and 'Abdu'l-Bahá had two "chosen Successors"?

4. "O ye the faithful loved ones of 'Abdu'l-Bahá! It is incumbent upon you to take the greatest care of Shoghi Effendi, the twig that hath branched from and the fruit given forth by the two hallowed and Divine Lote-Trees . . . .

"For he is, after 'Abdu'l-Bahá, the Guardian of the Cause of God, the Afnán, the Hands (pillars) of the Cause and the beloved of the Lord must obey him and turn unto him. He that obeyeth him not, hath not obeyed God; he that turneth away from him, hath turned away from God and he that denieth him, hath denied the True One."
(*Will and Testament of 'Abdu'l-Bahá*, p. 25)

How did 'Abdu'l-Bahá describe Shoghi Effendi?

Why did 'Abdu'l-Bahá equate disobedience to the Guardian as disobedience to God?

5. "Once the mind and heart have grasped the fact that God guides men through a Mouthpiece, a human being, a Prophet, infallible and unerring, it is only a logical projection of this acceptance to also accept the station of 'Abdu'l-Bahá and the Guardians. . . . If a person can accept Bahá'u'lláh's function, it should not present any difficulty to them to also accept what He has ordained in a Divinely guided individual in matters pertaining to the Faith."
(On behalf of Shoghi Effendi, *Directives from the Guardian*, p. 30)

Acceptance of the Guardian is a logical projection of what?

Why does acceptance of Bahá'u'lláh's function logically lead to acceptance of the station of the Guardian?

75

6. "He is the Guardian of the Cause in the very fullness of that term, and the appointed interpreter of its teachings, and is guided in his decisions to do that which protects it and fosters its growth and highest interests."

(On behalf of Shoghi Effendi, *Letters from the Guardian to Australia and New Zealand: 1923-1957*, p. 55)

In what ways were the Guardian's decisions guided?

Give an example of the way in which the Guardian's decisions protected the Faith and fostered its growth and highest interests.

Illustrations

What do the following illustrations teach about the attitude with which believers should view the guidance of the Guardian?

"The Guardian was the center of spiritual power in the world 'and that power continually radiated from him; it was a driving spiritual energy which impelled him forward'. To be close to that power, to live near that force, was not an easy thing; it was something to aspire to but he [Hand of the Cause of God Leroy Ioas] felt 'few of us achieved much in the way of nearness to the Guardian's spirit'. The Guardian could speak with such power that the very walls of the room seemed to vibrate and at such times 'you knew it was more than a man speaking', it was the power of the spirit speaking through him. . . .

"The unerring guidance of God encompassed Shoghi Effendi at all times, as promised by the Master, and to observe this mysterious process at work was a 'tremendous experience'. The Bahá'ís wondered if this guidance operated in all matters or only in regard to the Faith. Leroy said he frankly did not know where it began or ended; he had discussed the question with Rúḥíyyih Khánum, who has written that she herself did not know 'where Shoghi Effendi ended and the Guardian began'. Once Leroy even broached the subject to Shoghi Effendi. The Guardian opened his eyes very wide and looked at him: 'Leroy, have you not read the Will and Testament of the Master?' Leroy replied that he had read it many times, and the Guardian said: 'Well, what does it say?'

Leroy answered that while he knew what was said in the Will, he had been asked to write many letters to Bahá'ís wanting advice on personal matters and Shoghi Effendi almost always advised them to consult experts and follow the advice they received. 'Yes,' said the Guardian, 'this is in accordance with the teachings of Bahá'u'lláh, the Bahá'ís must consult experts at all times.' Leroy said this had led him to ask whether the Guardian was guided in all matters or only those relating to the Cause itself. The Guardian replied: 'In the Will and Testament, there are no limitations placed on the infallibility of the Guardian.' On another occasion the Guardian told Leroy: 'Bahá'u'lláh has conferred upon me a power that enables me to know what I need to know.'

"We don't understand, Leroy said, what this power is which flowed through the Guardian, but we constantly saw it in operation. We do know that when the Guardian decided upon a certain course of action for the good of the Faith, it was because he had been guided to do so. He confirmed this to us many times. Thus his insistence that the Bahá'ís act immediately to accomplish the things he knew must be done.

"There were constant small examples of this penetrating power. One night Shoghi Effendi was speaking of the manner in which the Universal House of Justice and the National Assemblies would function together in future. As he spoke, Leroy thought to himself that under certain circumstances what the Guardian was describing would not work, and he made a mental note to ask for further elucidation. When the Guardian had completed his thought, he took a sip of coffee and turned to Leroy: 'You wouldn't think this would work under certain circumstances, but I will explain to you how it does.'

"In another instance the Guardian was deeply concerned with the spirit behind an action taken by the U.S. National Assembly. He turned to Leroy and said, 'You were on the Assembly when this was first discussed; tell me what their thinking was.' As Leroy gave some details, the Guardian stopped him, saying, 'I will tell you what occurred.' He then explained what had happened as if he had been at the meeting, and asked whether he was right or wrong. You are exactly right, Shoghi Effendi, Leroy responded, even to the details."

(Anita Ioas Chapman, *Leroy Ioas: Hand of the Cause of God*, pp. 286-87)

"It is seven o'clock in the morning on a spring day in 1957. My brother, sister, and I are getting ready for school. My father [Hand of the Cause of God Zikrullah Khadem] is about to go to work. It is time for breakfast.

"There is a knock at the door. My younger brother answers. 'It is the cable [telegram] man!' he announces. We know this means that a cable has come from the beloved Guardian. We all know what to do when such a cable arrives.

"My brother receives the cable with respect, signs for it, and gives the messenger a generous tip. He carries the cable to my father and hands it over, using both hands, the Persian sign of respect.

"My father is already in another world. He has performed his ablutions and has been praying since the knock at the door to prepare himself for receiving the message. He seems to be in the presence of the beloved Guardian.

"My father kisses the cable and raises it to his forehead, indicating the utmost respect for the sacred communication. Then he opens the envelope, takes out the paper, and reads the message silently. We watch him with admiration and wait to see if there is something in the cable he feels he can share with us.

"My father's agenda for the day has just changed. He will attend to the cable received from the Guardian before doing anything else. He has just canceled all of the important meetings he had scheduled for the morning. We know what he is going to do when we go to school. He will be on his way downtown to the central post office, the only place from which one could send a telegram. The city is crowded. The traffic is heavy. It takes about an hour to go to the post office. He will stand in the post office queue. When his turn comes, he will submit a cable to the Holy Land indicating receipt of the Guardian's cable.

"He will then be relieved that he has performed part of his duty. Leaving the post office, he will then deliver the message to the person addressed by the Guardian. Having delivered the message, he will resume his other activities.

"What has happened today is not a rare occurrence. It happens several times a week, and often several times a day. I am fascinated by his consistency of approach every time. I marvel at his devotion to his job of serving as the messenger for the beloved Guardian."

(Riaz Khadem, "The Power of Example," in Javidukht Khadem, *Zikrullah Khadem*, pp. 205-06)

Analysis Questions

Answer the following questions. Suggested answers appear in Appendix A.

1. Which one of the following statements best describes the succession of authority in the Bahá'í Faith?

   A. Bahá'u'lláh was succeeded by the Administrative Order.

   B. Bahá'u'lláh was succeeded by 'Abdu'l-Bahá; 'Abdu'l-Bahá was succeeded by the Guardianship; and the Guardianship was succeeded by the Universal House of Justice.

   C. Bahá'u'lláh was succeeded by 'Abdu'l-Bahá; the twin institutions of the Guardianship and the Universal House of Justice were the successors of Bahá'u'lláh and 'Abdu'l-Bahá.

   D. Bahá'u'lláh was succeeded by 'Abdu'l-Bahá; 'Abdu'l-Bahá was succeeded by the Guardianship; and the Guardianship was succeeded by the Administrative Order.

2. Which of the following statements accurately describe the responsibilities conferred upon the Guardian. Circle all correct answers.

   A. The Guardian interpreted the Word of God.

   B. The Guardian enacted laws not expressly recorded in the Book.

   C. The Guardian applied the principles of the Faith and promulgated its laws.

   D. The Guardian administered the Faith's activities and coordinated its activities.

3. Which of the following statements accurately reflect the Bahá'í Teachings on the question of the station and function of Shoghi Effendi? Circle all correct answers.

   A. Shoghi Effendi was essentially human; therefore, his

interpretations have the same status as those of any other believer.
B. Shoghi Effendi was essentially human; however, he was infallibly guided by Bahá'u'lláh and the Báb in his interpretations.
C. Shoghi Effendi's interpretations of the Word of God were inspired, but believers can choose whether to obey the interpretations.
D. Shoghi Effendi's interpretations are equally binding as the Sacred Text.

Memorization and Presentation Exercises

A. Memorizing the Sacred and Authoritative Writings
Commit to memory the following quotations (or two of your choosing from this chapter):

"The world's equilibrium hath been upset through the vibrating influence of this most great, this new World Order. Mankind's ordered life hath been revolutionized through the agency of this unique, this wondrous System—the like of which mortal eyes have never witnessed."
(Bahá'u'lláh, *The Kitáb-i-Aqdas*, parag. 181)

"The sacred and youthful branch, the Guardian of the Cause of God, as well as the Universal House of Justice to be universally elected and established, are both under the care and protection of the Abhá Beauty, under the shelter and unerring guidance of the Exalted One . . . . Whatsoever they decide is of God."
(*Will and Testament of 'Abdu'l-Bahá*, p. 11)

B. Presenting the Themes of the Covenant

Prepare a brief presentation on the theme of Shoghi Effendi as Guardian of the Cause of God.

In your explanation, include discussion of:

1. how 'Abdu'l-Bahá formally established the Administrative Order and why the Administrative Order is unique;
2. the appointment and functions of Shoghi Effendi as Guardian of the Cause of God; and
3. the infallibility of the Guardian and the need for obedience to him.

Share your presentation with a partner or group.

CHAPTER 5
The Passing of Shoghi Effendi and the Ministry of the Hands of the Cause of God

Light and glory, greeting and praise
be upon the Hands of His Cause . . . .
— Bahá'u'lláh

Overview

A. The Requirements of Succession and the Passing of Shoghi Effendi

Further to appointing Shoghi Effendi as "the Guardian of the Cause of God,"[1] 'Abdu'l-Bahá's Will and Testament established the Guardianship as a hereditary institution: "after him [Shoghi Effendi] will succeed the first-born of his lineal descendents."[2] The Will and Testament set forth specific conditions for Shoghi Effendi's appointment of his successor:

> O ye beloved of the Lord! It is incumbent upon the Guardian of the Cause of God to appoint in his own life-time him that shall become his successor, that differences may not arise after his passing. He that is appointed must manifest in himself detachment from all worldly things, must be the essence of purity, must show in himself the fear of God, knowledge, wisdom and learning. Thus, should the first-born of the Guardian of the Cause of God not manifest in himself the truth of the words:—"The child is the secret essence of its sire," that is, should he not inherit of the spiritual within him (the Guardian of the Cause of God) and his glorious lineage not be matched with a goodly character, then must he, (the Guardian of the Cause of God) choose another branch to succeed him.

The Hands of the Cause of God must elect from their own number nine persons that shall at all times be occupied in the important services in the work of the Guardian of the Cause of God. The election of these nine must be carried either unanimously or by majority from the company of the Hands of the Cause of God and these, whether unanimously or by a majority vote, must give their assent to the choice of the one whom the Guardian of the Cause of God hath chosen as his successor. This assent must be given in such wise as the assenting and dissenting voices may not be distinguished (i.e., secret ballot).[3]

As these provisions of the Will and Testament make clear, 'Abdu'l-Bahá specified several requirements for the Guardian's appointment of his successor:

(1) It is "incumbent upon the Guardian of the Cause of God to appoint in his own life-time him that shall become his successor . . . ."[4]

(2) The appointee "must manifest in himself detachment from all worldly things, must be the essence of purity, must show in himself the fear of God, knowledge, wisdom and learning."[5]

(3) "[A]fter him [Shoghi Effendi] will succeed the first-born of his lineal descendents."[6] Should "the first-born of the Guardian of the Cause of God . . . not inherit of the spiritual" and not possess "a goodly character," then must the Guardian "choose another branch" (male descendent of Bahá'u'lláh) "to succeed him."[7]

(4) "The Hands of the Cause of God must elect from their own number nine persons . . . ."[8]

(5) And these nine elected Hands "must give their assent to the choice of the one whom the Guardian of the Cause of God hath chosen as his successor."[9]

84

Thus, 'Abdu'l-Bahá specified who could appoint the Guardian's successor (Shoghi Effendi could); when the appointment was to be made (in Shoghi Effendi's lifetime); what spiritual qualities the successor had to possess (detachment, fear of God, knowledge, etc.); who the successor could be (Shoghi Effendi's "first-born" or another "branch"); and who had to approve the choice of the successor (nine elected members from among the Hands of the Cause of God). Each of these conditions had to be satisfied for an individual to have become Shoghi Effendi's successor.

By the time of his passing in 1957, Shoghi Effendi had not, however, appointed a successor. The appointment of a successor was made impossible because Shoghi Effendi did not have any children and, therefore, no "first-born" child; nor was another "branch" (male descendent of Bahá'u'lláh) eligible for appointment inasmuch as all had broken the Covenant. Moreover, the other conditions for the appointment of a successor had not been satisfied: Shoghi Effendi had not "in his own life-time" appointed a successor; he had not pointed to a successor who had "inherit[ed] of the spiritual"; and the Hands of the Cause had not "elect[ed] from their own number nine persons" who had given "their assent to the choice of the one whom the Guardian of the Cause of God hath chosen as his successor." Thus, the requirements for the appointment of a successor, as delineated in the Will and Testament of 'Abdu'l-Bahá, could not be satisfied.

The death of Shoghi Effendi was a great shock to Bahá'ís around the world. In addition, the community had to cope with the fact that Shoghi Effendi had been unable to appoint a successor and had not left a will or other written instructions.[10] As the Universal House of Justice later observed, "appalling dangers . . . faced the infant Cause when it was suddenly deprived of . . . Shoghi Effendi."[11] Yet, the power of Bahá'u'lláh's Covenant soon became evident. As discussed below, following Shoghi Effendi's passing, the Faith maintained its unity and integrity under the leadership, and through the historic services, of the Hands of the Cause of God: "The entire history of religion shows no comparable record of such strict self-discipline, such absolute loyalty and such complete self-abnegation by the leaders of a religion finding themselves suddenly deprived of their divinely inspired guide."[12]

B. The Ministry of the Hands of the Cause of God

Although Shoghi Effendi had not appointed a successor, he had taken steps for the Bahá'í community to be led and protected by the institution of the Hands of the Cause of God. During His lifetime, Bahá'u'lláh created the institution of the Hands of the Cause of God[13] and appointed a few believers to the position.[14] Subsequently, 'Abdu'l-Bahá designated others as Hands of the Cause.[15] The institution was "formally defined and established by 'Abdu'l-Bahá in His Will and Testament,"[16] wherein He emphasized and clarified the responsibilities of the Hands of the Cause.[17] These responsibilities included protecting and propagating the Faith.[18]

'Abdu'l-Bahá wrote in His Will and Testament that the "body of the Hands of the Cause of God is under the direction of the Guardian of the Cause of God."[19] The Hands were to be "nominated and appointed by the Guardian."[20] In the course of his ministry, Shoghi Effendi appointed forty-two believers as Hands of the Cause of God.[21] From the early 1920's until the early 1950's, he posthumously designated ten individuals as Hands of the Cause. In the last six years of his ministry, he appointed thirty-two Bahá'ís, during their lifetimes, as Hands of the Cause. These included a contingent of twelve individuals appointed in 1951, a second contingent of seven appointed in 1952, and five others appointed between 1952 and 1957. On October 2, 1957, Shoghi Effendi appointed a final contingent of eight Hands. When he passed away in November 1957, there were twenty-seven Hands living.[22]

In making the appointments, Shoghi Effendi referred to the Hands of the Cause as an "august Institution" destined to assume "the dual sacred responsibility for protection and propagation of the Cause of Bahá'u'lláh."[23] In June 1957, he elaborated on the responsibilities of the institution of the Hands of the Cause:

> To its newly assured responsibility to assist National Spiritual Assemblies of the Bahá'í world in the specific purpose of effectively prosecuting the World Spiritual Crusade, the primary obligation to watch over and insure protection to the Bahá'í world community, in close collaboration with these same National Assemblies, is now added.[24]

Shoghi Effendi declared that the institutions of the Hands of the Cause and the National Spiritual Assemblies occupy "with the Universal House of Justice, next to the Institution of the Guardianship, foremost rank in the divinely ordained administrative hierarchy of the World Order of Bahá'u'lláh."[25] Moreover, he explained that "[t]he security of our precious Faith, the preservation of the spiritual health of the Bahá'í communities, the vitality of the faith of its individual members, the proper functioning of its laboriously erected institutions, the fruition of its worldwide enterprises, the fulfilment of its ultimate destiny, all are directly dependent upon the befitting discharge of the weighty responsibilities now resting upon the members of these two institutions" of the Hands and National Assemblies.[26] As between the Hands of the Cause and the National Spiritual Assemblies, the Hands occupied a "superior" "rank and position."[27] Just weeks before his passing, in announcing the appointment of the final contingent of the Hands of the Cause, Shoghi Effendi referred to the Hands as "one of the cardinal and pivotal institutions ordained by Bahá'u'lláh, and confirmed in the Will and Testament of 'Abdu'l-Bahá."[28] He further entitled them "the Chief Stewards of Bahá'u'lláh's embryonic World Commonwealth" and reiterated that they were invested with "the dual function of guarding over the security, and of insuring the propagation" of the Faith of Bahá'u'lláh.[29]

After the death of Shoghi Effendi on November 4, 1957, the Hands of the Cause assumed the international administration of the Faith. Based on the position and powers conferred upon them by Shoghi Effendi, the Hands concluded that among the then-existing institutions of the Faith, they were responsible for overseeing the worldwide affairs of the Faith. They determined that as "the Chief Stewards of Bahá'u'lláh's embryonic World Commonwealth,"[30] they would exercise leadership of the Faith until such time as the Universal House of Justice would be elected.[31] This was done with the "complete agreement and loyalty of the National Spiritual Assemblies and the body of the believers."[32] Shortly after assuming direction of the Faith, the Hands of the Cause announced that the election of the Universal House of Justice would take place in Riḍván 1963.[33]

"From the very outset of their custodianship of the Cause of God the Hands realized that since they had no certainty of divine guidance such as is incontrovertibly assured to the Guardian and to the Universal House of Justice, their one safe course was to follow with undeviating firmness the instructions and policies of Shoghi Effendi."[34] The Hands of the Cause did just that: They led the Bahá'í community in fulfilling the goals of the Ten Year Crusade, the plan that had been devised by Shoghi Effendi for the Bahá'í world. During the period of the Hands' ministry from 1957 to 1963, impressive victories were achieved in the expansion of the Faith. For example, the number of localities wherein Bahá'ís resided increased from some four thousand in 1957 to over eleven thousand in 1963, and the number of National Spiritual Assemblies more than doubled from twenty-six in 1957 to fifty-six in 1963.[35]

C. The Defection of Mason Remey

On November 25, 1957, all twenty-seven Hands of the Cause agreed to a resolution declaring that Shoghi Effendi "passed away in London (England) on the 4th of November, 1957, without having appointed his successor."[36] The Hands further resolved: "[I]t is now fallen upon us as Chief Stewards of the Bahá'í World Faith to preserve the unity, the security and the development of the Bahá'í World Community and all its institutions . . . ."[37] In a proclamation issued on that same day to the Bahá'ís of the East and West, the Hands unanimously stated that "the beloved Guardian had left no heir. The Aghsán (branches) one and all are either dead or have been declared violators of the Covenant by the Guardian for their faithlessness to the Master's Will and Testament and their hostility to him . . . . [N]o successor to Shoghi Effendi could have been appointed by him . . . ."[38]

Mason Remey was one of the Hands of the Cause who signed the above-referenced resolution and proclamation. Nevertheless, in April 1960, at the age of eighty-six, he "proclaimed" that he was the "second Guardian" of the Bahá'í Faith.[39] Remey asserted this claim despite the Will and Testament's clear authority to the contrary. As detailed above, the Will and Testament set forth certain objectively verifiable conditions for the appointment of Shoghi Effendi's successor. These conditions could not possibly have been fulfilled in the person of Mason Remey: (1) In no document had Remey been identified by Shoghi Effendi as his "successor";[40] (2) such an appointment had not occurred in the "life-time" of Shoghi Effendi;[41] (3) Remey was not among the Aghsán—the "first-born of the Guardian" or another "branch";[42] and (4) the Hands had not elected from among themselves nine persons who had given "their assent to the choice of the one whom the Guardian of the Cause of God hath chosen as his successor."[43]

Remey claimed that he was the second Guardian because Shoghi Effendi had in 1951 appointed him as the president of the International Bahá'í Council.[44] Remey's argument was as follows: Shoghi Effendi had indicated that the International Bahá'í Council was the forerunner of the Universal House of Justice.[45] Further, according to 'Abdu'l-Bahá's Will and Testament, the Guardian was the sacred head of the Universal House of Justice. Remey asserted that by virtue of his appointment to the position of president of the International Bahá'í Council, he was the president of the Universal House of Justice and, thus, the Guardian.[46]

Remey's argument was flawed for numerous reasons:

(1) It ignored the Will and Testament's explicit provisions regarding how Shoghi Effendi was to appoint his successor.

(2) There had never been a promise by Shoghi Effendi that the membership of the *appointed* International Bahá'í Council would carry over to the *elected* Universal House of Justice.[47] Indeed, 'Abdu'l-Bahá had provided instructions on how the membership of the Universal House of Justice was to be composed, namely, through election.[48] 'Abdu'l-Bahá had not indicated that a believer could be appointed to the Universal House of Justice.

(3) If the president of the International Bahá'í Council was to be the president of the Universal House of Justice (and, therefore, the Guardian), then Shoghi Effendi would have presumably named himself the president of the International Bahá'í Council.[49]

(4) Whereas the appointments of 'Abdu'l-Bahá and Shoghi Effendi had been explicit and in writing, Remey was incapable of offering a single written word in support of his claim. 'Abdu'l-Bahá had

counseled believers that should anyone claim to be the Center of the Faith, "ask him to produce a written proof of the authority he follows."[50] Remey could not offer any written proof.

(5) 'Abdu'l-Bahá had declared that "ere the expiration of a thousand years, no one has the right to utter a single word, even to claim the station of Guardianship."[51] Yet, Remey was asserting precisely such a claim.

(6) Finally, Remey's contentions contradicted his signed declarations that the "Guardian had left no heir," that the "Aghsán (branches) one and all are either dead or have been declared violators of the Covenant," and that "no successor to Shoghi Effendi could have been appointed by him . . . ."[52]

The other Hands of the Cause gave Remey every opportunity to abandon his claim, exposing the fallacies of his arguments and repeatedly warning him about the consequences of his actions.[53] When he persisted, the Hands were forced to declare him and the few who were misled by him as violators of the Covenant.[54]

Remey's subsequent actions showed the lengths to which he would go in attacking the Covenant and challenging the actions of Shoghi Effendi. For example, Remey announced that Shoghi Effendi had mistakenly formed the Administration upon the Bábí Faith, rather than the Bahá'í Faith. Therefore, the "only thing" for Remey to do as the second Guardian was to "set matters aright" and "discard all which Shoghi Effendi did and to institute a New Faith" that would lead to the establishment of the "TRUE Baha'i Faith," which had "not yet been established in the world."[55] Remey also referred to the "violations of the Faith that were made unwittingly by Shoghi Effendi."[56] Such statements further evidenced Remey's disregard of the Bahá'í Teachings. In a letter on his behalf, Shoghi Effendi had stated: "Future Guardians . . . cannot 'abrogate' the interpretations of former Guardians."[57]

The Hands of the Cause had the authority to expel Remey and others who followed in his path. The Will and Testament of 'Abdu'l-Bahá had given the Hands the authority to excommunicate those who would oppose the Guardian: "My object is to show that the Hands of the Cause of

God must be ever watchful and so soon as they find anyone beginning to oppose and protest against the Guardian of the Cause of God, cast him out from the congregation of the people of Bahá and in no wise accept any excuse from him."[58] 'Abdu'l-Bahá had even envisioned the possibility that one from "within" the company of the Hands could seek to create division in the Faith: "Should any, within or without the company of the Hands of the Cause of God disobey and seek division, the wrath of God and His vengeance will be upon him, for he will have caused a breach in the true Faith of God."[59]

The Hands of the Cause concluded that Remey's unfounded claim to the Guardianship was in conflict with the spirit and letter of the Will and Testament of 'Abdu'l-Bahá and a repudiation of that sacred document, the Charter on which the institution of the Guardianship rested. Remey had, in effect, opposed and protested against the Guardian and had sought to create division—a fact confirmed by Remey's own subsequent statement that he wished to "discard all which Shoghi Effendi did and to institute a New Faith."[60] In light of Remey's actions, he could, according to the Will and Testament of 'Abdu'l-Bahá, be "cast . . . out" by the Hands of the Cause "from the congregation of the people of Bahá."[61] In a cable dated July 26, 1960, the Hands announced Remey's excommunication.[62]

For the fourteen years following his excommunication, Remey continued to press his claim, but failed to attract any appreciable following or to create a division within the Faith. In 1974, in the one hundredth year of his life, he died and was buried without religious rites, having been abandoned by his one-time followers.[63] Since Remey's death, those who originally accepted his claims have become hopelessly divided and their groups have essentially disintegrated.[64] Remey's arrogant attempt to usurp the Guardianship and his utter failure to create division within the Faith provided yet another example of the futility of all efforts to undermine the impregnable Covenant of the Faith of Bahá'u'lláh.[65]

D. The Significance of the Services of the Hands of the Cause of God

The Hands of the Cause thus protected the Faith of God during the critical years following the passing of Shoghi Effendi. With absolute faith in the Writings and in accordance with the instructions in the Will and

Testament of 'Abdu'l-Bahá, the Hands called for the election of the Universal House of Justice. They "even went so far as to ask that they themselves be not voted for."[66] On April 21, 1963, on the occasion of the one hundredth anniversary of the Declaration of Bahá'u'lláh, the Universal House of Justice was elected.[67] Just days after its formation, the House of Justice described the significance of the services the Hands of the Cause had rendered in the preceding six years:

> The paeans of joy and gratitude, of love and adoration which we now raise to the throne of Bahá'u'lláh would be inadequate, and the celebrations of this Most Great Jubilee in which, as promised by our beloved Guardian, we are now engaged, would be marred were no tribute paid at this time to the Hands of the Cause of God. For they share the victory with their beloved commander, he who raised them up and appointed them. They kept the ship on its course and brought it safe to port. The Universal House of Justice, with pride and love, recalls on this supreme occasion its profound admiration for the heroic work which they have accomplished. We do not wish to dwell on the appalling dangers which faced the infant Cause when it was suddenly deprived of our beloved Shoghi Effendi, but rather to acknowledge with all the love and gratitude of our hearts the reality of the sacrifice, the labor, the self-discipline, the superb stewardship of the Hands of the Cause of God. We can think of no more fitting words to express our tribute to these dearly loved and valiant souls than to recall the Words of Bahá'u'lláh Himself: "Light and glory, greeting and praise be upon the Hands of His Cause, through whom the light of fortitude hath shone forth and the truth hath been established that the authority to choose rests with God, the Powerful, the Mighty, the Unconstrained, through whom the ocean of bounty hath surged and the fragrance of the gracious favors of God, the Lord of mankind, hath been diffused."[68]

Study Questions

Answer the following questions based on the above Overview:

Content Questions

1. What requirements did 'Abdu'l-Bahá set forth in His Will and Testament regarding Shoghi Effendi's appointment of a successor?

2. Why was it not possible for Shoghi Effendi to have appointed a successor in accordance with the provisions of the Will and Testament of 'Abdu'l-Bahá?

3. Who created the institution of the Hands of the Cause? Who formally defined and established the institution?

4. What were the "dual sacred" responsibilities the Hands of the Cause were destined to assume?

5. Shoghi Effendi described the Hands of the Cause as "the _____ Stewards of _____ embryonic World _____."

6. During what years were the Hands of the Cause leading the Faith? What were some of the victories of the Bahá'í world under the leadership of the Hands of the Cause during the Ten Year Crusade?

7. What was Mason Remey's argument in support of his assertion that he was the second Guardian? What were the flaws in this argument?

8. On what authority did the Hands of the Cause rely in expelling Mason Remey from the Faith?

9. What was the fate of Mason Remey?

Application/Discussion Questions

1. In describing the leadership of the Hands of the Cause following Shoghi Effendi's passing, the Universal House of Justice declared that the "entire

history of religion shows no comparable record of such strict self-discipline, such absolute loyalty and such complete self-abnegation by the leaders of a religion finding themselves suddenly deprived of their divinely inspired guide." Why were the services of the Hands of the Cause so distinctive?

2. After the passing of Shoghi Effendi, what were the qualities demonstrated by the Hands of the Cause in the face of their awesome responsibilities? How can believers today manifest these same qualities?

3. What were the attitudes of the Hands of the Cause toward the establishment of the Universal House of Justice? What lessons does their example offer for believers today?

4. What did Mason Remey's actions reveal about his attitude toward the Covenant? What lessons may be learned from the Remey episode?

Quotations for Reflection

Answer the questions following the quotations below:

1. "There is no doubt at all that in the Will and Testament of 'Abdu'l-Bahá Shoghi Effendi was the authority designated to appoint his successor, but he had no children and all the surviving Aghsán had broken the Covenant. Thus, as the Hands of the Cause stated in 1957, it is clear that there was no one he could have appointed in accordance with the provisions of the Will. To have made an appointment outside the clear and specific provisions of the Master's Will and Testament would obviously have been an impossible and unthinkable course of action for the Guardian, the divinely appointed upholder and defender of the Covenant. Moreover, that same Will had provided a clear means for the confirmation of the Guardian's appointment of his successor . . . . The nine Hands to be elected by the body of the Hands were to give their assent by secret ballot to the Guardian's choice. In 1957 the entire body of the Hands, after fully investigating the matter, announced that Shoghi Effendi had appointed no successor and left no will. This is documented and established.

"The fact that Shoghi Effendi did not leave a will cannot be adduced as evidence of his failure to obey Bahá'u'lláh—rather should we acknowledge that in his very silence there is a wisdom and a sign of his infallible guidance. We should ponder deeply the writings that we have, and seek to understand the multitudinous significances that they contain. Do not forget that Shoghi Effendi said two things were necessary for a growing understanding of the World Order of Bahá'u'lláh: the passage of time and the guidance of the Universal House of Justice."

(The Universal House of Justice, *Messages from the Universal House of Justice: 1963-1986*, pp. 83-84)

Could Shoghi Effendi have appointed a successor? If not, why not?

Shoghi Effendi did not leave a will. What might have been the wisdom of this action?

2. "The Hands of the Cause of God were individuals appointed by Bahá'u'lláh and charged with various duties, especially those of protecting and propagating His Faith. In *Memorials of the Faithful* 'Abdu'l-Bahá referred to other outstanding believers as Hands of the Cause, and in His Will and Testament He included a provision calling upon the Guardian of the Faith to appoint Hands of the Cause at his discretion. Shoghi Effendi first raised posthumously a number of the believers to the rank of Hands of the Cause, and during the latter years of his life appointed a total of 32 believers from all continents to this position. In the period between the passing of Shoghi Effendi in 1957 and the election of the Universal House of Justice in 1963, the Hands of the Cause directed the affairs of the Faith in their capacity as Chief Stewards of Bahá'u'lláh's embryonic World Commonwealth . . . . In November 1964, the Universal House of Justice determined that it could not legislate to make it possible to appoint Hands of the Cause."

(*The Kitáb-i-Aqdas*, Note # 183)

What were the duties of the Hands of the Cause? In what capacity did the Hands of the Cause lead the Faith between 1957 and 1963?

Can the Universal House of Justice appoint Hands of the Cause? If not, why not?

3. "Following the passing of Shoghi Effendi the international administration of the Faith was carried on by the Hands of the Cause of God with the complete agreement and loyalty of the National Spiritual Assemblies and the body of the believers. This was in accordance with the Guardian's designation of the Hands as the 'Chief Stewards of Bahá'u'lláh's embryonic World Commonwealth.'

"From the very outset of their custodianship of the Cause of God the Hands realized that since they had no certainty of divine guidance such as is incontrovertibly assured to the Guardian and to the Universal House of Justice, their one safe course was to follow with undeviating firmness the instructions and policies of Shoghi Effendi. The entire history of religion shows no comparable record of such strict self-discipline, such absolute loyalty and such complete self-abnegation by the leaders of a religion finding themselves suddenly deprived of their divinely inspired guide. The debt of gratitude which mankind for generations, nay, ages to come, owes to this handful of grief-stricken, steadfast, heroic souls is beyond estimation."

(The Universal House of Justice, *Messages from the Universal House of Justice: 1963-1986*, p. 51)

Following the passing of Shoghi Effendi, did the Hands of the Cause, in carrying out the international administration of the Faith, have the support of National Spiritual Assemblies and the body of the believers?

The Universal House of Justice declared that the "debt of gratitude which mankind for generations, nay, ages to come, owes" to the Hands of the Cause "is beyond estimation." Why?

4. ". . . when nearing the midway point of the Ten Year Crusade, the Bahá'í World found itself abruptly deprived of the guiding hand of its beloved Guardian. The anguish which then seized our hearts, far from paralyzing the progress of the Cause, stiffened our resolve and fired

96

our zeal to complete the tasks which God, through His Chosen Branch, had laid upon us. The august institution of the Hands of the Cause of God which he had, but recently, in compliance with the instructions of the Master's Will, raised up, kept the people of this Cause faithfully to the path which had been shown to us by the pen of divine guidance, and brought us not only to the triumphal conclusion of that Crusade but to the culminating point of the construction of the framework of Bahá'u'lláh's World Order."

(The Universal House of Justice, *Messages from the Universal House of Justice: 1963-1986*, p. 14)

What did the Hands of the Cause achieve during the second half of the Ten Year Crusade?

Why was it so important that the Ten Year Crusade initiated by the Guardian be fully carried out?

5. "My object is to show that the Hands of the Cause of God must be ever watchful and so soon as they find anyone beginning to oppose and protest against the Guardian of the Cause of God, cast him out from the congregation of the people of Bahá and in no wise accept any excuse from him. How often hath grievous error been disguised in the garb of truth, that it might sow the seeds of doubt in the hearts of men!"

(*Will and Testament of 'Abdu'l-Bahá*, p. 12)

Did the Will and Testament of 'Abdu'l-Bahá give the Hands of the Cause the authority to expel believers from the Faith?

What was the significance of the above passage in the period following Shoghi Effendi's passing?

6. "Having been in charge of the Cause of God for six years, the Hands, with absolute faith in the Holy Writings, called upon the believers to elect the Universal House of Justice, and even went so far as to ask that they themselves be not voted for. The sole, sad instance of anyone

succumbing to the allurements of power was the pitiful attempt of Charles Mason Remey to usurp the Guardianship."
(The Universal House of Justice, *Messages from the Universal House of Justice: 1963-1986*, p. 52)

". . . the Hands, with _____ faith in the _____
_____ , called upon the believers to elect the _____
_____ ___ _____ . . . ."

The Hands of the Cause asked that believers not vote for them in the election of the Universal House of Justice. What did this request reveal about the Hands?

Illustrations

What does the following illustration suggest about the challenges faced by the Hands of the Cause after the passing of Shoghi Effendi? How is the example of the Hands still relevant for Bahá'ís, particularly those serving in administrative capacities?

"The temporary headship of the Bahá'í Faith by the Hands of the Cause appointed by Shoghi Effendi commenced with his wholly unexpected and sudden passing through a heart attack in London, England, on November 4, 1957, after he had fully recovered from Asiatic flu, an event which shook the Bahá'í world to its roots. I sent a cable as follows . . . :

SHOGHI EFFENDI BELOVED OF ALL HEARTS SACRED TRUST GIVEN BELIEVERS BY MASTER PASSED AWAY SUDDEN HEART ATTACK IN SLEEP FOLLOWING ASIATIC FLU. URGE BELIEVERS REMAIN STEADFAST CLING INSTITUTION HANDS LOVINGLY REARED RECENTLY REINFORCED EMPHASIZED BELOVED GUARDIAN. ONLY ONENESS HEART ONENESS PURPOSE CAN BEFITTINGLY TESTIFY

LOYALTY ALL NATIONAL ASSEMBLIES
BELIEVERS DEPARTED GUARDIAN WHO
SACRIFICED SELF UTTERLY FOR SERVICE FAITH.
RUHIYYIH

. . . .

"This terrible news evoked throughout the Bahá'í world a passionate wave of response; cables and letters expressing the shock and sorrow of the believers and their firm loyalty to the Hands poured in after his passing. . . .

"The labours of the Hands of the Cause at the time of this unique crisis followed an unbroken pattern till the day the Universal House of Justice was elected on April 21, 1963. The Hands who had gathered in London met and, in spite of their shock and grief, decided not an instant's time must be lost in holding a plenary meeting of our entire body at our World Centre in the Holy Land. This was called for November 18th. Our first act was to choose a delegation to open the apartment of Shoghi Effendi which had been sealed by the International Bahá'í Council right after his passing (in addition to being locked by him when we left Haifa, as was his usual custom) and to make an exhaustive search for any document he might have left—a Will or otherwise. There was no such thing to be found.

"The general body of the Hands then met in the upper hall of the Mansion of Bahá'u'lláh at Bahjí, near His resting-place . . . . Of all our Conclaves—the only befitting term for such august gatherings—that first one was the most epoch-making. Not only were we dazed and grieving, we were orphans, deprived of our father. The responsibility for the entire Cause of God, to which each one of us was wholly consecrated, had been placed in our hands, with neither premonition, warning nor advice. Aside from the thought that we were now the only ones to direct the Bahá'ís of the world, to protect and guide them and to win the Crusade of our beloved Guardian, we were faced with problems of inconceivable magnitude. . . .

"When one adds to the staggering total of . . . problems the fact that all this rested on the shoulders of twenty-seven Hands, the first of whom had only been called to their high office six years previously and the last of whom were appointed a bare four weeks before Shoghi Effendi passed away, one gets some idea of the state and the burden of the Hands of the Cause of God. . . .

". . . The death of Shoghi Effendi had really been like an arrow shot into our hearts. Each one struggled with his bereavement in his own way. One of us, Mason Remey, one of the oldest and most distinguished, solved his personal dilemma by concluding that the Bahá'í Faith could not go on without a Guardian and that undoubtedly Shoghi Effendi's successor was himself—for various invalid and unprovable reasons, such as that he was one of the earliest, famous believers of the West, had been made a Hand of the Cause by Shoghi Effendi and President of the International Bahá'í Council. All this was true, but it still did not make him the second Guardian. Mason Remey's activities, beginning in 1960, when he 'proclaimed' himself the second Guardian, were a profound source of embarrassment to his fellow-Hands who, in addition to all their other heavy, heartbreaking responsibilities, now found themselves obliged to progressively remonstrate with, admonish, warn, expose and finally excommunicate him. This extraordinary and sudden display of unexpected pride and conceit passed over the Bahá'í world, producing a brief flutter in France, a passing ripple in Chile and sundry vibrations in the United States, Pakistan and one or two other countries, and was soon gone forever. For those who, like myself and Paul Haney, had known and loved him all our lives, and Milly Collins, who had been a particularly old friend and co-worker, it was a very bitter and tragic experience. Unfollowed and unmourned, alone and isolated in his old age, when he died he was buried by his young secretary who was not a Bahá'í. Although this whole episode had no effect on the Faith, it added to the burdens of the Custodians, consumed hours of consideration better spent on constructive matters, and saddened our hearts. Like any branch cut from the root, the Remey incident withered away."

(Amatu'l-Bahá Rúḥíyyih Khánum, Introduction, *The Ministry of the Custodians: 1957-1963*, pp. 7-9, 16)

Analysis Questions

Answer the following questions. Suggested answers appear in Appendix A.

1. Which of the following statements regarding Shoghi Effendi's appointment of a successor are true? Circle all correct answers.

> A. Shoghi Effendi could have guaranteed that the Faith would have had a second Guardian if he had left a will that appointed a successor.
>
> B. Shoghi Effendi had no children, and all the surviving Aghṣán had broken the Covenant.
>
> C. The Will and Testament of 'Abdu'l-Bahá had provided a means for the confirmation of the Guardian's appointment of his successor.
>
> D. Shoghi Effendi could not have appointed a successor in accordance with the provisions of the Will and Testament of 'Abdu'l-Bahá.

2. Which of the following choices accurately describe the assumption of the leadership of the Faith by the Hands of the Cause in the period following Shoghi Effendi's passing? Circle all correct answers.

> A. In his letters, Shoghi Effendi had explicitly appointed the body of the Hands of the Cause as his successor.
>
> B. Aside from the Guardian and the Universal House of Justice, the Hands of the Cause occupied the foremost rank in the Bahá'í Administrative Order and were the Chief Stewards of Bahá'u'lláh's embryonic World Commonwealth.
>
> C. Shoghi Effendi had assured the Hands that they would be divinely guided to lead the Faith following his passing.
>
> D. The Hands assumed the leadership of the Faith with the full support of all National Spiritual Assemblies around the world.

3. Why could Mason Remey not be, as he claimed, the second Guardian of the Faith? Circle all correct answers.

> A. He was not appointed by Shoghi Effendi.
>
> B. He was not appointed in the life-time of Shoghi Effendi.
>
> C. He was not among the Aghṣán– "the first-born of the Guardian" or another "branch"–and, therefore, was not qualified for this hereditary office.
>
> D. The Hands of the Cause had not elected from their own number

nine persons who had given their assent to the choice of Remey as Shoghi Effendi's successor.

Memorization and Presentation Exercises

A. Memorizing the Sacred and Authoritative Writings
Commit to memory the following quotations (or two of your choosing from this chapter):

"It is incumbent upon the Guardian of the Cause of God to appoint in his own life-time him that shall become his successor . . . ."
(*Will and Testament of 'Abdu'l-Bahá*, p. 12)

"My object is to show that the Hands of the Cause of God must be ever watchful and so soon as they find anyone beginning to oppose and protest against the Guardian of the Cause of God, cast him out from the congregation of the people of Bahá and in no wise accept any excuse from him."
(*Will and Testament of 'Abdu'l-Bahá*, p. 12)

B. Presenting the Themes of the Covenant
Prepare a brief presentation on the theme of the passing of Shoghi Effendi and the ministry of the Hands of the Cause of God.

In your explanation, include discussion of:

1. the requirements of succession and the passing of Shoghi Effendi;
2. the ministry of the Hands of the Cause and the authority for their assumption of international leadership of the Faith; and
3. the defection of Mason Remey.

Share your presentation with a partner or group.

CHAPTER 6
The Universal House of Justice:
Significance, Origin, Authority,
and Election

Unto the Most Holy Book every one must turn,
and all that is not expressly recorded therein
must be referred to the Universal House of Justice.
— 'Abdu'l-Bahá

Overview

A. The Significance of the Universal House of Justice

"Through His Covenant, Bahá'u'lláh has provided an unfailing source of divine guidance that will endure throughout the Dispensation."[1] Such divine guidance was transmitted first through 'Abdu'l-Bahá, then through the Guardian, and since 1963, through the Universal House of Justice—a council brought into being through the "free and democratic election by the mass of the faithful."[2] That God's Manifestation has ensured the continuity of divine guidance through an elected council is one of the most striking and inspiring features of Bahá'u'lláh's Covenant, a feature finding no parallel in the world's recorded religious history.

Also wondrous is the vision, set forth in the Bahá'í Writings, of the significance and purpose of the Universal House of Justice. Bahá'u'lláh wrote: "It is incumbent upon the men of God's House of Justice to fix their gaze by day and by night upon that which hath shone forth from the Pen of Glory for the training of peoples, the upbuilding of nations, the protection of man and the safeguarding of his honour."[3] 'Abdu'l-Bahá further declared that "God hath ordained" the Universal House of Justice as "the source of all good."[4] Shoghi Effendi alluded to the glories of the day when the Universal House of Justice would be established:

. . . God's Supreme House of Justice shall be erected and firmly established in the days to come. When this most great edifice shall be reared on such an immovable foundation, God's purpose, wisdom, universal truths, mysteries and realities of the Kingdom, which the mystic Revelation of Bahá'u'lláh has deposited within the Will and Testament of 'Abdu'l-Bahá, shall gradually be revealed and made manifest.[5]

Shoghi Effendi further explained that the Universal House of Justice—the "supreme legislative body of the future Bahá'í Commonwealth"[6]—is "to be the exponent and guardian of that Divine Justice which can alone insure the security of, and establish the reign of law and order in, a strangely disordered world."[7] It is an institution that "posterity will regard as the last refuge of a tottering civilization."[8]

B. The Scriptural Origin of the Universal House of Justice

The Universal House of Justice finds its scriptural origin in Bahá'u'lláh's Kitáb-i-Aqdas and in His subsequent Tablets. In the Most Holy Book, Bahá'u'lláh formally ordained the institution of the "House of Justice,"* defined its functions, fixed its revenues, and designated its members as the "Men of Justice," the "Deputies of God," and the "Trustees of the All-Merciful."[9] In Tablets revealed after the Kitáb-i-Aqdas, Bahá'u'lláh made the following statements regarding the House of Justice:

It is incumbent upon the Trustees of the House of Justice to take counsel together regarding those things which have not outwardly been revealed in the Book, and to enforce that which is agreeable to them.[10]

This passage, now written by the Pen of Glory, is accounted as part of the Most Holy Book: The men of God's House of Justice have been charged with the affairs of the people. They, in truth, are the Trustees of God among His

---

*The terms "House of Justice," "Supreme House of Justice," and "International House of Justice" are, at times, used in the Bahá'í Writings to refer to the Universal House of Justice.

servants and the daysprings of authority in His countries.

. . . Inasmuch as for each day there is a new problem and for every problem an expedient solution, such affairs should be referred to the House of Justice that the members thereof may act according to the needs and requirements of the time.[11]

'Abdu'l-Bahá expounded upon Bahá'u'lláh's establishment of the Universal House of Justice: "He [Bahá'u'lláh] has ordained and established the House of Justice, which is endowed with a political as well as a religious function, the consummate union and blending of church and state. . . . Its rulings shall be in accordance with the commands and teachings of Bahá'u'lláh, and that which the Universal House of Justice ordains shall be obeyed by all mankind. This international House of Justice shall be appointed and organized from the Houses of Justice of the whole world . . . ."[12] 'Abdu'l-Bahá explained that the "Universal House of Justice, likewise, wardeth off all differences and whatever it prescribeth must be accepted and he who transgresseth is rejected."[13] During His lifetime, He indicated that "this Universal House of Justice" had "not yet been instituted,"[14] but referred to its future establishment: "After 'Abdu'l-Bahá, whenever the Universal House of Justice is organized it will ward off differences."[15] Likewise, Shoghi Effendi referred to the future establishment of the Universal House of Justice.[16]

C. The Authority of the Universal House of Justice to Legislate and Elucidate

Bahá'u'lláh and 'Abdu'l-Bahá defined the authority of the Universal House of Justice. The House of Justice has been invested with the authority to legislate on those matters not explicitly and outwardly recorded in Bahá'u'lláh's Writings: "Unto the Most Holy Book every one must turn, and all that is not expressly recorded therein must be referred to the Universal House of Justice."[17] For example, the Kitáb-i-Aqdas prohibits theft, but does not specify the degrees of penalties for the offense. When asked about this matter, Bahá'u'lláh responded that the "determination of the degrees of these penalties rests with the House of Justice."[18] Thus, the House of Justice has been "invested by Bahá'u'lláh with the authority to legislate whatsoever has not been explicitly and outwardly recorded in His holy Writ."[19]

'Abdu'l-Bahá commented upon the wisdom of the legislative authority of the Universal House of Justice:

> Those matters of major importance which constitute the foundation of the Law of God are explicitly recorded in the Text, but subsidiary laws are left to the House of Justice. The wisdom of this is that the times never remain the same, for change is a necessary quality and an essential attribute of this world, and of time and place. Therefore the House of Justice will take action accordingly.[20]

The Universal House of Justice "can supplement but never invalidate or modify in the least degree what has already been formulated by Bahá'u'lláh."[21] It can, however, alter its own laws: It has "the right and power to abrogate, according to the changes and requirements of the time, whatever has been already enacted and enforced by a preceding House of Justice."[22] In this connection, 'Abdu'l-Bahá wrote:

> Inasmuch as the House of Justice hath power to enact laws that are not expressly recorded in the Book and bear upon daily transactions, so also it hath power to repeal the same. Thus for example, the House of Justice enacteth today a certain law and enforceth it, and a hundred years hence, circumstances having profoundly changed and the conditions having altered, another House of Justice will then have power, according to the exigencies of the time, to alter that law. This it can do because these laws form no part of the divine explicit Text. The House of Justice is both the initiator and the abrogator of its own laws.[23]

In discussing the principle that the Universal House of Justice may not alter Bahá'u'lláh's revealed Word, but may legislate only on matters not in the Book, Shoghi Effendi asserted: "Such is the immutability of His revealed Word. Such is the elasticity which characterizes the functions of His appointed ministers. The first preserves the identity of His Faith, and guards the integrity of His law. The second enables it, even as a living organism, to expand and adapt itself to the needs and requirements of an ever-changing society."[24]

As explained by 'Abdu'l-Bahá and Shoghi Effendi, the Universal House of Justice also has the power of elucidation, which is related to legislation. 'Abdu'l-Bahá's Will and Testament declared: "It is incumbent upon these members (of the Universal House of Justice) to . . . deliberate upon all problems which have caused difference, questions that are obscure and matters that are not expressly recorded in the Book."[25] Shoghi Effendi, in response to a question about "the nature and scope of the Universal Court of Arbitration," made clear that "this and other similar matters will have to be explained and elucidated by the Universal House of Justice, to which, according to the Master's explicit instructions, all important and fundamental questions must be referred."[26] The Universal House of Justice "makes deductions on the basis of the revealed Texts and their authorized interpretations."[27] Although it may elucidate, the House of Justice "will not engage in interpreting the Holy Writings."[28]

What is the difference between the function of interpretation carried out by the Guardian and that of elucidation exercised by the Universal House of Justice? The House of Justice has explained that there is a "profound difference" between the two functions.[29] The "interpretations of the Guardian represent the true intent inherent in the Sacred Texts."[30] "The divinely inspired legislation of the Universal House of Justice does not attempt to say what the revealed Word means—it states what must be done in cases where the revealed Text or its authoritative interpretation is not explicit."[31] "The major distinction between the two functions is that legislation with its resultant outcome of elucidation is susceptible of amendment by the House of Justice itself, whereas the Guardian's interpretation is a statement of truth which cannot be varied."[32]

D. Other Rights, Duties, and Responsibilities of the Universal House of Justice

"While ultimately the major function of the Universal House of

Justice will be that of legislation, it has continuing responsibility for executive and judicial functions of the institution."[33] The Universal House of Justice has "the responsibility for the application of the revealed word, the protection of the Faith, as well as the duty 'to insure the continuity of that divinely-appointed authority which flows from the Source of our Faith, to safeguard the unity of its followers, and to maintain the integrity and flexibility of its Teachings.'"[34] The House of Justice has the authority to "administer" the Faith's "affairs, coordinate its activities, promote its interests, execute its laws and defend its subsidiary institutions."[35] Additionally, it has the prerogative to "apply the principles, promulgate the laws, protect the institutions, adapt loyally and intelligently the Faith to the requirements of progressive society, and consummate the incorruptible inheritance which the Founders of the Faith have bequeathed to the world."[36]

In outlining the responsibilities of the Universal House of Justice, 'Abdu'l-Bahá's Will and Testament provided: "Unto this body all things must be referred. . . . By this body all the difficult problems are to be resolved . . . ."[37] As noted above, the members of the Universal House of Justice are to "deliberate upon all problems which have caused difference,"[38] so the House of Justice has the responsibility for "settling differences."[39] When there exist differences of opinion on "fundamental questions," such matters should be referred to the House of Justice.[40] In "the process of translating the Teachings into practice, the final arbiter is, by the explicit authority of the Revealed Text, the Universal House of Justice."[41]

Other responsibilities of the Universal House of Justice include "administering the worldwide affairs of the Cause and directing the course of the implementation of the Divine Plan."[42] Shoghi Effendi indicated that the House of Justice would "launch enterprises embracing" the "whole Bahá'í world."[43] He wrote that it would "devise and carry out important undertakings, world-wide activities and the establishment of glorious institutions."[44] Further, he explained that the House of Justice would "guide, organize and unify the affairs of the Movement throughout the world"[45] and would outline the steps "necessary to establish the World Order of Bahá'u'lláh on this earth."[46] The Guardian thus called upon believers to look to "the guidance of God's Universal House of Justice, to obtain a clearer and fuller understanding" of the "provisions and implications" of Bahá'u'lláh's new World Order.[47]

Finally, in relation to the Universal House of Justice, the Guardian foresaw that "as the Bahá'í Faith permeates the masses of the peoples of East and West, and its truth is embraced by the majority of the peoples of a number of the Sovereign States of the world," the Universal House of Justice will "attain the plenitude of its power, and exercise, as the supreme organ of the Bahá'í Commonwealth, all the rights, the duties, and responsibilities incumbent upon the world's future super-state."[48]

E. The Election of the Universal House of Justice

In addition to establishing the Universal House of Justice and defining its authority, the Bahá'í Writings also set out the method for its election. In His Will and Testament, 'Abdu'l-Bahá stated that the House of Justice "must be elected by universal suffrage, that is, by the believers. . . . By this House is meant the Universal House of Justice, that is, in all countries a secondary House of Justice must be instituted, and these secondary Houses of Justice must elect the members of the Universal one."[49]

The following elaboration upon this electoral process appears in one of 'Abdu'l-Bahá's Tablets:

> At whatever time all the beloved of God in each country appoint their delegates, and these in turn elect their representatives, and these representatives elect a body, that body shall be regarded as the Supreme House of Justice.
>
> The establishment of that House is not dependent upon the conversion of all the nations of the world. For example, if conditions were favorable and no disturbances would be caused, the friends in Persia would elect their representatives, and likewise the friends in America, in India, and other areas would also elect their representatives, and these would elect a House of Justice. That House of Justice would be the Supreme House of Justice. That is all.[50]

In interpreting the first sentence of the above-quoted passage, Shoghi Effendi explained: "These words clearly indicate that a three-stage election has been provided by 'Abdu'l-Bahá for the formation of the International House of Justice, and as it is explicitly provided in His Will and Testament that the 'Secondary House of Justice (*i.e.*, National Assemblies) must elect the members of the Universal One,' it is obvious that the members of the National Spiritual Assemblies will have to be indirectly elected by the body of the believers in their respective provinces."[51] In summary, in this "three-stage" election, first, the believers elect their delegates; second, the delegates elect the members of the National Spiritual Assemblies; and third, the members of the National Spiritual Assemblies elect the Universal House of Justice. Accordingly, at "whatever time" such a three-stage election takes place, the body elected "shall be regarded as the Supreme House of Justice."[52]

'Abdu'l-Bahá "contemplated the possibility of the formation of the Universal House of Justice in His own lifetime, and but for the unfavorable circumstances prevailing under the Turkish régime, would have, in all probability, taken the preliminary steps for its establishment."[53] In "the darkest moments" of 'Abdu'l-Bahá's life, when the enemies of the Faith were threatening to deport Him "to the most inhospitable regions of Northern Africa,"[54] and when His life was in danger, 'Abdu'l-Bahá communicated with Ḥájí Mírzá Taqí Afnán, the cousin of the Báb, and directed him to "arrange for the election of the Universal House of Justice should the threats against the Master materialize."[55] The threats against 'Abdu'l-Bahá were not carried out, so the election of the Universal House of Justice did not take place at that time.

Shortly after assuming the office of the Guardian of the Faith, Shoghi Effendi considered the possibility of calling for the election of the Universal House of Justice, but decided against it so that an adequate administrative foundation could first be developed at the local and national levels of the Bahá'í community.[56] In 1923, Shoghi Effendi wrote: "With these Assemblies, local as well as national, harmoniously, vigorously, and efficiently functioning throughout the Bahá'í world, the only means for the establishment of the Supreme House of Justice will have been secured."[57] Eighteen years later, he explained: "At this time when the National Assemblies in the Cause are not yet functioning sufficiently or

110

fully representative of all the various important elements within it, and when some of the Bahá'ís are not even free to practice their faith, despite their numbers, it is quite impracticable to seek to establish the Universal House of Justice. Whenever conditions permit, it will be established."[58] He further stated that "that which is very important now is the consolidation of the Spiritual Assemblies in every centre, because on these fortified and unshakeable foundations, God's Supreme House of Justice shall be erected and firmly established in the days to come."[59]

During his thirty-six year ministry, Shoghi Effendi encouraged Bahá'í communities to raise up and consolidate Spiritual Assemblies—local and national. In 1921, when Shoghi Effendi assumed the mantle of the Guardianship, there were no National Spiritual Assemblies in existence.[60] By 1957, there were twenty-six.[61] Following Shoghi Effendi's passing, through the execution of the Ten Year Crusade under the leadership of the Hands of the Cause, the process of developing Spiritual Assemblies continued. By 1963, the number of National Spiritual Assemblies in the world had increased to fifty-six.[62] Also by that year, hundreds of Local Spiritual Assemblies had been brought into being, and believers resided in over eleven thousand localities around the world.[63] Moreover, building on what the Guardian had established, the Hands of the Cause took steps internationally to prepare for the formation of the Universal House of Justice.[64] A strong foundation was thus laid for the election of the Universal House of Justice.

There were other reasons that made the election of the Universal House of Justice not only timely, but necessary, by 1963. As the Universal House of Justice itself has explained:

> At the time of our beloved Shoghi Effendi's death it was evident, from the circumstances and from the explicit requirements of the Holy Texts, that it had been impossible for him to appoint a successor in accordance with the provisions of the Will and Testament of 'Abdu'l-Bahá. This situation, in which the Guardian died without being able to appoint a successor, presented an obscure question not covered by the explicit Holy Text, and had to be referred to the Universal House of Justice.[65]

Before the Universal House of Justice was formed and had the opportunity to consider the question, it was not known whether the House of Justice could appoint or legislate to make it possible to appoint a second Guardian to succeed Shoghi Effendi:

> The friends should clearly understand that before the election of the Universal House of Justice there was no knowledge that there would be no Guardian. There could not have been any such foreknowledge, whatever opinions individual believers may have held. Neither the Hands of the Cause of God, nor the International Bahá'í Council, nor any other existing body could make a decision upon this all-important matter. Only the House of Justice had authority to pronounce upon it. This was one urgent reason for calling the election of the Universal House of Justice as soon as possible.[66]

Following the passing of Shoghi Effendi, the Hands of the Cause carried out the international administration of the Faith. However, they were aware that "since they had no certainty of divine guidance such as is incontrovertibly assured to the Guardian and to the Universal House of Justice, their one safe course was to follow with undeviating firmness the instructions and policies of Shoghi Effendi."[67] The Guardian had given believers detailed plans covering the period through Riḍván 1963. "From that point onward, unless the Faith were to be endangered, further divine guidance was essential."[68] This was another "pressing reason" in calling for the election of the Universal House of Justice. As such, the Hands of the Cause invited National Spiritual Assemblies to elect the Universal House of Justice on April 21, 1963. On that date, the election of the House of Justice was carried out in accordance with the instructions and procedures set forth by 'Abdu'l-Bahá.[69]

There was nothing in the Bahá'í Writings mandating that the election of the Universal House of Justice only be called by the Guardian. As discussed above, 'Abdu'l-Bahá had many years earlier contemplated the formation of the Universal House of Justice when He had asked the cousin of the Báb to arrange for its election should the threats against

'Abdu'l-Bahá materialize. Furthermore, 'Abdu'l-Bahá had declared: "At *whatever time* all the beloved of God in each country appoint their delegates, and these in turn elect their representatives, and these representatives elect a body, that body shall be regarded as the Supreme House of Justice."[70] This is precisely what occurred in 1963. Elected in a three-stage election by Bahá'ís throughout the world, God's House of Justice came into being and assumed its seat on Mt. Carmel in Haifa, Israel. Since the inaugural election of the Universal House of Justice in 1963, and its subsequent elections every five years since then,[71] believers have begun to witness the fulfillment of Shoghi Effendi's promises regarding this sacred institution:

> . . . the mighty edifice, the Universal House of Justice, will be erected, raising high its noble frame above the world of existence. The unity of the followers of Bahá'u'lláh will thus be realized and fulfilled from one end of the earth to the other. The explicit ordinances of His Most Holy Book will be promulgated, applied and carried out most befittingly in the world of creation, and the living waters of everlasting life will stream forth from that fountain-head of God's World Order upon all the warring nations and peoples of the world, to wash away the evils and iniquities of the realm of dust, heal man's age-old ills and ailments.[72]

Study Questions

Answer the following questions based on the above Overview:

CONTENT QUESTIONS

1. ". . . that Universal House of Justice which, as its title implies, is to be the _____ and guardian of that Divine _____ which can alone insure the security of, and establish the reign of _____ and _____ in, a strangely disordered world."

2. In what documents did Bahá'u'lláh ordain the Universal House of Justice?

3. "Unto the Most Holy Book _____ one must turn and all that is not _____ _____ therein must be referred to the Universal House of Justice."

4. What is the difference between the function of "elucidation" exercised by the Universal House of Justice and the function of "interpretation" carried out by the Guardian?

5. List five major responsibilities of the Universal House of Justice.

6. "At whatever time all the beloved of God in each country appoint their _____, and these in turn elect their _____, and these _____ elect a body, that body shall be regarded as the Supreme _____ __ _____."

7. Did 'Abdu'l-Bahá envision that the Universal House of Justice might be elected in His lifetime?

8. Identify two reasons why the election of the Universal House of Justice was essential by 1963.

9. Was there a requirement in the Bahá'í Writings that the election of the Universal House of Justice be called by the Guardian?

APPLICATION/DISCUSSION QUESTIONS
1. 'Abdu'l-Bahá declared that "God hath ordained" the Universal House of Justice as "the source of all good." What does it mean that the Universal House of Justice is "the source of all good"? What are the implications of 'Abdu'l-Bahá's statement for how believers should view the guidance of the Universal House of Justice?

2. Would the Universal House of Justice be able to change a law revealed by Bahá'u'lláh because, for instance, the law was not popular in society (e.g., Bahá'u'lláh's law prohibiting the consumption of alcohol)? If not, why not?

3. One of the responsibilities of the Universal House of Justice is to "deliberate upon all problems which have caused difference." How does the discharge of this responsibility preserve the unity of the Bahá'í community? Under what circumstances should believers approach the Universal House of Justice about resolving "problems which have caused difference"?

4. 'Abdu'l-Bahá wrote: "At whatever time all the beloved of God in each country appoint their delegates, and these in turn elect their representatives, and these representatives elect a body, that body shall be regarded as the Supreme House of Justice." If, God forbid, by some catastrophic event (e.g., natural disaster, war), none of the members of the Universal House of Justice were able to serve, could the Bahá'í community elect new members to the Universal House of Justice? How does the process established by 'Abdu'l-Bahá for the election of the Universal House of Justice ensure that the Bahá'í community will be able to reconstitute this institution's membership whenever necessary?

Quotations for Reflection
Answer the questions following the quotations below:

1. "When that central pivot of the people of Bahá [the Universal House of Justice] shall be effectively, majestically and firmly established, a new era will dawn, heavenly bounties and graces will pour out from that Source, and the all-encompassing promises will be fulfilled."
(Shoghi Effendi, *The Compilation of Compilations*, vol. I, p. 329)

The Universal House of Justice is that "central _____ of the people of Bahá . . . ."

What are some of the "heavenly bounties and graces" that have poured out from the Universal House of Justice since its establishment?

2. "It [the Universal House of Justice] enacteth all ordinances and regulations that are not to be found in the explicit Holy Text. By this body all the difficult problems are to be resolved . . . ."
(*Will and Testament of 'Abdu'l-Bahá*, p. 14)

"Severed from the no less essential institution of the Universal House of Justice this same System of the Will of 'Abdu'l-Bahá would be paralyzed in its action and would be powerless to fill in those gaps which the Author of the Kitáb-i-Aqdas has deliberately left in the body of His legislative and administrative ordinances. . . .

"'It is incumbent upon the members of the House of Justice,' Bahá'u'lláh . . . declares in the Eighth Leaf of the Exalted Paradise, 'to take counsel together regarding those things which have not outwardly been revealed in the Book, and to enforce that which is agreeable to them. God will verily inspire them with whatsoever He willeth, and He verily is the Provider, the Omniscient.'. . .

"Not only does 'Abdu'l-Bahá confirm in His Will Bahá'u'lláh's above-quoted statement, but invests this body with the additional right and power to abrogate, according to the exigencies of time, its own enactments, as well as those of a preceding House of Justice. 'Inasmuch as the House of Justice,' is His explicit statement in His Will, 'hath power to enact laws that are not expressly recorded in the Book and bear upon daily transactions, so also it hath power to repeal the same . . . This it can do because these laws form no part of the divine explicit text.'"
(Shoghi Effendi, *The World Order of Bahá'u'lláh*, pp. 148-49)

What are among the responsibilities and powers of the Universal House of Justice?

Why is the Universal House of Justice such a critical institution in the Bahá'í Administrative Order?

3. "It is incumbent upon these members (of the Universal House of Justice) to gather in a certain place and deliberate upon all problems which have caused difference, questions that are obscure and matters that are not expressly recorded in the Book."
(*Will and Testament of 'Abdu'l-Bahá*, p. 20)

"The Universal House of Justice, beyond its function as the enactor of legislation, has been invested with the more general functions of protecting and administering the Cause, solving obscure questions and deciding upon matters that have caused difference."

(The Universal House of Justice, *Messages from the Universal House of Justice: 1963-1986*, p. 157)

"The Guardian has in his writings specified for the House of Justice such fundamental functions as the formulation of future worldwide teaching plans, the conduct of the administrative affairs of the Faith, and the guidance, organization and unification of the affairs of the Cause throughout the world."

(The Universal House of Justice, *Messages from the Universal House of Justice: 1963-1986*, p. 89)

Beyond its legislative responsibility, what other responsibilities does the Universal House of Justice carry out?

At this time, the discharge of which duties by the Universal House of Justice appear to have the highest priority and urgency?

4. "Briefly, this is the wisdom of referring the laws of society to the House of Justice. In the religion of Islam, similarly, not every ordinance was explicitly revealed; nay not a tenth part of a tenth part was included in the Text; although all matters of major importance were specifically referred to, there were undoubtedly thousands of laws which were unspecified. These were devised by the divines of a later age according to the laws of Islamic jurisprudence, and individual divines made conflicting deductions from the original revealed ordinances. All these were enforced. Today this process of deduction is the right of the body of the House of Justice, and the deductions and conclusions of individual learned men have no authority, unless they are endorsed by the House of Justice. The difference is precisely this, that from the conclusions and endorsements of the body of the House of Justice whose members are elected by and known to the worldwide Bahá'í community, no differences will arise; whereas the conclusions of individual divines and scholars

would definitely lead to differences, and result in schism, division, and dispersion. The oneness of the Word would be destroyed, the unity of the Faith would disappear, and the edifice of the Faith of God would be shaken."

> ('Abdu'l-Bahá, quoted in the Universal House of Justice, *Messages from the Universal House of Justice: 1963-1986*, p.86)

What is the wisdom of referring the laws of society to the Universal House of Justice?

How does the Universal House of Justice preserve the unity of the Bahá'í community?

5. "There is a profound difference between the interpretations of the Guardian and the elucidations of the House of Justice in exercise of its function to 'deliberate upon all problems which have caused difference, questions that are obscure and matters that are not expressly recorded in the Book.' The Guardian reveals what the Scripture means; his interpretation is a statement of truth which cannot be varied. Upon the Universal House of Justice, in the words of the Guardian, 'has been conferred the exclusive right of legislating on matters not expressly revealed in the Bahá'í writings.' Its pronouncements, which are susceptible of amendment or abrogation by the House of Justice itself, serve to supplement and apply the Law of God."

> (The Universal House of Justice, *Messages from the Universal House of Justice: 1963-1986*, p. 56)

"The divinely inspired legislation of the House of Justice does not attempt to say what the revealed Word means—it states what must be done in cases where the revealed Text or its authoritative interpretation is not explicit; and in this context it offers explanations."

> (On behalf of the Universal House of Justice, to an individual believer, August 27, 1998)

What is the difference between the interpretations of the Guardian and the elucidations of the Universal House of Justice?

If a believer wishes to know the intent of a mystical passage in Bahá'u'lláh's Writings, would the Universal House of Justice be able to offer its own explanation? What if the believer wishes to know what to do in relation to a situation not covered by Bahá'í law?

6. "It must be pointed out . . . that . . . the establishment of the Supreme House of Justice is in no way dependent upon the adoption of the Bahá'í Faith by the mass of the peoples of the world, nor does it presuppose its acceptance by the majority of the inhabitants of any one country. In fact, 'Abdu'l-Bahá, Himself, in one of His earliest Tablets, contemplated the possibility of the formation of the Universal House of Justice in His own lifetime, and but for the unfavorable circumstances prevailing under the Turkish régime, would have, in all probability, taken the preliminary steps for its establishment."

(Shoghi Effendi, *The World Order of Bahá'u'lláh*, p. 7)

'Abdu'l-Bahá contemplated the formation of which institution in His own lifetime?

'Abdu'l-Bahá and Shoghi Effendi chose not to call for the election of the Universal House of Justice in their lifetimes. What may have been the wisdom of this decision?

Illustrations

Reflect on the following excerpts. What is unique about the Universal House of Justice? How significant will be the role of the Universal House of Justice in the future?

". . . when you come to the institutions of the Faith, we have to remember that in the Bahá'í Dispensation, we are living in a new kind of dispensation because this is the coming of the Kingdom of God on earth. It is 'the Day that shall not be followed by night.'. . .

"After Bahá'u'lláh, we had 'Abdu'l-Bahá and the Guardian. There, at the head of the Faith was one individual who was divinely-guided, who was infallible, who had all authority. This was difficult enough for mankind as a whole, but one is used to that: One is used to having Prophets in the world; it is not an unusual thing for mankind to have the experience of divinely-guided individuals. But previously, it's always come to an end.

"But in the Bahá'í Faith, God has done a most extraordinary thing, and that is, given human beings the possibility of bringing a divinely-guided institution into being, so it cannot be completely destroyed. Where you had a hereditary line—as even with the Guardianship—events can break the line. . . . If the coming into being is dependent on something before, it can be broken. It happened with the Imamate and, as we all know, Shoghi Effendi died without a successor. But in the Bahá'í Faith, if we need the Universal House of Justice, we know how to elect it. . . . And because it is so clear in the Writings, the Bahá'ís have no doubt that if they held certain elections and followed the pattern that 'Abdu'l-Bahá had laid down, the nine people who would be elected would become a divinely-guided body."

(Ian Semple, "Infallibility of the Universal House of Justice" (lecture, Haifa, Israel, May 31, 1989))

"In my present functioning as a member of the Universal House of Justice, I find myself at times meditating on a statement which appears in the writings of the Guardian and it appears without conditionality—I find no conditionality attached to it. It is rather a definite statement without any maybes or possiblies or perhapses.

"And in that statement, the Guardian refers to . . . the Universal House of Justice. And he says that 'this House is one which posterity will regard as the last refuge of a tottering civilization.'

"When I read that passage, I say to myself, 'What does it mean about the future condition of mankind?' I sometimes sit in the council chamber in the Seat of the Universal House of Justice, I look at my eight colleagues seated around the table, I realize that we nine are not the House of Justice. It is a great, magnificent spiritual entity of which we are simply the weak and feeble outward expression.

"But I say to myself, 'This institution, this Universal House of Justice . . ., the Guardian tells us definitely, categorically, without conditionality, will be such that posterity will look upon it as the 'last refuge of a tottering civilization.'

"I offer this passage to you simply as an indication of the great changes that are coming to humanity.

"When they will come—in which decade, in which century—we know not. But we do know that they will come—that the Cause of which we are all members is destined to play a major transforming, revolutionizing role in the history of humanity on this planet."

(Peter Khan, "Mental Tests," *The American Bahá'í*, December 31, 1995 (lecture, Wilmette, Illinois, September 23, 1995))

Analysis Questions

Answer the following questions. Suggested answers appear in Appendix A.

1. Which of the following accurately describe the authority and duties of the Universal House of Justice? Circle all correct answers.

> A. The Universal House of Justice legislates on matters not expressly provided in Bahá'u'lláh's Writings.
> B. The Universal House of Justice deliberates upon problems which have caused difference and questions that are obscure.
> C. The Universal House of Justice interprets the Word of God.
> D. The Universal House of Justice guides, organizes, and unifies the affairs of the Faith throughout the world.

2. Which of the following were requirements for the election of the Universal House of Justice? Circle all correct answers.

> A. The Universal House of Justice had to be elected through a three-stage electoral process.
> B. The Universal House of Justice had to be elected by the members of National Spiritual Assemblies.
> C. The Universal House of Justice had to be elected after the adoption of the Bahá'í Faith by the mass of the peoples of the world.

D. The Guardian had to call the election of the Universal House of Justice.

3. Which of the following were pressing reasons for electing the Universal House of Justice in 1963? Circle all correct answers.

A. The Guardian had said 1963 was the only year the Universal House of Justice could be elected.

B. The Ten Year Crusade had ended, and the Bahá'í world was in need of further divine guidance.

C. The Universal House of Justice was the only body that could resolve the obscure question of what was to be done in the situation of the Guardian having passed away without having been able to appoint a successor.

D. The year 1963 was the one hundredth anniversary of the Declaration of Bahá'u'lláh.

Memorization and Presentation Exercises

A. Memorizing the Sacred and Authoritative Writings

Commit to memory the following quotations (or two of your choosing from this chapter):

"It is incumbent upon the Trustees of the House of Justice to take counsel together regarding those things which have not outwardly been revealed in the Book, and to enforce that which is agreeable to them."

(*Tablets of Bahá'u'lláh*, p. 68)

"At whatever time all the beloved of God in each country appoint their delegates, and these in turn elect their representatives, and these representatives elect a body, that body shall be regarded as the Supreme House of Justice."

('Abdu'l-Bahá, quoted in the Universal House of Justice, *Messages from the Universal House of Justice: 1963-1986*, p. 53)

B. Presenting the Themes of the Covenant

Prepare a brief presentation on the theme of the significance, origin, authority, and election of the Universal House of Justice.

In your explanation, include discussion of:

1. the significance and scriptural origin of the Universal House of Justice;
2. the authority, rights, duties, and responsibilities of the Universal House of Justice; and
3. the election of the Universal House of Justice.

Share your presentation with a partner or group.

CHAPTER 7

The Twin Institutions
of the Guardianship
and the Universal House of Justice

. . . they supplement each other's authority and functions,
and are permanently and fundamentally united in their aims.
— Shoghi Effendi

Overview

A. Duties and Functions of the Guardianship
and the Universal House of Justice

The Guardianship[1] and the Universal House of Justice are the "twin institutions"[2] of the Administrative Order of Bahá'u'lláh. These "twin pillars that support this mighty Administrative Structure" are "divine in origin, essential in their functions and complementary in their aim and purpose."[3] "The Guardian and the Universal House of Justice have certain duties and functions in common . . . ."[4] Their "common, their fundamental object is to insure the continuity of that divinely-appointed authority which flows from the Source of our Faith, to safeguard the unity of its followers and to maintain the integrity and flexibility of its teachings."[5]

In addition to sharing certain duties and functions, each of the institutions of the Guardianship and the Universal House of Justice "operates within a separate and distinct sphere."[6] The Guardian was designated by 'Abdu'l-Bahá as "the Interpreter of the Word of God."[7] The Universal House of Justice was invested by Bahá'u'lláh with the function of "legislating on matters not expressly revealed in the teachings."[8] The two institutions "supplement each other's authority and functions, and are permanently and fundamentally united in their aims."[9]

In His Will and Testament, 'Abdu'l-Bahá declared that the

Guardian of the Cause of God was the "sacred head and the distinguished member for life" of the Universal House of Justice.[10] The Guardian was to participate in the deliberations of the House of Justice. He could not "override the decision of the majority of his fellow-members," but could advise on the meaning and spirit of Bahá'u'lláh's utterances and could define the scope of the legislation of the Universal House of Justice.[11]

B. The Breaking of the Line of Guardians

Although the Bahá'í Writings envisioned the Guardian and the Universal House of Justice functioning together, and future Guardians are "envisaged and referred to in the Writings," there is "nowhere any promise or guarantee that the line of Guardians would endure forever . . . ."[12] On the contrary, there are "clear indications" that the line of Guardians "could be broken."[13] One of the most significant passages alluding to the possibility of a break in the line of Guardians appears in the Kitáb-i-Aqdas:

> Endowments dedicated to charity revert to God, the Revealer of Signs. None hath the right to dispose of them without leave from Him Who is the Dawning-place of Revelation. After Him, this authority shall pass to the Aghsán, and after them to the House of Justice —should it be established in the world by then—that they may use these endowments for the benefit of the Places which have been exalted in this Cause, and for whatsoever hath been enjoined upon them by Him Who is the God of might and power. Otherwise, the endowments shall revert to the people of Bahá who speak not except by His leave and judge not save in accordance with what God hath decreed in this Tablet . . . .[14]

In this passage, Bahá'u'lláh decreed that charitable endowments revert to "the Revealer of Signs," and no one may "dispose of them" without permission from "Him Who is the Dawning-place of Revelation." After "Him," this authority passes to the "Aghsán"—Bahá'u'lláh's male descendents. And after "them," the authority passes to "the House of Justice," "should it be established in the world by then." "Otherwise, the endowments shall revert to the people of Bahá who speak not except by His leave . . . ."[15]

These verses of the Kitáb-i-Aqdas anticipated the succession of chosen Aghsán and thus the institution of the Guardianship, given that the Guardians were to be appointed from among the Aghsán. This passage also envisaged a break in the line of the Aghsán: "After Him, this authority shall pass to the Aghsán [Branches], and *after them* to the House of Justice—*should it be established in the world by then.*"[16] "The passing of Shoghi Effendi in 1957 precipitated the very situation provided for in this passage, in that the line of Aghsán ended before the House of Justice had been elected."[17]

As previously discussed in Chapter 5, there was no one who could have been appointed as Shoghi Effendi's successor because the specific requirements of succession, set forth in the Will and Testament of 'Abdu'l-Bahá, could not be fulfilled. After its formation in 1963, the Universal House of Justice consulted on the question of whether it could legislate to make it possible to appoint a successor to Shoghi Effendi. "After long and prayerful consultation, the House of Justice . . . found that there is no way in which it can legislate for a second Guardian to succeed Shoghi Effendi."[18] Therefore, Shoghi Effendi was not succeeded by another Guardian.

Although Bahá'u'lláh anticipated the ending of the line of the Aghsán, yet there is a "repeated insistence in the Writings on the indestructibility of the Covenant."[19] Bahá'u'lláh categorically stated: "The Hand of Omnipotence hath established His Revelation upon an unassailable, an enduring foundation."[20] 'Abdu'l-Bahá confirmed: "Everything is subject to corruption; but the Covenant of thy Lord shall continue to pervade all regions."[21] "Verily, God effecteth that which He pleaseth; naught can annul His Covenant; naught can obstruct His favor nor oppose His Cause!"[22]

'Abdu'l-Bahá further explained: "The tests of every dispensation are in direct proportion to the greatness of the Cause, and as heretofore such a manifest Covenant, written by the Supreme Pen, hath not been entered upon, the tests are proportionately more severe."[23] The following text from the Universal House of Justice sheds further light on the tests facing the Cause:

> The Cause of God is organic, growing and developing like a living being. Time and again it has faced crises which have perplexed the believers, but each time the Cause, impelled by the immutable purpose of God, overcame the crisis and went on to greater heights.
>
> However great may be our inability to understand the mystery and the implications of the passing of Shoghi Effendi, the strong cord to which all must cling with assurance is the Covenant. The emphatic and vigorous language of 'Abdu'l-Bahá's Will and Testament is at this time, as at the time of His own passing, the safeguard of the Cause: "Unto the Most Holy Book every one must turn and all that is not expressly recorded therein must be referred to the Universal House of Justice. That which this body, whether unanimously or by a majority doth carry, that is verily the truth and the purpose of God Himself. . . ."[24]

Though we may not fully understand at this time why the line of Guardians was broken, we do know that the Faith emerged from this severe test undivided, having demonstrated the power of Bahá'u'lláh's Covenant. In addressing the issue of the break in the line of Guardians, the Universal House of Justice has observed that "we must never underestimate the grievous loss that the Faith has suffered"; however, "God's purpose for mankind remains unchanged . . ., and the mighty Covenant of Bahá'u'lláh remains impregnable."[25]

C. The Principle of Inseparability

If the Bahá'í Writings describe the Guardianship and the Universal House of Justice as "twin institutions" and envision the Guardian serving as a member and as head of the Universal House of Justice, can the House of Justice function in the absence of a living Guardian? This question is resolved through an understanding of the principle of inseparability. Shoghi Effendi characterized the Guardianship and the Universal House of Justice as "inseparable institutions."[26] In a letter entitled "The Dispensation of Bahá'u'lláh," Shoghi Effendi offered the following explanation on the relationship of the institution of the Guardianship to the World Order of Bahá'u'lláh:

> Divorced from the institution of the Guardianship the World Order of Bahá'u'lláh would be mutilated and permanently deprived of that hereditary principle which, as 'Abdu'l-Bahá has written, has been invariably upheld by the Law of God. . . . Without such an institution the integrity of the Faith would be imperiled, and the stability of the entire fabric would be gravely endangered. Its prestige would suffer, the means required to enable it to take a long, an uninterrupted view over a series of generations would be completely lacking, and the necessary guidance to define the sphere of the legislative action of its elected representatives would be totally withdrawn.[27]

In the very next paragraph of "The Dispensation of Bahá'u'lláh," Shoghi Effendi analogously characterized the relationship of the Universal House of Justice to the World Order—"this same System of the Will of 'Abdu'l-Bahá":

> Severed from the no less essential institution of the Universal House of Justice this same System of the Will of 'Abdu'l-Bahá would be paralyzed in its action and would be powerless to fill in those gaps which the Author of the Kitáb-i-Aqdas has deliberately left in the body of His legislative and administrative ordinances.[28]

The above passages make clear that both the Guardianship and the Universal House of Justice are vital to the World Order of Bahá'u'lláh. The Guardianship cannot be "[d]ivorced" from the World Order, and the

Universal House of Justice cannot be "[s]evered" from it. However, these passages do not dictate that each institution can only function in the presence of the other.

Whereas Shoghi Effendi envisaged the Guardianship and the Universal House of Justice functioning together, "it cannot logically be deduced from this that one is unable to function in the absence of the other."[29] In fact, from 1921 until 1957, Shoghi Effendi discharged his responsibilities as Guardian without the presence of the Universal House of Justice. Despite the fact that the Universal House of Justice had not yet been elected and was not functioning during the entire period of Shoghi Effendi's ministry, he, nevertheless, described the Guardianship and the Universal House of Justice as "inseparable institutions."[30] Similarly, the Universal House of Justice is now functioning without the presence of a living Guardian, "but the principle of inseparability remains."[31]

The Universal House of Justice has cautioned that the "Guardianship does not lose its significance nor position in the Order of Bahá'u'lláh merely because there is no living Guardian. We must guard against two extremes: one is to argue that because there is no Guardian all that was written about the Guardianship and its position in the Bahá'í World Order is a dead letter and was unimportant; the other is to be so overwhelmed by the significance of the Guardianship as to underestimate the strength of the Covenant, or to be tempted to compromise with the clear texts in order to find somehow, in some way, a 'Guardian.'"[32] The "Institution of the Guardianship exerts a continuing influence on the operation of the House of Justice through the existence of the vast body of interpretations written by the beloved Guardian during the thirty-six years of his ministry and through the Guardian's assigned role of defining the sphere of the legislative action of the Universal House of Justice."[33]

D. The Universal House of Justice Functioning Infallibly in the Absence of a Living Guardian

It may be asked whether in the absence of a living Guardian the Universal House of Justice functions infallibly and whether there exists any danger that it might stray into the jurisdiction of the Guardian. A study of the authoritative Writings of the Faith clarifies these questions.

Bahá'u'lláh, 'Abdu'l-Bahá, and Shoghi Effendi confirmed that the Universal House of Justice would be infallibly guided.[34] This assurance was never contingent on the presence of a Guardian among the membership of the Universal House of Justice. Regarding the Universal House of Justice, Bahá'u'lláh proclaimed: "God will verily inspire them with whatsoever He willeth . . . ."[35] 'Abdu'l-Bahá affirmed: "That which this body, whether unanimously or by a majority doth carry, that is verily the truth and the purpose of God Himself."[36] He further referred to the "House of Justice whose members are elected by and known to the worldwide Bahá'í community" as taking decisions and establishing laws "through the inspiration and confirmation of the Holy Spirit."[37] Additionally, Shoghi Effendi stated, in relation to "the members of the Universal House of Justice," that "[t]hey . . . have thus been made the recipients of the divine guidance which is at once the life-blood and ultimate safeguard of this Revelation."[38] These and other passages confirm that it is "the elected members of the Universal House of Justice" who "in consultation are recipients of unfailing Divine Guidance."[39]

As the Universal House of Justice itself has elucidated, the "infallibility of the Universal House of Justice, operating within its ordained sphere, has not been made dependent upon the presence in its membership of the Guardian of the Cause. Although in the realm of interpretation the Guardian's pronouncements are always binding, in the area of the Guardian's participation in legislation it is always the decision of the House itself which must prevail."[40] "The absence of the Guardian, while a great deprivation, does not impair the conferred ability of the Universal House of Justice to make infallible decisions."[41] Thus, "the infallibility of the Universal House of Justice . . . is conferred by God, and it is in no way dependent upon the presence of a living Guardian."[42]

In the absence of a living Guardian, will the Universal House of Justice ever infringe upon the sphere of jurisdiction of the Guardian? Several reasons establish that the Universal House of Justice will not infringe upon "the sacred and prescribed domain"[43] of the Guardian. First, Shoghi Effendi wrote that the "sphere of jurisdiction" of the institutions of the Guardianship and the Universal House of Justice is "clearly defined."[44] Bahá'u'lláh's Writings (revealed over His forty-year ministry), as well as 'Abdu'l-Bahá's and Shoghi Effendi's interpretations (set forth respectively during twenty-nine-year and thirty-six-year ministries), provide ample guidance on the sphere of jurisdiction of the Universal House of Justice.

Second, as discussed above, the Universal House of Justice is itself guaranteed divine guidance. Such divine guidance safeguards the institution from infringing upon the Guardian's jurisdiction.

Third, Shoghi Effendi gave the assurance that the Guardian and the Universal House of Justice "[n]either can, nor will ever, infringe upon the sacred and prescribed domain of the other. Neither will seek to curtail the specific and undoubted authority with which both have been divinely invested."[45] "Each exercises, within the limitations imposed upon it, its powers, its authority, its rights and prerogatives. These are neither contradictory, nor detract in the slightest degree from the position which each of these institutions occupies. Far from being incompatible or mutually destructive, they supplement each other's authority and functions, and are permanently and fundamentally united in their aims."[46]

Finally, the Universal House of Justice itself has made clear that "[n]either the Universal House of Justice, nor any other institution, person or group of persons can assume" the Guardian's function of making "authoritative interpretations of the Teachings."[47]

As the Universal House of Justice has further explained, the "fact that the Guardian has the authority to define the sphere of the legislative action of the Universal House of Justice does not carry with it the corollary that without such guidance the Universal House of Justice might stray beyond the limits of its proper authority; such a deduction would conflict with all the other texts referring to its infallibility, and specifically with the Guardian's own clear assertion that the Universal House of Justice never can or will infringe on the sacred and prescribed domain of the Guardianship."[48]

The Universal House of Justice has commented on its prerogatives and duties in relation to those of the Guardian:

> In the specific sense of referring to the office and function of the Guardian himself, the House of Justice finds that the prerogatives and duties vested in him are of three kinds. First, . . . there are a number of functions and objects which the Guardianship shares with the Universal

House of Justice and which the House of Justice must continue to pursue. Secondly, there are other functions of the Guardianship which, in the absence of a Guardian, devolve upon the Universal House of Justice, for example, the Headship of the Faith, the responsibility for directing the work of the Institution of the Hands of the Cause of God[49] and of ensuring the continuing discharge of the functions of protection and propagation vested in that Institution, and the right to administer the Ḥuqúqu'lláh.[50] Thirdly, there are those prerogatives and duties which lie exclusively within the sphere of the Guardian himself and, therefore, in the absence of a Guardian, are inoperative except insofar as the monumental work already performed by Shoghi Effendi continues to be of enduring benefit to the Faith. Such a function is that of authoritative interpretation of the Teachings.[51]

Accordingly, the Universal House of Justice can infallibly function in the absence of a Guardian and discharge those duties that are not within the exclusive sphere of jurisdiction of the Guardian.

"The Universal House of Justice, which the Guardian said would be regarded by posterity as 'the last refuge of a tottering civilization,' is now, in the absence of the Guardian, the sole infallibly guided institution in the world to which all must turn, and on it rests the responsibility for ensuring the unity and progress of the Cause of God in accordance with the revealed Word."[52]

Study Questions

Answer the following questions based on the above Overview:

CONTENT QUESTIONS

1. As to the Guardianship and the Universal House of Justice, what is their "common, their fundamental object"?

2. Is there any promise or guarantee in the Bahá'í Writings that the line of Guardians would endure forever?

3. Could the Universal House of Justice legislate for a second Guardian to succeed Shoghi Effendi?

4. "The _____ of every dispensation are in direct proportion to the _____ of the Cause, and as heretofore such a manifest _____, written by the Supreme Pen, hath not been entered upon, the _____ are proportionately more severe."

5. The Bahá'í Writings envisaged that the Guardianship and the Universal House of Justice would function together. Can it be logically deduced from this that one institution is unable to function in the absence of the other? If not, why not?

6. Was the infallibility of the Universal House of Justice ever made dependent upon the presence in its membership of the Guardian?

7. The Guardian and the Universal House of Justice "[n]either can, nor will ever, _____ upon the sacred and prescribed _____ of the other."

8. The Guardian had the authority to define the sphere of the legislative action of the Universal House of Justice. Does this fact carry with it the corollary that without such guidance the Universal House of Justice might stray beyond the limits of its proper authority?

9. Which of the Guardian's prerogatives and duties can the Universal House of Justice carry out?

APPLICATION/DISCUSSION QUESTIONS

1. Draw two overlapping circles, one of which represents the sphere of jurisdiction of the Guardian, and the second of which represents the sphere of jurisdiction of the Universal House of Justice. What duties should be listed in the overlapping part of the circles? What duties should be listed in each of the non-overlapping parts?

2. Explain how the passage from the Kitáb-i-Aqdas referring to

endowments dedicated to charity (*see* section B of the Overview) anticipated a break in the line of Guardians.

3. The Faith successfully passed the test of the break in the line of Guardians. What does this suggest about the power of the Covenant? What types of tests could the Faith face in the future, and what will be the role of the Covenant in relation to those tests?

4. How does distinguishing between the institution of the Guardianship and the person of the Guardian help to resolve questions about whether the Universal House of Justice can continue to function without the presence of a living Guardian? How does the principle of inseparability help us to understand the functioning of the Universal House of Justice in the absence of a living Guardian?

Quotations for Reflection

Answer the questions following the quotations below:

1. "It must always be remembered that authoritative interpretation of the Teachings was, after 'Abdu'l-Bahá, the exclusive right of the Guardian, and fell within the 'sacred and prescribed domain' of the Guardianship, and therefore the Universal House of Justice cannot and will not infringe upon that domain. The exclusive sphere of the Universal House of Justice is to 'pronounce upon and deliver the final judgment on such laws and ordinances as Bahá'u'lláh has not expressly revealed'. Apart from this fundamental difference in the functions of the twin pillars of the Order of Bahá'u'lláh, insofar as the other duties of the Head of the Faith are concerned, the Universal House of Justice shares with the Guardian the responsibility for the application of the revealed word, the protection of the Faith, as well as the duty 'to insure the continuity of that divinely-appointed authority which flows from the Source of our Faith, to safeguard the unity of its followers, and to maintain the integrity and flexibility of its Teachings.'"

    (On behalf of the Universal House of Justice, *Lights of Guidance*, p. 312)

What are the exclusive responsibilities of the Guardianship and the Universal House of Justice? What responsibilities do they share?

What are implications of the fact that the Guardianship and the Universal House of Justice share certain responsibilities?

2. "After prayerful and careful study of the Holy Texts bearing upon the question of the appointment of the successor to Shoghi Effendi as Guardian of the Cause of God, and after prolonged consultation which included consideration of the views of the Hands of the Cause of God residing in the Holy Land, the Universal House of Justice finds that there is no way to appoint or to legislate to make it possible to appoint a second Guardian to succeed Shoghi Effendi."
(The Universal House of Justice, *Wellspring of Guidance*, p. 11)

Could the Universal House of Justice appoint or legislate to make it possible to appoint a second Guardian to succeed Shoghi Effendi?

What is the significance of the above passage?

3. "We are glad that you have brought to our attention the questions perplexing some of the believers. It is much better for these questions to be put freely and openly than to have them, unexpressed, burdening the hearts of devoted believers. Once one grasps certain basic principles of the Revelation of Bahá'u'lláh such uncertainties are easily dispelled. This is not to say that the Cause of God contains no mysteries. Mysteries there are indeed, but they are not of a kind to shake one's faith once the essential tenets of the Cause and the indisputable facts of any situation are clearly understood."
(The Universal House of Justice, *Messages from the Universal House of Justice: 1963-1986*, p. 50)

Does the Cause have mysteries? What kind of mysteries does the Cause not have?

How should questions perplexing believers be handled?

136

4. "Nowhere is it stated that the infallibility of the Universal House of Justice is by virtue of the Guardian's membership or presence on that body. Indeed, 'Abdu'l-Bahá in His Will and Shoghi Effendi in his 'Dispensation of Bahá'u'lláh' have both explicitly stated that the elected members of the Universal House of Justice in consultation are recipients of unfailing Divine Guidance. Furthermore the Guardian himself in *The World Order of Bahá'u'lláh* asserted that 'It must be also clearly understood by every believer that the institution of Guardianship does not under any circumstances abrogate, or even in the slightest degree detract from, the powers granted to the Universal House of Justice by Bahá'u'lláh in the Kitábu'l-Aqdas, and repeatedly and solemnly confirmed by 'Abdu'l-Bahá in His Will. It does not constitute in any manner a contradiction to the Will and Writings of Bahá'u'lláh, nor does it nullify any of His revealed instructions.'"

(The Universal House of Justice, *Messages from the Universal House of Justice: 1963-1986*, p. 157)

Is the infallibility of the Universal House of Justice dependent upon the Guardian's membership or presence on that body?

What are implications of the statement that the institution of the Guardianship does not detract from the powers granted to the Universal House of Justice by Bahá'u'lláh?

5. "However, quite apart from his function as a member and sacred head for life of the Universal House of Justice, the Guardian, functioning within his own sphere, had the right and duty 'to define the sphere of the legislative action' of the Universal House of Justice. In other words, he had the authority to state whether a matter was or was not already covered by the Sacred Texts and therefore whether it was within the authority of the Universal House of Justice to legislate upon it. No other person, apart from the Guardian, has the right or authority to make such definitions. The question therefore arises: In the absence of the Guardian, is the Universal House of Justice in danger of straying outside its proper sphere and thus falling into error? Here we must remember three things: First, Shoghi Effendi, during the thirty-six years of his Guardianship,

has already made innumerable such definitions, supplementing those made by 'Abdu'l-Bahá and by Bahá'u'lláh Himself. As already announced to the friends, a careful study of the Writings and interpretations on any subject on which the House of Justice proposes to legislate always precedes its act of legislation. Second, the Universal House of Justice, itself assured of divine guidance, is well aware of the absence of the Guardian and will approach all matters of legislation only when certain of its sphere of jurisdiction, a sphere which the Guardian has confidently described as 'clearly defined.' Third, we must not forget the Guardian's written statement about these two Institutions: 'Neither can, nor will ever, infringe upon the sacred and prescribed domain of the other.'"

(The Universal House of Justice, *Messages from the Universal House of Justice: 1963-1986*, pp. 84-85)

In the absence of the Guardian, is the Universal House of Justice in danger of straying outside its proper sphere and thus falling into error? If not, why not?

How does the institution of the Guardianship continue "to define the sphere of the legislative action" of the Universal House of Justice?

6. "In the Order of Bahá'u'lláh there are certain functions which are reserved to certain institutions, and others which are shared in common, even though they may be more in the special province of one or the other. For example, although the Hands of the Cause of God have the specific functions of protection and propagation, and are specialized for these functions, it is also the duty of the Universal House of Justice and the Spiritual Assemblies to protect and teach the Cause—indeed teaching is a sacred obligation placed upon every believer by Bahá'u'lláh. Similarly, although after the Master authoritative interpretation was exclusively vested in the Guardian, and although legislation is exclusively the function of the Universal House of Justice, these two Institutions are, in Shoghi Effendi's words, 'complementary in their aim and purpose.' 'Their common, their fundamental object is to ensure the continuity of that divinely appointed authority which flows from the Source of our Faith,

to safeguard the unity of its followers and to maintain the integrity and flexibility of its teachings.' Whereas the Universal House of Justice cannot undertake any function which exclusively appertained to the Guardian, it must continue to pursue the object which it shares in common with the Guardianship."

(The Universal House of Justice, *Messages from the Universal House of Justice: 1963-1986*, p. 86)

What functions of the Guardian can the Universal House of Justice not undertake?

What is the wisdom of institutions sharing certain functions, but possessing other specialized functions?

Illustrations

Reflect on the implications of the following excerpt on the functioning of the Universal House of Justice in the absence of a living Guardian:

"Even a cursory review of the workings of the House of Justice since its establishment in 1963 makes it clear to a believer that every directive issued by that body has been divinely inspired, that every plan it devised and every act it carried out has been blessed by Providence. Its achievements and victories, both at the World Centre of the Faith and around the world, and the progress it has made during the last three decades despite its modest resources, have been miraculous. In circumstances of crisis as well as of triumph, the House of Justice has been enabled to steer the Bahá'í community on the course set for it by the hand of the Almighty. All these accomplishments are entirely due to the assistance and confirmations of Bahá'u'lláh which have reached it continuously at all times, and guided every step it has taken in the execution of God's plan for mankind.

"It is natural that the members of the House of Justice are always conscious of that outpouring of divine assistance; they know only too well that the decisions of the House are guided by Bahá'u'lláh. They have openly declared before their electors their sense of unworthiness to serve on that august institution, but have confidently taken on the burden of such immense responsibility in the assurance of the protection, guidance and confirmations of Bahá'u'lláh which reach them during their deliberations.

"One of the most important decisions which the Universal House of Justice made soon after its election was the question of the Guardianship. Since Shoghi Effendi could not have appointed a successor to himself, the decision regarding this important matter had to be taken by this body, as there was nothing in the *Will and Testament* of 'Abdu'l-Bahá to show how to resolve a situation where there was no one to succeed Shoghi Effendi. The following statement was issued by the House of Justice on this vital matter:

> After prayerful and careful study of the Holy Texts bearing upon the question of the appointment of the successor to Shoghi Effendi as Guardian of the Cause of God, and after prolonged consultation which included consideration of the views of the Hands of the Cause of God residing in the Holy Land, the Universal House of Justice finds that there is no way to appoint or [to] legislate to make it possible to appoint a second Guardian to succeed Shoghi Effendi.

". . . in the absence of the Guardian, the Universal House of Justice, apart from turning to the Holy Text, consults the writings of Shoghi Effendi when it begins the process of legislation, or prepares its general communications, or makes decisions on various subjects. In this way, it ensures that its pronouncements are not in conflict with the meaning of the Holy Text and do not depart from the spirit of Bahá'u'lláh's revealed utterances. In the absence of the Guardian who was to have been its permanent head, the Universal House of Justice has no officers, all members having equal responsibility in consultation and other functions."

(Adib Taherzadeh, *The Covenant of Bahá'u'lláh*, pp. 398-400)

Analysis Questions

Answer the following questions. Suggested answers appear in Appendix A.

1. Which of the following statements about the Guardianship are correct? Circle all correct answers.

    A. Future Guardians are envisaged and referred to in the Bahá'í Writings.

    B. The Bahá'í Writings promise that the line of Guardians would endure forever.

    C. There are clear indications that the line of Guardians could be broken at some point.

    D. The Kitáb-i-Aqdas anticipates a break in the line of Guardians.

2. Which of the following statements accurately explain the relationship of the Guardianship and the Universal House of Justice? Circle all correct answers.

    A. The Bahá'í Writings envisaged the Guardian and the Universal House of Justice functioning together.

    B. The Guardian could not function in the absence of the Universal House of Justice.

    C. The Universal House of Justice could not function in the absence of a living Guardian.

    D. The inseparability of the Guardianship and the Universal House of Justice does not mean that both must function simultaneously.

3. Which of the following statements accurately describe the prerogatives and duties of the Guardian and the Universal House of Justice? Circle all correct answers.

    A. The Universal House of Justice must continue to pursue those functions the Guardian shared with the Universal House of Justice.

    B. The Universal House of Justice has the right to administer the Ḥuqúqu'lláh.

    C. The Guardian's function of interpretation has devolved upon the Universal House of Justice.

    D. Even though the Universal House of Justice may not appoint

Hands of the Cause, it must ensure the continuing discharge of the functions of protection and propagation vested in the institution of the Hands of the Cause.

Memorization and Presentation Exercises

A. Memorizing the Sacred and Authoritative Writings

Commit to memory the following quotations (or two of your choosing from this chapter):

"The tests of every dispensation are in direct proportion to the greatness of the Cause, and as heretofore such a manifest Covenant, written by the Supreme Pen, hath not been entered upon, the tests are proportionately more severe."

(*Selections from the Writings of 'Abdu'l-Bahá*, p. 210)

"Neither can, nor will ever, infringe upon the sacred and prescribed domain of the other. Neither will seek to curtail the specific and undoubted authority with which both have been divinely invested."

(Shoghi Effendi, *The World Order of Bahá'u'lláh*, p. 150)

B. Presenting the Themes of the Covenant

Prepare a brief presentation on the theme of the twin institutions of the Guardianship and the Universal House of Justice.

In your explanation, include discussion of:

1. the institutions of the Guardianship and the Universal House of Justice and the principle of inseparability;
2. the breaking of the line of Guardians; and
3. the Universal House of Justice functioning infallibly in the absence of a living Guardian.

Share your presentation with a partner or group.

CHAPTER 8
The Infallibility
of the Universal House of Justice

That which this body,
whether unanimously or by a majority doth carry,
that is verily the truth and the purpose of God Himself.
— 'Abdu'l-Bahá

Overview

A. The Guarantee of the Infallibility of the Universal House of Justice

One of the essential features of Bahá'u'lláh's Covenant is the infallibility of the Universal House of Justice. Bahá'u'lláh and 'Abdu'l-Bahá have explicitly guaranteed divine inspiration and infallible guidance for the Universal House of Justice. In His Tablets, Bahá'u'lláh declared:

> It is incumbent upon the Trustees of the House of Justice to take counsel together regarding those things which have not outwardly been revealed in the Book, and to enforce that which is agreeable to them. God will verily inspire them with whatsoever He willeth, and He, verily, is the Provider, the Omniscient.[1]

> Inasmuch as for each day there is a new problem and for every problem an expedient solution, such affairs should be referred to the Ministers of the House of Justice that they may act according to the needs and requirements of the time. They that, for the sake of God, arise to serve His Cause, are the recipients of divine inspiration from the unseen Kingdom. It is incumbent upon all to be obedient unto them.[2]

The guarantee of divine guidance for the Universal House of Justice has been repeatedly confirmed by 'Abdu'l-Bahá. In His Will and Testament, 'Abdu'l-Bahá referred to the Universal House of Justice as the institution "which God hath ordained as the source of all good and freed from all error."[3] 'Abdu'l-Bahá's Will and Testament further provided: "That which this body, whether unanimously or by a majority doth carry, that is verily the truth and the purpose of God Himself."[4] The Guardian and the Universal House of Justice are protected and unerringly guided by Bahá'u'lláh and the Báb: "The sacred and youthful branch, the Guardian of the Cause of God, as well as the Universal House of Justice . . ., are both under the care and protection of the Abhá Beauty, under the shelter and unerring guidance of the Exalted One . . . . Whatsoever they decide is of God."[5] 'Abdu'l-Bahá likewise made evident that the House of Justice "is under the protecting power of Bahá'u'lláh Himself."[6] "A universal, or international, House of Justice shall . . . be organized. Its rulings shall be in accordance with the commands and teachings of Bahá'u'lláh . . . ."[7]

B. The Nature of the Infallibility of the Universal House of Justice

According to 'Abdu'l-Bahá, "infallibility is of two kinds: essential infallibility and acquired infallibility."[8] "Essential infallibility is peculiar to the supreme Manifestation, for it is His essential requirement, and an essential requirement cannot be separated from the thing itself. The rays are the essential necessity of the sun and are inseparable from it."[9] Whatever emanates from the Manifestations of God "is identical with the truth, and conformable to reality."[10] "Whatever They say is the word of God, and whatever They perform is an upright action."[11] Thus, Bahá'u'lláh, like all the Manifestations of God, possessed essential infallibility.

In contrast to essential infallibility, "acquired infallibility is not a natural necessity; on the contrary, it is a ray of the bounty of infallibility which shines from the Sun of Reality upon hearts, and grants a share and portion of itself to souls. Although these souls have not essential infallibility, still they are under the protection of God—that is to say, God preserves them from error."[12] 'Abdu'l-Bahá affirmed that the

Universal House of Justice possesses "acquired infallibility":

> For instance, the Universal House of Justice, if it be
> established under the necessary conditions—with
> members elected from all the people—that House of
> Justice will be under the protection and the unerring
> guidance of God. If that House of Justice shall decide
> unanimously, or by a majority, upon any question not
> mentioned in the Book, that decision and command
> will be guarded from mistake.[13]

Infallibility has been conferred on the body of the Universal
House of Justice, not its individual members: "Now the members of
the House of Justice have not, individually, essential infallibility; but
the body of the House of Justice is under the protection and unerring
guidance of God: this is called conferred infallibility."[14]

It should be noted that there exists a difference between
omniscience (possessing all knowledge) and infallibility (being guarded
from mistake). The Manifestations of God are "omniscient at will."[15]
The following excerpt from Bahá'u'lláh's Writings illustrates this truth:
"[W]henever We desire to quote the sayings of the learned and of the
wise, presently there will appear before the face of thy Lord in the form
of a tablet all that which hath appeared in the world and is revealed in
the Holy Books and Scriptures."[16] Unlike Bahá'u'lláh, "the Universal
House of Justice is not omniscient...."[17] Like the Guardian, the House
of Justice "wants to be provided with facts when called upon to render
a decision, and like him it may well change its decision when new
facts emerge."[18]

C. The Scope of the Infallibility of the Universal House of Justice

Because, as human beings, we are limited by finite understandings
and traditional knowledge,[19] it may well be impossible for us to fully
comprehend the character and scope of the Universal House of Justice's
infallibility—a divine bounty that transcends human experience. In an
analogous context, Shoghi Effendi stated that it is "not for individual

145

believers to limit the sphere of the Guardian's authority."[20] Nevertheless, although a complete and exact understanding of the infallibility of the House of Justice may be beyond the reach of our minds, by examining the authoritative Writings of the Faith, it may still be possible to gain some sense of the general features of this infallibility.

The Bahá'í Writings addressing the issue of infallibility indicate that the Universal House of Justice is infallibly guided in any decision it makes in the discharge of its responsibilities. Referring to the Universal House of Justice (as well as the Guardian), 'Abdu'l-Bahá declared: "Whatsoever they decide is of God."[21] He further wrote: "Whatever will be its decision, by majority vote, shall be the real truth, inasmuch as that House is under the protection, unerring guidance and care of the one true Lord. He shall guard it from error and will protect it under the wing of His sanctity and infallibility."[22] Moreover, the House of Justice is "the source of all good and freed from all error."[23]

'Abdu'l-Bahá specifically confirmed that the Universal House of Justice is divinely guided in legislating on matters not outwardly revealed in the Book: "Unto the Most Holy Book every one must turn, and all that is not expressly recorded therein must be referred to the Universal House of Justice. That which this body, whether unanimously or by a majority doth carry, that is verily the truth and the purpose of God Himself."[24] Likewise, "[i]f that House of Justice shall decide unanimously, or by a majority, upon any question not mentioned in the Book, that decision and command will be guarded from mistake."[25]

Although the Writings at times refer to the infallibility of the Universal House of Justice in the context of its legislative function, the House of Justice's infallibility is not strictly limited to making laws. Several reasons suggest this. As noted above, 'Abdu'l-Bahá stated "[w]hatsoever" the House of Justice decides "is of God,"[26] and "[w]hatever will be its decision . . . shall be the real truth."[27] In these passages, 'Abdu'l-Bahá placed no limitations on the types of decisions in which the House of Justice would be divinely guided.

Moreover, that the infallibility of the Universal House of Justice extends to the discharge of all of its responsibilities is confirmed by examination of the purposes of the Covenant. "The essence of the Covenant is the continuation of divine guidance after the Ascension of the Prophet through the presence in this world of an institution to which all the friends turn and which can indisputably state what is the Will of God. After 'Abdu'l-Bahá the Guardianship and the Universal House of Justice are such institutions."[28] The "continuation of divine guidance" through the Universal House of Justice and its expression of "the Will of God" are manifest, for example, as it acts to "administer" the Faith's "affairs, coordinate its activities, promote its interests, execute its laws and defend its subsidiary institutions."[29] The Universal House of Justice itself has explained, in a letter written on its behalf, that as one of the "infallible Institutions which lie at the heart of the Covenant," it has the task of "applying the laws," in addition to "making laws."[30] The House of Justice is "invested" with the "inspiration required to enable it to guide the Cause of God."[31] It receives "divine guidance" in formulating teaching plans[32] and is conferred "unerring guidance" as it directs the development of the Administrative Order.[33] In "The Dispensation of Bahá'u'lláh," Shoghi Effendi clearly implied that the divine guidance received by the Universal House of Justice extends to "the conduct of the administrative affairs of the Faith."[34]

Further, one of 'Abdu'l-Bahá's writings specifically refers to the infallibility of the House of Justice not only in establishing laws, but also in making decisions:

> Let it not be imagined that the House of Justice will take any decision according to its own concepts and opinions. God forbid! The Supreme House of Justice will *take decisions* and *establish laws* through the inspiration and confirmation of the Holy Spirit, because it is in the safekeeping and under the shelter and protection of the Ancient Beauty . . . .[35]

One of the areas in which the Universal House of Justice may make decisions is in solving problems that have caused difference. 'Abdu'l-Bahá made clear that the House of Justice is unerringly guided in the discharge of this responsibility:

> Beware, beware lest anyone create a rift or stir up sedition.

147

> Should there be differences of opinion, the Supreme House of Justice would immediately resolve the problems. Whatever will be its decision, by majority vote, shall be the real truth, inasmuch as that House is under the protection, unerring guidance and care of the one true Lord.[36]

The above references demonstrate that the infallibility of the Universal House of Justice extends to "any decision" it makes. The House of Justice has "found nothing in the writings of Shoghi Effendi which suggests that the House of Justice would on any occasion reach a 'wrong decision'."[37] Furthermore, "although National and Local Spiritual Assemblies can receive divine guidance if they consult in the manner and spirit described by 'Abdu'l-Bahá, they do not share in the explicit guarantees of infallibility conferred upon the Universal House of Justice."[38] As the House of Justice has observed, "'Abdu'l-Bahá in His Will and Shoghi Effendi in his 'Dispensation of Bahá'u'lláh' have both explicitly stated that the elected members of the Universal House of Justice in consultation are recipients of unfailing Divine Guidance."[39]

D. Obedience to the Universal House of Justice

Bahá'u'lláh commanded His followers to obey "the Ministers of the House of Justice": "It is incumbent upon all to be obedient unto them."[40] 'Abdu'l-Bahá expanded upon the significance and dimensions of such obedience. He explained that obedience to the decisions of the Universal House of Justice "is a bounden and essential duty and an absolute obligation, and there is no escape for anyone."[41] God "has commanded the firm believers to obey that blessed, sanctified and all-subduing body, whose sovereignty is divinely ordained and of the Kingdom of Heaven and whose laws are inspired and spiritual."[42]

In relation to both the Universal House of Justice and the Guardian, 'Abdu'l-Bahá's Will and Testament pronounced:

> Whatsoever they decide is of God. Whoso obeyeth him not, neither obeyeth them, hath not obeyed God; whoso

rebelleth against him and against them hath rebelled against God; whoso opposeth him hath opposed God; whoso contendeth with them hath contended with God; whoso disputeth with him hath disputed with God; whoso denieth him hath denied God; whoso disbelieveth in him hath disbelieved in God; whoso deviateth, separateth himself and turneth aside from him hath in truth deviated, separated himself and turned aside from God. May the wrath, the fierce indignation, the vengeance of God rest upon him![43]

Not only must believers obey the Universal House of Justice, but they are also enjoined to seek its guidance: "All must seek guidance and turn unto . . . the House of Justice. And he that turneth unto whatsoever else is indeed in grievous error."[44] With regard to Bahá'u'lláh's new World Order, Shoghi Effendi wrote: "We must trust to time, and the guidance of God's Universal House of Justice, to obtain a clearer and fuller understanding of its provisions and implications."[45]

"The unchallengeable authority and assurance of divine guidance conferred upon the Universal House of Justice in the sacred Scriptures make it, at this time, the supreme and central institution of the Faith to which all must turn, and also the one body invested with the authority and inspiration required to enable it to guide the Cause of God and maintain unbroken the Covenant of Bahá'u'lláh."[46] Bahá'ís "can have complete confidence in the ability of the Universal House of Justice to function 'under the care and protection of the Abhá Beauty, under the shelter and unerring guidance of His Holiness, the Exalted One.'"[47]

Study Questions

Answer the following questions based on the above Overview:

CONTENT QUESTIONS

1. ". . . the House of Justice which God hath ordained as the source of all _____ and freed from all _____."

149

2. "That which this body, whether unanimously or by a _____ doth carry, that is verily the _____ and the purpose of _____ Himself."

3. What are the two kinds of infallibility described by 'Abdu'l-Bahá, and what is the nature of each?

4. Why does the Universal House of Justice want to be provided with facts before rendering a decision?

5. Are the members of the Universal House of Justice individually infallible?

6. "Whatever will be its [the Universal House of Justice's] decision, by _____ vote, shall be the real _____, inasmuch as that House is under the _____, _____ _____ and _____ of the one true Lord."

7. Is the infallibility of the Universal House of Justice confined to the exercise of its legislative function? If not, what Writings would support a broader view of the House of Justice's infallibility?

8. What is the difference between the divine guidance received by National and Local Spiritual Assemblies and that received by the Universal House of Justice?

9. "All must seek _____ and turn unto . . . the House of Justice. And he that turneth unto whatsoever else is indeed in _____ _____."

APPLICATION/DISCUSSION QUESTIONS
1. How does the guarantee of infallibility conferred on the Universal House of Justice by Bahá'u'lláh and 'Abdu'l-Bahá instill confidence in believers about the direction and destiny of the Cause?

2. As to the Universal House of Justice, 'Abdu'l-Bahá wrote: "That which this body, whether unanimously or by a majority doth carry, that is verily the truth and the purpose of God Himself." What are the implications of this statement for how believers should regard the letters of the Universal House of Justice addressed to the Bahá'ís of the world? How would we respond if we received a letter personally addressed to us from God?

3. In relation to "the Ministers of the House of Justice," Bahá'u'lláh declared: "It is incumbent upon all to be obedient unto them." How can believers express their obedience in relation to the teaching plans of the Universal House of Justice? Are there degrees of such obedience?

4. How can one strive to obey a decision of the Universal House of Justice even if one does not immediately understand the wisdom of that decision?

Quotations for Reflection

Answer the questions following the quotations below:

1. "Say, O people: Verily the Supreme House of Justice is under the wings of your Lord, the Compassionate, the All-Merciful, that is, under His protection, His care, and His shelter; for He has commanded the firm believers to obey that blessed, sanctified and all-subduing body, whose sovereignty is divinely ordained and of the Kingdom of Heaven and whose laws are inspired and spiritual."

('Abdu'l-Bahá, quoted in the Universal House of Justice, *Messages from the Universal House of Justice: 1963-1986*, p. 85)

What is the relationship of the Universal House of Justice to God?

How is the Universal House of Justice distinctive in comparison with the institutions of previous religions?

2. "Whatever will be its decision, by majority vote, shall be the real truth, inasmuch as that House is under the protection, unerring guidance and care of the one true Lord. He shall guard it from error and will protect it under the wing of His sanctity and infallibility."

('Abdu'l-Bahá, quoted in the Universal House of Justice, *Messages from the Universal House of Justice: 1963-1986*, p. 53)

How should any decision of the Universal House of Justice be viewed? Why?

3. "Unto the Most Holy Book every one must turn, and all that is not expressly recorded therein must be referred to the Universal House of Justice. That which this body, whether unanimously or by a majority doth carry, that is verily the truth and the purpose of God Himself. . . . It is incumbent upon these members (of the Universal House of Justice) to gather in a certain place and deliberate upon all problems which have caused difference, questions that are obscure and matters that are not expressly recorded in the Book. Whatsoever they decide has the same effect as the Text itself."

(*Will and Testament of 'Abdu'l-Bahá*, pp. 19-20)

What is the effect of that which the Universal House of Justice decides?

How can believers (or anyone else) come to know the purpose of God in this day?

4. "All must consider themselves to be of the order of subjects, submissive and obedient to the commandments of God and the laws of the House of Justice. Should any deviate by so much as a needle's point from the decrees of the Universal House of Justice, or falter in his compliance therewith, then is he of the outcast and rejected."

(*Selections from the Writings of 'Abdu'l-Bahá*, p. 68)

How should believers relate to the Universal House of Justice?

Why is it that if any "deviate by so much as a needle's point from the decrees of the Universal House of Justice, or falter in his compliance therewith, then is he of the outcast and rejected"?

5. "The Universal House of Justice, beyond its function as the enactor of legislation, has been invested with the more general functions of protecting and administering the Cause, solving obscure questions and deciding upon matters that have caused difference. . . . 'Abdu'l-Bahá in His Will and Shoghi Effendi in his 'Dispensation of Bahá'u'lláh' have both explicitly stated that the elected members of the Universal House of Justice in consultation are recipients of unfailing Divine Guidance."

(The Universal House of Justice, *Messages from the Universal House of Justice: 1963-1986*, p. 157)

Beyond its function as the enactor of legislation, what other functions does the Universal House of Justice carry out?

Is the Universal House of Justice divinely guided in the exercise of functions other than legislation?

6. "When the Universal House of Justice shall have stepped forth from the realm of hope into that of visible fulfilment and its fame be established in every corner and clime of the world, then that august body—solidly grounded and founded on the firm and unshakeable foundation of the entire Bahá'í community of East and West, and the recipient of the bounties of God and His inspiration—will proceed to devise and carry out important undertakings, world-wide activities and the establishment of glorious institutions. By this means the renown of the Cause of God will become world-wide and its light will illumine the whole earth."

(Shoghi Effendi, *The Compilation of Compilations*, vol. I, p. 329)

By what means will the renown of the Cause of God become world-wide and its light illumine the whole earth?

What are some of the "important undertakings" and "world-wide activities" the Universal House of Justice has devised and carried out? What are some of the "glorious institutions" the Universal House of Justice has established?

Illustrations

What do the following illustrations convey about why believers should obey the Universal House of Justice?

"Now, regarding the future of the Faith, 'Abdu'l-Bahá suddenly began to continually emphasize the need for the Universal House of Justice and the significance of its establishment. In clearly defined statements, He made us understand that the friends should not assume that after the setting of the Sun of the Covenant, the Cause of God would fall into the hands of the wicked and the corrupt. He emphasized this point repeatedly; one night He instructed us thus: 'Write down My words, and communicate them to all parts of the world. Commit them to memory and mention them to anyone with whom you come into contact, so that no doubt may remain that after Me the Faith will be in the hands of the Universal House of Justice.'

"Since He had instructed that we should record His words, that night in the pilgrim house everyone wrote down whatever they could remember of His utterances. My notes are as follows:

"The night of Monday, the 16th day of Jamádí'u'lláh, A.H. 1319 A.H. [31 August 1903] we were in the presence of 'Abdu'l-Bahá. He made certain remarks regarding the Universal House of Justice, which in accordance with His instructions are recorded as follows:

"He stated: 'Nothing causes me more unhappiness than disunity, and this can only be remedied by obedience to the command of the Universal House of Justice. Even before the establishment of the House of Justice, the friends must be obedient to the existing Spiritual Assemblies even if they know of a certainty that their judgement is flawed. If this were not complied with, the mighty citadel of the Faith of God would not be safeguarded. All must obey the Universal House of Justice. Obedience to it is obedience to the Cause. Opposition to it is opposition to the Blessed Beauty. Denial of it is denial of God, the True One. Renouncing any word of the House of Justice is like unto the renunciation of a word from the Kitáb-i-Aqdas. Observe, how important this matter is! The Blessed Beauty has ordained the House of Justice as the law-maker. If the votes of the members are not unanimous and there are differences of views, then the vote of the majority is the vote of the Blessed Beauty.'

"He then added: 'Take this very moment. Should the Universal House of Justice be operating, by the one True God, beside Whom there is no God, I would have been the first to obey its decree, even if it should be against me. . . . Its command is the Blessed Command. Discuss this matter amongst yourselves, so that it may not be forgotten. Speak of it to one another; even make a written note of it.'. . .

"'Abdu'l-Bahá used to talk mostly (in those days) about the importance of the House of Justice. One night, when He spoke on this subject again He said, 'If the House of Justice had been operating in this day and pronounced my death sentence, all would have to obey.'

"The late Muḥammad Riḍáy-i-Qannád was disturbed at this statement by the Master, and he asked, 'Is the House of Justice of God, or is it not?'

"'Of course it is,' replied the Master.

"'How then is it possible for that which is of God to condemn He Who is of God?' asked he.

"'My object', 'Abdu'l-Bahá replied, 'is that you may know that on that day the House of Justice is the true one of God, for the Blessed Beauty has ordained it to be the law-maker.'"

(Youness Afroukhteh, *Memories of Nine Years in 'Akká*, pp. 169-72)

"The authority of the Guardian and the Universal House of Justice go back to the authority of Bahá'u'lláh Himself, so similar principles apply. One should obey them because one *knows* that they are divinely guided. I can recall more than one occasion on which I found myself either unable to understand a decision of the Universal House of Justice or in disagreement with it. You know, the House of Justice doesn't always have unanimous decisions; it has majority decisions sometimes. Such a situation is not surprising of course. The House of Justice is infallible, but individual human beings aren't, so it's only logical that sometimes one should initially disagree with a decision that is reached. In all cases, naturally, I have accepted the decision and after a lapse of time I have always found why the House of Justice was right and I was wrong. The interesting thing is that it isn't only that it was for reasons that I didn't recognize at the time—'All right, that was what I misunderstood in the consultation, I now know what was right'—but sometimes even because of things that I could not have known at the time the decision was made. The ways of God . . . are mysterious, even when they come through His institutions."

(Ian Semple, "Obedience" (lecture, Haifa, Israel, July 26, 1991))

Analysis Questions

Answer the following questions. Suggested answers appear in Appendix A.

1. Which one of the following statements regarding infallibility is correct?
> A. The Universal House of Justice possesses essential infallibility.
> B. The members of the Universal House of Justice possess essential infallibility.
> C. The members of the Universal House of Justice possess conferred infallibility.
> D. The Universal House of Justice possesses conferred infallibility.

2. Which of the following statements accurately describe the nature of the infallibility of the Universal House of Justice? Circle all correct answers.
> A. Because the Universal House of Justice is infallible, it is omniscient.
> B. The Universal House of Justice wants to be provided with facts when called upon to render a decision.
> C. The Universal House of Justice may change its decision if new facts emerge.
> D. The Universal House of Justice is guarded from mistake.

3. Which of the following statements accurately describe the scope of the infallibility of the Universal House of Justice? Circle all correct answers.

> A. Whatever is the decision of the Universal House of Justice is the real truth.
> B. If the Universal House of Justice decides upon any question not mentioned in the Book, that decision is guarded from mistake.
> C. The Universal House of Justice is infallible in interpreting the Writings.
> D. The Universal House of Justice is guided by God in the implementation of the laws of the Kitáb-i-Aqdas.

Memorization and Presentation Exercises

A. Memorizing the Sacred and Authoritative Writings

Commit to memory the following quotations (or two of your choosing from this chapter):

"Unto the Most Holy Book every one must turn, and all that is not expressly recorded therein must be referred to the Universal House of Justice. That which this body, whether unanimously or by a majority doth carry, that is verily the truth and the purpose of God Himself."
(*Will and Testament of 'Abdu'l-Bahá*, p. 19)

"All must consider themselves to be of the order of subjects, submissive and obedient to the commandments of God and the laws of the House of Justice. Should any deviate by so much as a needle's point from the decrees of the Universal House of Justice, or falter in his compliance therewith, then is he of the outcast and rejected."
(*Selections from the Writings of 'Abdu'l-Bahá*, p. 68)

B. Presenting the Themes of the Covenant

Prepare a brief presentation on the theme of the infallibility of the Universal House of Justice.

In your explanation, include discussion of:

1. the guarantee of the infallibility of the Universal House of Justice;
2. the nature and scope of the infallibility of the Universal House of Justice; and
3. the importance of obedience to the Universal House of Justice.

Share your presentation with a partner or group.

CHAPTER 9

The Protection of the Cause of God

. . . Guard ye the Cause of God,
protect His law and have the utmost fear of discord.
— 'Abdu'l-Bahá

Overview

A. Internal Attacks and the Importance
of the Protection of the Cause of God

"The Bahá'í Faith has not lacked for ambitious men" who have sought to "seize the reins of authority and distort the Faith for their own ends . . . ."[1] Individuals who have attempted to create division within the Cause of God have included some of its "most powerful and renowned" adherents, some of its "ablest propagators, champions, and administrators,"[2] and even some of the "most highly placed amongst the kith and kin"[3] of Bahá'u'lláh, 'Abdu'l-Bahá, and Shoghi Effendi. In "every case," however, such individuals "have broken themselves and dashed their hopes on the rock of the Covenant."[4] 'Abdu'l-Bahá explained that were it not for "the protecting power of the Covenant to guard the impregnable fort of the Cause of God, there would arise among the Bahá'ís, in one day, a thousand different sects as was the case in former ages."[5] Since the Faith's inception, for more than a century and half,[6] every attempt to create a "permanent cleavage"[7] within the Cause has resulted in failure. This is a proof of "the supreme gift" of Bahá'u'lláh's "incomparable Covenant."[8]

What principles have guarded the Cause of God from schism? How has the Faith maintained its unity, despite repeated attempts to shatter that unity? And what should be the response of Bahá'ís to those who seek to violate the Faith's integrity? The features of the Covenant discussed in previous chapters bear on these questions. Also relevant are other principles, discussed below, that specifically address how the Faith should be protected and what should be the response to those who seek to impair its unity and integrity.

'Abdu'l-Bahá referred to the supreme importance of protecting God's Cause: "The greatest of all things is the protection of the True Faith of God, the preservation of His Law, the safeguarding of His Cause and service unto His Word."[9] The responsibility to protect the Faith rests with the institutions of the Administrative Order.[10] Additionally, 'Abdu'l-Bahá exhorted the "beloved of the Lord" to strive to "shield the Cause of God from the onslaught of the insincere" who "cause the straight to become crooked and all benevolent efforts to produce contrary results."[11] He counseled: "Guard ye the Cause of God, protect His law and have the utmost fear of discord."[12]

B. Meaning of Covenant-breaking

A principle of paramount importance in the protection of the Faith is avoidance of those who have broken Bahá'u'lláh's Covenant: "[O]ne of the greatest and most fundamental principles of the Cause of God is to shun and avoid entirely the Covenant-breakers, for they will utterly destroy the Cause of God, exterminate His Law and render of no account all efforts exerted in the past."[13] A "Covenant-breaker . . . is one who disobeys and turns away from the Center of the Covenant."[14] The Universal House of Justice has further elucidated the meaning of Covenant-breaking:

> Every Bahá'í is at liberty, nay is urged, to freely express his opinion and his understanding of the Teachings, but all this is in a totally different category from that of a Bahá'í who opposes the clear Teachings of Bahá'u'lláh or who asserts his own opinion as an authoritative and correct interpretation of the Teachings, and attacks or opposes the very Institutions which Bahá'u'lláh has created to protect His Covenant. When a person declares his acceptance of Bahá'u'lláh as a Manifestation of God he becomes a party to the Covenant and accepts the totality of His Revelation. If he then turns round and

attacks Bahá'u'lláh or the central Institution of the Faith he violates the Covenant. If this happens every effort is made to help that person to see the illogicality and error of his actions, but if he persists he must, in accordance with the instructions of Bahá'u'lláh Himself, be shunned as a Covenant-breaker.[15]

Expounding on the causes of Covenant-breaking, 'Abdu'l-Bahá wrote that Covenant-breakers are "lost in passion and self."[16] They are motivated by "personal desires and the achievement of leadership."[17] In essence, Covenant-breakers are afflicted with the spiritual illness of "soaring ambition and deep self-love."[18] They "do not doubt the validity of the Covenant but selfish motives have dragged them to this condition. It is not that they do not know what they do—they are perfectly aware and still they exhibit opposition."[19] There is "absolutely nothing keeping those who have broken the Covenant . . . out of the Cause of God except their *own inner spiritually sick* condition."[20]

In "seeking leadership," Covenant-breakers instill "doubts among the friends that they may cause differences, and that these differences may result in their drawing a party to themselves."[21] Such enemies of the Faith attempt to authoritatively interpret the Writings, color the meaning according to their own capacity, and collect around them a following, promoting their own station and attempting to make a division in the Cause.[22] In His Will and Testament, 'Abdu'l-Bahá warned: "No doubt every vainglorious one that purposeth dissension and discord will not openly declare his evil purposes, nay rather, even as impure gold, will he seize upon divers measures and various pretexts that he may separate the gathering of the people of Bahá."[23] Covenant-breakers "outwardly . . . assert their firmness and steadfastness in the Covenant but when they come across responsive ears they secretly sow the seeds of suspicion."[24] "Probably no group of people in the world have softer tongues, or proclaim more loudly their innocence, than those who in their heart of hearts, and by their every act, are enemies of the Center of the Covenant."[25]

In addition to understanding who are Covenant-breakers, it is important to comprehend who are *not* Covenant-breakers. Those "who have withdrawn from the Cause because they no longer feel that they can support its Teachings and Institutions sincerely, are not Covenant-breakers—they are non-Bahá'ís and should just be treated as such."[26] "In general, . . . a person who has withdrawn from the Faith is regarded as being among the generality of humankind with whom the Bahá'ís are enjoined to associate 'in joy and fragrance'."[27] Moreover, believers who have flagrantly violated the laws of the Faith and who have been sanctioned through the removal of their administrative (voting) rights are not considered Covenant-breakers. "There is a sharp distinction between depriving a believer of his voting rights, which is a severe disciplinary measure and not a spiritual sanction, and pronouncing a former believer to be a truly spiritually diseased soul . . . ."[28] Additionally, a "believer failing in his duties in living the Bahá'í life" would not be "a Covenant-breaker of Bahá'u'lláh's Lesser Covenant deserving to be identified and declared as such."[29] Finally, there may be those believers who due to "ignorance or lack of proper training"[30] may have misunderstood some fundamental teaching of the Faith; such individuals are also not Covenant-breakers. Only a Bahá'í who, after counseling and exhortation, persists in attacking or disobeying the Faith's central Institution is deemed a Covenant-breaker.

In principle, only the Head of the Faith (in this day, the Universal House of Justice) may designate someone as a Covenant-breaker.[31] In the process of determining whether an individual has broken the Covenant, the Universal House of Justice has been assisted by the Hands of the Cause of God and, more recently, by the International Teaching Centre.[32] Today, the International Teaching Centre "must investigate all cases of incipient Covenant-breaking—employing, as necessary, the services of the Continental Counsellors and their auxiliaries and evaluating their reports—and decide whether the offender should be expelled from the Cause, submitting the decision to the Universal House of Justice for its consideration."[33] The International Teaching Centre "follows a similar procedure for the reinstatement of a contrite Covenant-breaker."[34]

C. Avoidance of Covenant-breakers

'Abdu'l-Bahá provided guidance on how believers should relate to Covenant-breakers: "[T]he beloved of the Lord must entirely shun them . . . ."[35] He explained that "Bahá'u'lláh, in all the Tablets and Epistles, forbade the true and firm friends from associating and meeting the violators of the Covenant of His Holiness, the Báb, saying that no one should go near them because their breath is like the poison of the snake that kills instantly."[36] "In the Holy Writings of His Holiness, Bahá'u'lláh, in a thousand places at least, the violators of the Covenant are execrated and condemned."[37] Thus, both "Bahá'u'lláh and the Master in many places and very emphatically have told us to shun entirely all Covenant breakers as they are afflicted with what we might try and define as a contagious spiritual disease . . . ."[38] It is because of the contagious nature of the spiritual ailment of Covenant-breaking that believers are directed to avoid those so afflicted: "The believers are commanded to shun Covenant-breakers for the same reason as healthy people do not associate with a person suffering from a serious contagious illness. A contagiously sick person cannot catch health from a thousand healthy people, but, on the contrary, he can infect them with his illness. Therefore such a person is quarantined and only those few people qualified to attend him do so."[39]

"The Master and Bahá'u'lláh have taught us that associating with these souls is not likely to heal them at all, but on the contrary exposes one to grave danger of contagion. The history of the Faith has proved this over and over again. The only way we can prove to such people that they are wrong is to censure their conduct; if we sympathise with them we only fortify their perversity and waywardness."[40] Accordingly, believers are "strictly forbidden" from having "personal contact or entering into correspondence" with Covenant-breakers.[41] "Bahá'ís must cease to have any association" with a Covenant-breaker "until such time as he repents when, of course, he can be accepted back into the community."[42] "These souls are not lost forever."[43] For instance, one of the most notorious Covenant-breakers in the history of the Faith was Mírzá Yaḥyá—Bahá'u'lláh's treacherous half-brother.[44] Yet, in the Kitáb-i-Aqdas, Bahá'u'lláh observed that God would even forgive Mírzá Yaḥyá if he repented.[45] "It follows, therefore, that God will forgive any soul *if he repents*."[46]

Is the shunning of Covenant-breakers consistent with the Bahá'í principles of love and unity? 'Abdu'l-Bahá set forth the general principle that believers should "treat compassionately all humankind—except for those who have some selfish, private motive, or some disease of the soul," for kindness "far from awakening them to the error of their ways, . . . maketh them to continue in their perversity as before."[47] In a letter on his behalf, Shoghi Effendi explained that "it is not personal ill-will, or lack of love, which leads to the excommunication of a person, but rather the fact that he has become like a cancer which must be removed before the entire body is destroyed."[48] If "a man cuts a cancer out of his body to preserve his health and very life, no one would suggest that for the sake of unity it should be reintroduced into the otherwise healthy organism. On the contrary, what was once a part of him has so radically changed as to have become a poison."[49] By shunning Covenant-breakers, believers serve to preserve the unity of the Cause: "[W]e must all turn our faces to the appointed Center" in order that Bahá'í unity "might be preserved"; otherwise, 'Abdu'l-Bahá warned, "in one year" the Bahá'ís would be "divided into a thousand sects."[50] "The seriousness of Covenant-breaking is that it strikes at the very centre and foundation of the unity of mankind. If God were to allow the instrument to be divided and impaired, how then would His purpose be achieved?"[51]

It may be asked whether avoiding contact with Covenant-breakers conflicts with the principle of independent investigation of the truth. The Universal House of Justice has written that "Bahá'ís themselves are commanded by Bahá'u'lláh to investigate truth independently, to 'see with' their 'own eyes, and not through the eyes of others'. Every Bahá'í is at liberty, nay is urged, to freely express his opinion and his understanding of the Teachings, but all this is in a totally different category from that of a Bahá'í who opposes the clear Teachings of Bahá'u'lláh."[52] By definition, the "most important and fundamental qualification" for being a Bahá'í is "recognition of the station of Bahá'u'lláh" as the Manifestation of God.[53] Because Bahá'u'lláh is God's Manifestation for this day, "whatever emanates" from Him is "identical with the truth."[54] Among the truths that have emanated from Bahá'u'lláh is the injunction that for their personal spiritual health and the spiritual health of the Bahá'í community, believers should shun Covenant-breakers. To disregard this injunction in the name of "independent investigation of the truth" is to imply that Bahá'u'lláh's Teachings are not, in fact, true and that truth must be found elsewhere. For a Bahá'í, this would be a logical and moral contradiction.

It is important to remember two qualifications in relation to the principle of non-association with Covenant-breakers:

> First, the civil rights of Covenant-breakers must be scrupulously upheld. For example, if a Bahá'í owes a debt to a person who breaks the Covenant he must be sure that it is repaid and that his obligations are met.
>
> Secondly, although the believers are required to avoid, if possible, all contact with Covenant-breakers it sometimes happens that contact on business matters cannot be avoided. For example, in one city the head of the rate collection department was a Covenant-breaker. In such situations the believers should restrict their contact with the Covenant-breaker to a purely formal business level and to an absolute minimum.[55]

As noted earlier, in this day, only the Universal House of Justice may designate an individual as a Covenant-breaker. If a Bahá'í encounters persons who seek to "sow the seeds of doubt in the minds of the friends and undermine the Faith,"[56] the believer should refer the matter to the appropriate Bahá'í institutions. Whenever "believers become aware of such problems, they should immediately contact whatever institution they feel moved to turn to, whether it be a Counsellor, an Auxiliary Board member, the National Spiritual Assembly or their own Local Assembly. It then becomes the duty of that institution to ensure that the report is fed into the correct channels and that all the other institutions affected are promptly informed."[57] If "a person evinces the Covenant-breaking spirit," the "Counsellors, and others who are appointed for the service, do all they can to rid him of it."[58]

D. Covenant-breaker Writings and Electronic Communications

Bahá'ís are prohibited from having personal contact with Covenant-breakers, but are believers also forbidden from reading the writings of Covenant-breakers? The Universal House of Justice has explained:

To read the writings of Covenant-breakers is not forbidden to the believers and does not constitute in itself an act of Covenant-breaking. Indeed, some of the Bahá'ís have the unpleasant duty to read such literature as part of their responsibilities for protecting the Cause of Bahá'u'lláh. However, the friends are warned in the strongest terms against reading such literature because Covenant-breaking is a spiritual poison and the calumnies and distortions of the truth which the Covenant-breakers give out are such that they can undermine the faith of the believer and plant the seeds of doubt unless he is forearmed with an unshakable belief in Bahá'u'lláh and His Covenant and a knowledge of the true facts.[59]

"It is better not to read books by Covenant Breakers because they are haters of the Light, sufferers from a spiritual leprosy, so to speak. But books by well meaning yet unenlightened enemies of the Cause can be read so as to refute their charges."[60] As to texts written by Covenant-breakers, "the friends should be advised to ignore these books . . . . There should certainly be no attempt made to destroy or remove such books from libraries. On the other hand there is no need at all for the friends to acquire them and, indeed, the best plan is to ignore them entirely."[61]

Because the number of Covenant-breakers in the world is minuscule in comparison to the size of the Bahá'í community, most believers may never personally meet a Covenant-breaker. However, in recent years, with the advent and growth of the Internet, it is now possible for Covenant-breakers to attempt to communicate with believers all over the world. Thus, today, believers may well encounter websites, chat rooms, or emails containing writings of Covenant-breakers. In response to inquiries by believers as to such encounters, the Universal House of Justice has, in letters written on its behalf, provided the following guidance:

The House of Justice is aware of such activities on the part of Covenant-breakers, and while it is closely following this issue, it sees no cause for undue concern. The friends should, of course, ignore any materials produced by Covenant-breakers which they may receive unsolicited by email or happen on while exploring the World Wide Web. . . .

The best countermeasure to Covenant-breaker initiatives and the greatest protection for the Cause is for the believers to acquire a deeper appreciation of the station and purpose of Bahá'u'lláh and to become well-grounded in His Covenant.[62]

The House of Justice feels that, when Bahá'ís are teaching in an online "chat room" and Covenant-breakers intrude upon the discussion, the friends should not feel obliged to sign off simply because Covenant-breakers are present in this virtual space. They should, however, refrain from knowingly engaging the Covenant-breakers in discussions and, in any case, should avoid being drawn into contentious or disputatious situations.[63]

With the establishment of websites providing authentic materials on the Faith,[64] sites maintained by Covenant-breaker groups "will have a diminishing impact" in the context of the information deluge on the Internet and against the background of the authorized Bahá'í sources now available.[65]

E. Recent Internal Opposition

During the 1990's, the Universal House of Justice noted the emergence of a new form of internal opposition to the Faith. Using the Internet, a small number of individuals began engaging in a campaign to question the integrity of the Faith's Teachings and to undermine the authority of its institutions. Unlike opposition in the past, this new form has generally not explicitly attacked the central Institution of the Faith, but rather subtly attempted to cast doubt on the authority of the Covenant and the nature of the Teachings. For example, "while purporting to accept the legitimacy of the Guardianship and the Universal House of Justice as twin successors of Bahá'u'lláh and the Centre of His Covenant," such opposition has attempted to "cast doubt on the nature and scope of the authority conferred on them in the Writings."[66]

"When other Bahá'ís have pointed out that such arguments contradict explicit statements of the Master, persons behind the scheme have responded by calling into question the soundness of 'Abdu'l-Bahá's own judgement and perspective. Gradually, these arguments have exposed the view of those involved that Bahá'u'lláh Himself was not the voice of God to our age but merely a particularly enlightened moral philosopher, one whose primary concern was to reform existing society."[67] "The purpose of some of those responsible would seem to be that, by diminishing the station of Bahá'u'lláh—a disservice done to previous Manifestations by people similarly inclined —, by casting doubt on the authority conferred on 'Abdu'l-Bahá, the Guardian and the Universal House of Justice, and by calling into question the integrity of Bahá'í administrative processes, they would be able to persuade a number of unwary followers that the Bahá'í Faith is in fact not a Divine Revelation but a kind of socio-political system being manipulated by ambitious individuals."[68]

This campaign has promoted, in place of the "institutional authority" established by Bahá'u'lláh's Covenant, "a kind of interpretive authority" that is attributed "to the views of persons technically trained in Middle East studies."[69] It has been argued that only those with training in Middle East studies can truly understand and interpret the Writings and Teachings of Bahá'u'lláh, Who was responding to the historical circumstances of the nineteenth century. Of course, this argument contradicts the principle that "the function of making authoritative interpretations of the Teachings is confined solely and exclusively to the Guardian" and that no "other institution, person or group of persons can assume that function."[70] Moreover, the argument rests on the false assumption that religion is a social creation of man, rather than a revelation from God: "It . . . ignores the issues of God's continuous relationship with His creation and His intervention in human life and history. Yet, from a Bahá'í point of view, it is precisely this intervention that is the central theme of the Teachings of the Founders of the revealed religions . . . ."[71]

Among the strategies of those engaged in this scheme of

opposition has been "to sow the seeds of doubt among believers about the Faith's teachings and institutions by appealing to unexamined prejudices that Bahá'ís may have unconsciously absorbed from non-Bahá'í society."[72] For example, Bahá'u'lláh's law limiting membership of the Universal House of Justice to men—a law explicitly confirmed by the interpretations of 'Abdu'l-Bahá and the Guardian[73]—is "misrepresented as merely a 'temporary measure' subject to eventual revision if sufficient pressure is brought to bear."[74] "Similarly, Shoghi Effendi's explanation of Bahá'u'lláh's vision of the future Bahá'í World Commonwealth that will unite spiritual and civil authority is dismissed in favour of the assertion that the modern political concept of 'separation of church and state' is somehow one that Bahá'u'lláh intended as a basic principle of the World Order He has founded."[75] Another strategy has been to denounce the integrity of Bahá'í elections, particularly that of the Universal House of Justice. All of these efforts have been aimed at undermining the confidence of believers in the Administrative Order.

Typically, when the above arguments have been challenged, the response of those behind the campaign of opposition has been that such challenges constitute infringement of their civil rights, including their free speech rights. Such a response is "meaningless in the light of the purely voluntary nature of Bahá'í membership."[76] As the Universal House of Justice has explained in a letter on its behalf:

> One is entirely free to accept or reject the system of belief Bahá'u'lláh teaches. The Bahá'í Faith is a religion which believes ardently in freedom of spiritual choice. No one is—or can ever be—compelled to be a Bahá'í, nor does any discredit attach to one who, having decided, for whatever reason, that he or she cannot continue to accept the Teachings, may decide to renounce them. What one cannot properly do is to behave in a way that undermines the unity of the Bahá'í community, by challenging the institutional authority that is an integral part of the Faith one professes to have accepted.[77]

"Discussion with those who sincerely raise problematic issues . . . can be beneficial and enlightening. However, to continue dialogue with those who have shown a fixed antagonism to the Faith, and have demonstrated their imperviousness to any ideas other than their own, is usually fruitless and, for the Bahá'ís who take part, can be burdensome and even spiritually corrosive."[78] "When we encounter minds that are closed and hearts that are darkened by evident malice, Bahá'u'lláh urges that we leave such persons to God and turn our attention to the opportunities which multiply daily for the promotion of the truths which He teaches."[79] Thus, "the friends should be advised to just leave these people alone, for their influence can be nothing but negative and destructive. . . ."[80]

The significance of this recent campaign of opposition is not its potential for success. It has already failed, as have all previous attempts, when faced with the clarity and power of Bahá'u'lláh's Covenant. Most of the principal actors are no longer Bahá'ís. Moreover, the Bahá'í community has not been persuaded by arguments that have contradicted the authoritative Writings of the Faith. This latest campaign has been discussed here because it lends perspective to a "new kind of internal opposition to Bahá'u'lláh's Mission," an "opposition that takes aim directly at Bahá'u'lláh's assertion of the spiritual nature of reality and of humanity's dependence on the interventions of Divine Revelation."[81]

Such opposition also serves as a reminder of the critical role of knowledge in the protection of the Faith: "The Cause of God must be protected from the enemies of the Faith, and from those who sow seeds of doubt in the hearts of the believers, and the greatest of all protections is knowledge . . . ."[82] Knowledge and appreciation of the Covenant is "the stronghold of the faith of every Bahá'í, and that which enables him to withstand every test and the attacks of the enemies outside the Faith, and the far more dangerous, insidious, lukewarm people inside the Faith who have no real attachment to the Covenant, and consequently uphold the intellectual aspect of the teachings while at the same time undermining the spiritual foundation upon which the whole Cause of God rests."[83] Knowledge of the Covenant must also be coupled with the spiritual qualities of humility and selflessness.[84] In referring to internal enemies of the Faith, 'Abdu'l-Bahá wrote: "They gave up everlasting glory in exchange for human pride . . . ."[85] The underlying spiritual cause of much of the internal opposition faced by the Faith appears to be egotism, pride, and self-glorification—allowing one's lower nature to develop into "a monster of selfishness."[86] Bahá'ís must, therefore, ever strive to purge themselves of self and ego.[87]

Accordingly, through continual efforts to obtain a deeper understanding of the Covenant and to develop the virtues of humility and selflessness, every believer can contribute to "the protection of the True Faith of God, the preservation of His Law, the safeguarding of His Cause and service unto His Word."[88]

Study Questions

Answer the following questions based on the above Overview:

CONTENT QUESTIONS

1. "And now, one of the greatest and most fundamental _____ of the Cause of God is to _____ and avoid _____ the _____, for they will utterly _____ the Cause of God, _____ His Law and render of ____ account all efforts exerted in the past."

2. What is the definition of a Covenant-breaker? Are those who have withdrawn from the Faith Covenant-breakers? Are those who have failed in their duties to live the Bahá'í life Covenant-breakers?

3. Are Covenant-breakers aware of what they are doing? If so, why do they oppose the Covenant?

4. Who investigates cases of potential Covenant-breaking? In this day, no person can be considered a Covenant-breaker unless he has been so designated by what institution?

5. What kind of contact should believers have with Covenant-breakers?

6. What should believers do when they become aware of individuals who are sowing the seeds of doubt in the minds of the friends and undermining the Faith?

7. How should believers treat Covenant-breaking materials encountered on the Internet or elsewhere?

8. The "new kind of internal opposition to Bahá'u'lláh's Mission" takes aim "directly at Bahá'u'lláh's assertion of the _____ nature of reality and of humanity's dependence on the interventions of _____ _____."

9. What is "the greatest of all protections" in safeguarding the Cause of God from the enemies of the Faith and those who sow seeds of doubt in the hearts of believers?

APPLICATION/DISCUSSION QUESTIONS

1. Why is Covenant-breaking so serious? What does the metaphor of a contagious disease teach about the nature of Covenant-breaking? What does the metaphor of cancer teach about the nature of Covenant-breaking?

2. How should a believer respond if he receives a communication from a Covenant-breaker? What if the Covenant-breaker is just requesting help to better understand the Bahá'í Teachings? What if the Covenant-breaker is someone whom the believer once admired or even personally knew?

3. What were the characteristics and approaches of the campaign of internal opposition to the Cause that emerged in the 1990's? Why is it a logical and moral contradiction to claim to accept Bahá'u'lláh but to reject the authority of the Administrative Order?

4. Why is egotism a major cause of internal opposition to the Faith? How can believers cultivate humility in themselves? How can believers discourage egotism in others?

Quotations for Reflection

Answer the questions following the quotations below:

1."Ex-communication is a spiritual thing . . . . Only actual enemies of the Cause are ex-communicated. On the other hand, those who conspicuously disgrace the Faith or refuse to abide by its laws can be deprived, as a punishment, of their voting rights . . . ."
(On behalf of Shoghi Effendi, *Lights of Guidance*, p. 185)

"Those people who have withdrawn from the Faith, though critical of it and disgruntled, are not necessarily Covenant-breakers."
(On behalf of Shoghi Effendi, *Messages to Canada*, p. 66)

> *Are those who have withdrawn from the Faith considered Covenant-breakers?*

> *Why is there a great difference between Covenant-breakers and those whose voting (administrative) rights have been removed?*

2. "These agitations of the violators are no more than the foam of the ocean, which is one of its inseparable features; but the ocean of the Covenant shall surge and shall cast ashore the bodies of the dead, for it cannot retain them. Thus it is seen that the ocean of the Covenant hath surged and surged until it hath thrown out the dead bodies—souls that are deprived of the Spirit of God and are lost in passion and self and are seeking leadership. This foam of the ocean shall not endure and shall soon disperse and vanish, while the ocean of the Covenant shall eternally surge and roar. . . ."
(*Selections from the Writings of 'Abdu'l-Bahá*, pp. 210-11)

". . . the Cause of God has always been attacked from within, and . . . beginning in the days of the Báb, the 'Sea of Truth' has over and over cast out its spiritually dead. It must do this, even as the body seeks to rid itself of poisons so as to preserve the health of the entire organism."
(On behalf of Shoghi Effendi, *The Light of Divine Guidance*, vol. 1, p. 136)

"Thus it is seen that the ocean of the Covenant hath surged and surged until it hath thrown out the dead bodies—_____ that are deprived of the _____ of _____ and are lost in _____ and _____ and are seeking _____."

Why can the ocean of the Covenant not "retain" the "bodies of the dead"? Who are "the dead"?

3. ". . . man should associate with people who are firm in the Covenant and Testament, and befriend the pure ones; because bad associates bring about infection of bad qualities. It is like leprosy; it is impossible for a man to associate and befriend a leper and not be infected. This command is for the sake of protection and to safeguard.

". . . Just as in bodily diseases we must prevent intermingling and infection and put into effect sanitary laws—because the infectious physical diseases uproot the foundation of humanity; likewise one must protect and safeguard the blessed souls from the breaths and fatal spiritual diseases; otherwise violation, like the plague, will become a contagion and all will perish. In the early days, after the Ascension of the Blessed Beauty, the center of violation was alone; little by little the infection spread; and this was due to companionship and association."

('Abdu'l-Bahá, *Bahá'í World Faith*, pp. 437-38)

"To be the enemy of the enemies of God is a good characteristic. We are not against them personally, just as any intelligent man is not personally against a man who has a dangerous contagious disease. But he carefully isolates the sick individual so that the contagion will not spread. So we shun the spiritually sick, wishing for their cure, but keeping clear of them."

(On behalf of Shoghi Effendi, *Lights of Guidance*, p. 187)

"The Master . . . said we must shun their company, but pray for them. If you put a leper in a room with healthy people, he cannot catch their health; on the contrary they are very likely to catch his horrible ailment."

(On behalf of Shoghi Effendi, *Lights of Guidance*, p. 188)

How should believers relate to Covenant-breakers?

Why should believers not associate with Covenant-breakers?

4. ". . . certain believers have the unpleasant duty of having to read such works [of Covenant-breakers] in the course of their duty to protect the Faith—but the friends are warned, in the strongest terms, of the danger of reading such literature. Unless one is very well informed of the history of the Faith and is deeply confirmed in one's belief, the calumnies and distortions of truth contained in such literature can undermine one's faith."

(The Universal House of Justice, quoted in *The Power of the Covenant*, Part Two, p. 39)

". . . the friends should not answer queries from individuals who obviously seek to draw them into the consideration of the spurious claims and logic of the Covenant-breakers."

(On behalf of the Universal House of Justice, to an individual, July 3, 1997)

How should believers regard the literature and communications of Covenant-breakers?

Why is it dangerous to read the writings of Covenant-breakers?

5. "Through the Covenant, which is a distinguishing feature of His Revelation, He has specified in unmistakable terms the means by which He wills to preserve the integrity of His message and to guide the implementation of His prescriptions for humankind. If one accepts the Bahá'í Teachings, one cannot, in good conscience, claim to be studying the Faith while ignoring the centrality of Bahá'u'lláh's Covenant to all aspects of the religion He has established."

(On behalf of the Universal House of Justice, *Issues Related to the Study of the Bahá'í Faith*, # 9)

"If one accepts the Bahá'í Teachings, one cannot, in good _____, claim to be studying the Faith while ignoring

the _____ of Bahá'u'lláh's _____ to all aspects of the religion He has established."

Provide an example of a statement about the Bahá'í Teachings that appears to ignore the centrality of the Covenant. How can the same statement be reframed to take into account the centrality of the Covenant?

6. ". . . the greatest protection to the Cause will be through ongoing deepening of the Bahá'í community in the Covenant and the history and teachings of the Faith."

(On behalf of the Universal House of Justice, to an individual, December 19, 1997)

What is the greatest protection to the Cause?

What is one way you may systematically increase your knowledge and appreciation of the Covenant and the history and teachings of the Faith?

Illustrations

Reflect on how the following illustrate the manner in which believers should relate to Covenant-breakers:

"Elizabeth and Charles Greenleaf . . . were members of that group which began with Thornton Chase in the latter years of the 1890's in Chicago. The group was led by Dr. Ibráhím Khayr'ulláh, sent by the Master to America to teach and nurture those interested in the Faith. . . .

"As letters from Haifa took six weeks or more to arrive in America, a delay causing anxiety to many eager hearts, Dr. Khayr'ulláh suggested what he considered a practical solution which he presented to the class. He who had been praised by 'Abdu'l-Bahá for his magnificent services, now took the first step towards becoming a Covenant-breaker. This was his suggestion: that he write a letter to the Master explaining the difficulties of communications and asking Him to retain His station of Infallibility for the believers in the East and to confer Infallibility on him (Dr. Khayr'ulláh) for the believers in the West. He asked the friends to think, to meditate and pray about this, then come to the next Sunday meeting to sign the letter. It would then be sent to the Master.

"Grave misgivings entered Elizabeth's heart but as Charles seemed to think it quite a sensible suggestion she tried to drown such thoughts. But they continued to trouble her until she had to tell Charles she could never sign such a letter. Charles felt impatient with such unfounded fears and the first coolness in all their married life grew between them. On the night before the meeting called to sign the letter, Elizabeth tried to ease her troubled heart with prayer. In the early morning, she awoke with a voice calling out within her, 'Tell Charles to beware of the white ram!'

"After a silent, unhappy breakfast, Charles prepared to go along to meet the friends. As he went to open the front door, Elizabeth could not contain herself any longer and called out that—to her—meaningless phrase: 'Charles, beware of the white ram!' Immediately he was stilled, and turning to her a face white with shock, asked, 'What do you know of the white ram?' 'Nothing,' she replied, 'nor do I wish to know unless you wish to tell me, except a voice told me to say these words to you.'

"Then Charles proceeded to tell her of a recurring dream telling of his danger, though the dream recurred in slightly different forms. The past night he had dreamed he was walking on a high plateau. Across a deep, rocky ravine was a beautiful meadow, the deep green grass blossomed with flowers. Connecting the plateau with this lovely meadow was a narrow, unguarded bridge. As Charles reached the middle of the bridge, a sleek, white-haired ram would step from the deep grass to meet him on the bridge. Charles stooped to touch the silky coat of the beautiful beast. The ram would put down his head to butt him off the bridge down into the rocky ravine. That morning the ram's eyes became the lustrous eyes of Khayr'ulláh! The Greenleafs went to the meeting to give a warning to the friends, without fully relating their dreams. Those who signed the letter disappeared from the history of the Faith. The faithful few became the bedrock of the Faith."

(Emeric Sala, *The Greenleafs: an eternal union*, Bahá'í News, September 1973, pp. 8-9)

"'Abdu'l-Bahá's admonitions typically included the necessity of shunning the dangers of moral corruption inherent in any association with the violators of the Covenant. He would say, 'Covenant-breaking has an adverse effect on public morals. The result of sowing such seeds of corruption will incline the people of the world towards ungodliness and atheism. . . .

"In this vein, He would offer examples supported by verses from the Qur'án, presenting logical proofs and reminding the friends of their unequivocal duty to prevent the Covenant-breakers from penetrating the Bahá'í community. He would give the same examples that the Blessed Beauty used to offer about the followers of Yaḥyá. One of these stressed the fact that in whatever city a follower of Yaḥyá had lived, his foul odour would persist for a long time, slowing down the teaching work . . . .

"One morning in the *bírúní* reception room, 'Abdu'l-Bahá was addressing me on this very subject, only two other people being present. I was reminded of a certain story which I wished to tell in support of 'Abdu'l-Bahá's words . . . . So I remarked, 'In Tehran, a school was established and Ḥubbu'lláh [a Covenant-breaker] . . . was a candidate for a teaching position there. As soon as we heard the news, the Hands of the Cause, along with two others and myself, met and consulted on ways to block his acceptance by the school. Finally, it was decided that Mr. . . . . should meet with the school authorities and persuade them to reject Ḥubbu'lláh.'

"I expected to receive 'Abdu'l-Bahá's praise and encouragement confirming our great service, but even before I had completed my remarks, He interrupted: 'What! You consulted on how to prevent a Covenant-breaker from earning a living? This is not how the Faith is served. In matters of earning a livelihood there is no difference between a believer and a Covenant-breaker. . . .'

"In short, He continued in this vein for some time, while I felt deep pangs of shame and remorse for my actions and words."

(Youness Afroukhteh, *Memories of Nine Years in 'Akká*, pp. 263-64)

Analysis Questions

Answer the following questions. Suggested answers appear in Appendix A.

1. Which one of the following choices best defines a Covenant-breaker?
   A. Someone who is not a Bahá'í.
   B. Someone who has withdrawn from the Faith.
   C. Someone who after accepting Bahá'u'lláh has turned round and attacked the central Institution of the Faith.
   D. Someone who has failed in his duties in living a Bahá'í life.

2. Which of the following are true statements about the relationship of believers to Covenant-breakers? Circle all correct answers:
   A. Believers should, for the sake of unity, strive to communicate with and show kindness to Covenant-breakers in order to persuade them to rejoin the Faith.
   B. Believers are strictly forbidden from having personal contact with Covenant-breakers.
   C. Believers are strictly forbidden from entering into correspondence with Covenant-breakers.
   D. Believers are warned in the strongest terms against reading Covenant-breaker literature.

3. While browsing the Internet, a believer encounters a website referring to the "Third Guardian of the Bahá'í Faith" and immediately suspects it is the website of Covenant-breakers. Which one of the following choices would be the best response to such a situation?
   A. The believer should thoroughly study the website so as to be able to refute the arguments presented.
   B. The believer should email the contact persons listed on the website and attempt to convince them that they are wrong and should rejoin the Faith.
   C. The believer should ignore the website.
   D. The believer should email other Bahá'í friends and invite them to see the website for themselves.

Memorization and Presentation Exercises

A. Memorizing the Sacred and Authoritative Writings
Commit to memory the following quotations (or two of your choosing from this chapter):

"O ye beloved of the Lord! The greatest of all things is the protection of the True Faith of God, the preservation of His Law, the safeguarding of His Cause and service unto His Word."
(Will and Testament of 'Abdu'l-Bahá, p. 4)

"And now, one of the greatest and most fundamental principles of the Cause of God is to shun and avoid entirely the Covenant-breakers, for they will utterly destroy the Cause of God, exterminate His Law and render of no account all efforts exerted in the past."
(Will and Testament of 'Abdu'l-Bahá, p. 20)

B. Presenting the Themes of the Covenant
Prepare a brief presentation on the theme of protection of the Cause of God.

In your explanation, include discussion of:

1. the importance of protection of the Faith and the meaning of Covenant-breaking;
2. the significance of shunning Covenant-breakers and avoiding their literature and communications; and
3. the nature of the campaign of internal opposition against the Faith that emerged in the 1990's.

Share your presentation with a partner or group.

CHAPTER 10
The Individual and the Covenant

Let not the means of order be made the cause of confusion
and the instrument of union an occasion for discord.
— Bahá'u'lláh

Overview

A. The Two Authoritative Centers and the Administrative Order

"In the Bahá'í Faith there are two authoritative centers appointed to which the believers must turn"—"the Book with its Interpreter" and "the Universal House of Justice."[1] "The Book" refers to "the Word" or "the record of the utterance of Bahá'u'lláh."[2] The "Interpreter of the Word is an extension of that center which is the Word," for "it is he and he alone who can authoritatively state what the Book means."[3] According to "the explicit texts of the Kitáb-i-Aqdas and the Kitáb-i-'Ahd," 'Abdu'l-Bahá was the "Interpreter of the Word of God."[4] In turn, the Will and Testament of 'Abdu'l-Bahá conferred on Shoghi Effendi, as Guardian of the Faith, the role of the "Interpreter of the Word of God."[5] The authority of the Words of Bahá'u'lláh and the interpretations of 'Abdu'l-Bahá and the Guardian "is absolute and immutable until such time as Almighty God shall reveal His new Manifestation to Whom will belong all authority and power."[6]

The Faith's second authoritative center, the Universal House of Justice, is "guided by God to decide on whatever is not explicitly revealed in the Book."[7] "The provenance, the authority, the duties, the sphere of action of the Universal House of Justice all derive from the revealed Word of Bahá'u'lláh which, together with the interpretations and expositions of the Centre of the Covenant and of the Guardian of the Cause . . . constitute the binding terms of reference of the Universal House of Justice and are its bedrock foundation."[8] In His Will and Testament, 'Abdu'l-Bahá referred believers to the authoritative centers of the Book and the Universal House of Justice: "Unto the Most Holy Book every one must turn, and all that is not expressly recorded therein must be referred to the Universal House of Justice."[9] He further declared: "All must seek guidance and turn unto the Center of the Cause and the House of Justice. And he that turneth unto whatsoever else is indeed in grievous error."[10]

The soul's obligations toward the two authoritative centers—the Book along with its authorized interpretations and the Universal House of Justice—lie at the very heart of the Covenant. In a real sense, today, firmness in the Covenant is dependent on the degree of one's faithfulness to these two authoritative centers. The individual's relationship to the Book and, more broadly, to the Faith's authoritative Writings is explored in sections B and C below. The believer's relationship to the Universal House of Justice was discussed in Chapter 8.

The implications of the Covenant are not, however, confined to the authoritative centers of the Book and the Universal House of Justice. The Covenant is also related to the whole of the Administrative Order, which is intimately linked to the two authoritative centers. The Administrative Order finds its origin and principles in the Book and the Book's authorized interpretations: "This Administrative Order . . . rests securely on the laws, the precepts, the ordinances and institutions which the Founder of the Faith has Himself specifically laid down and unequivocally established, and functions in strict accordance with the interpretations of the authorized Interpreters of its holy scriptures."[11] Moreover, the second authoritative center, the Universal House of Justice, is the "supreme institution"[12] and "central governing body"[13] of the Administrative Order. The "Covenant has given birth" to the Administrative Order upon which has been conferred the authority to "administer the affairs of the community and to ensure both the integrity of the Word of God and the promotion of the Faith's message."[14]

"This Administrative Order consists, on the one hand, of a series of elected councils, universal, secondary and local, in which are vested legislative, executive and judicial powers over the Bahá'í community and, on the other, of eminent and devoted believers appointed for the specific purposes of protecting and propagating the Faith of Bahá'u'lláh under the guidance of the Head of that Faith."[15] Under the guidance of the Universal House of Justice, "legislative, executive and judicial authority over the affairs of the Bahá'í community is exercised by Local and National Spiritual Assemblies."[16] As such, Bahá'ís are called to observe "the principle of complete, and immediate obedience to the Assemblies, both local and national."[17] Though they are to be obeyed as a matter of principle, Spiritual Assemblies are not guaranteed infallibility like the Universal House of Justice: "National and Local Spiritual Assemblies can receive divine guidance if they consult in the manner and spirit described by 'Abdu'l-Bahá," but "they do not share in the explicit guarantees of infallibility conferred upon the Universal House of Justice."[18] The members of the Administrative Order's other branch— Counsellors and their auxiliaries—"have no legislative, executive or judicial authority" and "are entirely devoid of priestly functions or the right to make authoritative interpretations," yet they play "a vital role in advancing the interests of the Faith"[19] through the "spiritual, moral and intellectual influence" of their services.[20] How the Covenant affects the relationship of believers to the subsidiary institutions of the Administrative Order is the subject of the discussion in sections D and E that follow in this chapter.

B. The Individual's Relationship to the Authoritative Writings

The Covenant has profound implications for the individual believer's relationship to the authoritative Writings of the Bahá'í Faith. These implications include recognizing what constitutes the authoritative Writings of the Faith, acquiring the spiritual qualities of reliance and humility in relation to the Writings, and appreciating the principle within the Writings that God's Manifestation does whatever He wills.

As the existence of the two authoritative centers implies, only the "Writings of the Báb and Bahá'u'lláh, those of 'Abdu'l-Bahá, the letters of the Guardian and the decisions of the Universal House of Justice . . . are authoritative . . . ."[21] With regard to "the writings of the beloved Guardian and the pronouncements of the Universal House of Justice, though they are not regarded as sacred texts nor are of the same station as the Writings of the Central Figures of the Faith, nevertheless . . . they are authoritative statements of guidance and direction for the friends."[22]

Two additional points bear emphasis. First, only writings, not oral statements, are considered authoritative: "Bahá'u'lláh has made it clear enough that only those things that have been revealed in the form of Tablets have a binding power over the friends. Hearsays may be matters of interest but can in no way claim authority."[23] 'Abdu'l-Bahá explained that "[a]ny narrative that is not authenticated by a Text should not be trusted. . . . For the people of Bahá, the Text, and only the Text, is authentic."[24] Second, no other writings related to the Faith have authority. "[W]ritings by Bahá'ís . . . have no authority at all apart from their own internal reasonableness,"[25] and "the deductions and conclusions of individual learned men have no authority, unless they are endorsed by the House of Justice."[26]

For believers, the Faith's authoritative Writings provide the standard of truth in this day. The Guardian wished "the friends to always bear in mind and to conscientiously and faithfully follow" "the principle of unqualified and whole-hearted loyalty to the revealed Word."[27] The "Book of God is the standard by which to weigh all forms of behavior."[28] The "Revelation of Bahá'u'lláh is the standard of truth against which all other views and conclusions are to be measured."[29] That which Bahá'u'lláh has revealed is "identical with the truth,"[30] "identical with the Will of God Himself."[31] Accordingly, any meaningful exploration of the beliefs and practices of the Bahá'í Faith can only be carried out within the framework of the authoritative Writings of the Faith. In discussions about the Bahá'í Teachings, "Bahá'ís will . . . wish to assist the consultative processes by sharing and discussing relevant Bahá'í texts. This will itself have the further effect of drawing attention back to the framework of Bahá'í belief."[32]

The Covenant calls for an attitude of humility on the part of those seeking to understand the Faith's Writings. The "Manifestation of God is of a higher realm and has a perception far above that of any human being."[33] Therefore, "no human being can have a full and correct understanding of the revelation of God . . . ."[34] Because an "exact and thorough comprehension of so vast a system, so sublime a revelation, so sacred a trust, is for obvious reasons beyond the reach and ken of our finite minds,"[35] a believer may well encounter Bahá'í laws or principles whose wisdom may not be immediately clear to that individual. For instance, one may initially be challenged in understanding Bahá'u'lláh's prescription of a daily obligatory prayer, or His prohibition against homosexual relations, or His restriction of the membership of the Universal House of Justice to men. The difficulty in understanding the meaning or wisdom of any Bahá'í precept can only be overcome by first attaining a measure of intellectual humility. We cannot be "overanxious to encompass the Divine Message within the framework" of our "limited understanding,"[36] but "must have the humility to appreciate the limitations of our own knowledge and outlook, and strive always to understand the purpose of Bahá'u'lláh" in setting forth His Teachings.[37]

Related to the spiritual quality of humility is recognition of the divine principle that the Manifestation of God does whatever He wills in setting forth His ordinances. Bahá'u'lláh declared that were God "to decree as lawful the thing which from time immemorial had been forbidden, and forbid that which had, at all times, been regarded as lawful, to none is given the right to question His authority."[38] 'Abdu'l-Bahá used the following analogy to explain this principle: The skilled physician (whose ability has been ascertained) possesses knowledge lacked by the patient; therefore, "the patient has no right to object" inasmuch as "whatever the doctor says and does is right."[39] Whoever has failed to recognize the principle that God's Manifestation does whatever He wills, "the winds of doubt will agitate him, and the sayings of the infidels will distract his soul."[40] But whoever "hath acknowledged this principle will be endowed with the most perfect constancy."[41]

C. The Individual's Interpretation of the Authoritative Writings

Because the individual believer's understanding of God's revelation can never be complete, his interpretations of the Writings cannot be authoritative. The Bahá'í Writings distinguish between the authoritative interpretations of 'Abdu'l-Bahá and the Guardian and the personal interpretations of believers:

A clear distinction is . . . drawn in the Bahá'í Writings between authoritative interpretation and the

> understanding that each individual arrives at from a study
> of its Teachings. Individual interpretations based on a
> person's understanding of the Teachings constitute the
> fruit of man's rational power and may well contribute to
> a greater comprehension of the Faith. Such views,
> nevertheless, lack authority. In presenting their personal
> ideas, individuals are cautioned not to discard the
> authority of the revealed words, not to deny or contend
> with the authoritative interpretation, and not to engage
> in controversy . . . .[42]

Thus, in studying the Teachings, a believer is free to come to his or her own understandings; however, there is an "absolute prohibition against anyone propounding 'authoritative' or 'inspired' interpretations or usurping the function of Guardian."[43]

The prohibition against individuals propounding authoritative interpretations of the Teachings bears on how believers should share their views with others. The Universal House of Justice has encouraged an "atmosphere of mutual respect and tolerance" as Bahá'ís grow in their understanding of the Faith.[44] Because the personal interpretations of believers "lack authority," in "presenting their personal ideas, individuals . . . should offer their thoughts as a contribution to knowledge, making it clear that their views are merely their own."[45] Believers are free to "express their own views without pressing them on their fellow Bahá'ís."[46] "Individual interpretations continually change as one grows in comprehension of the teachings. . . . So, although individual insights can be enlightening and helpful, they can also be misleading. The friends must therefore learn to listen to the views of others without being over-awed or allowing their faith to be shaken . . . ."[47]

The Universal House of Justice has observed that some Bahá'ís, "imbued by what they conceive to be loyalty to Bahá'u'lláh, cling to blind acceptance of what they understand to be a statement of the Sacred Text. . . . The danger of such an attitude is that it exalts personal understanding of some part of the Revelation over the whole, leads to illogical and internally inconsistent applications of the Sacred Text, and provides fuel to those who would mistakenly characterize loyalty to the

Covenant as 'fundamentalism.'"[48] Such insistence on one's personal understanding of the Teachings can lead to contention and conflict, which, Bahá'u'lláh declared, "are categorically forbidden in His Book."[49]

"Beyond contention, moreover, is the condition in which a person is so immovably attached to one erroneous viewpoint that his insistence upon it amounts to an effort to change the essential character of the Faith. This kind of behavior, if permitted to continue unchecked, could produce disruption in the Bahá'í community, giving birth to countless sects as it has done in previous Dispensations."[50] Individual investigation of the truth "cannot and must not . . . produce 'sects' in relation to the Teachings of the Faith; the Covenant provides the centre of guidance which is to prevent such a degeneration."[51] It is "ultimately the responsibility of the Universal House of Justice, in watching over the security of the Cause and upholding the integrity of its Teachings, to require the friends to adhere to standards" defined by the Writings.[52]

D. The Individual's Relationship to the Institutions of the Administrative Order

In addition to framing the individual's relationship to the authoritative Writings, the Covenant also guides the believer's relationship to the institutions of the Administrative Order. To properly relate to these institutions, a believer must appreciate the Administrative Order's unique nature and features. In emphasizing the distinctiveness of the Administrative Order, Shoghi Effendi pointed out that it is "fundamentally different from anything that any Prophet has previously established, inasmuch as Bahá'u'lláh has Himself revealed its principles, established its institutions, appointed the person to interpret His Word and conferred the necessary authority on the body designed to supplement and apply His legislative ordinances."[53] Lacking an appreciation of the Administrative Order's divinely-conceived nature "will detract from the perspective of anyone who measures Bahá'í administrative processes against practices prevalent in today's society. For notwithstanding its inclination to democratic methods in the administration of its affairs, and regardless of the resemblance of some of its features to those of other systems, the Administrative Order is not to be viewed merely as an improvement on past and existing systems; it represents a departure both in origin and in concept."[54]

The Administrative Order is not merely a system for decision-making and the exercise of authority within the Bahá'í Faith. Rather, this Order is "the channel, the instrument, the embodiment" of the spirit of the Faith.[55] The Administrative Order is based on spiritual principles, operates on spiritual powers, and is concerned with spiritual relationships. For example, the spiritual principle of unity constitutes the "guarantee of well-being and success" in the endeavors of Bahá'í administrative institutions.[56] The spiritual "power of Bahá'u'lláh to reinforce the efforts of those who serve Him" must be taken into account in the plans of Bahá'í institutions.[57] And the spiritual qualities of "love, respect and courtesy" are requisites for "successful Bahá'í relationships" within the Administrative Order.[58] As the Universal House of Justice has observed, "occupation with the mechanics of Bahá'í Administration, divorced from the animating spirit of the Cause, leads to a distortion, to an arid secularization foreign to the nature of the Administration."[59] Bahá'u'lláh counseled: "Let not the means of order be made the cause of confusion and the instrument of union an occasion for discord."[60]

The Universal House of Justice has cautioned that if Bahá'ís overlook the spiritual nature of the Administrative Order, the style of administration within the Bahá'í community will become infected with materialistic and secular tendencies that will negatively impact the effectiveness of Bahá'í institutions. For instance, in 1994, the Universal House of Justice addressed these words to the National Spiritual Assembly of the Bahá'ís of the United States: "The corrosive influence of an overbearing and rampant secularization is infecting the style of administration of the Faith in your community and threatening to undermine its efficacy."[61] The House of Justice identified within American society certain "unsavoury characteristics" resulting from the neglect of spiritual principles: "aggressiveness and competitiveness," "partisanship," "suspicion of public-policy institutions," "skepticism towards established authority," and "cynical disregard of the moderating principles and rules of civilized human relationships."[62] Over time, these unhealthy and "entrenched habits of American life" had come to exert "too great a sway over the manner of management of the Bahá'í community and over the behaviour of portions of its rank and file in relation to the Cause."[63] An "immediate, deliberate effort," urged the House of Justice, was required to arrest this "unwholesome influence."[64]

As indicated above, one of the unhealthy attitudes prevalent in many parts of the world, particularly in the West, is the "inordinate skepticism regarding authority."[65] If such an attitude of mistrust toward those in authority were to infect the Bahá'í community, then the very effectiveness of the Administrative Order would be jeopardized. Such a sobering reality demands that each believer personally reflect on such questions as: Do I view the exercise of authority within the Bahá'í community in the same way as most people view the workings of governmental institutions? Do I regard decisions or requests of Spiritual Assemblies—National and Local—with skepticism? Do I whole-heartedly support the plans of Bahá'í administrative bodies, though I may not completely understand the wisdom of the plans? Do I uphold and abide by the decisions of Bahá'í institutions, even when I personally disagree with their judgment?

"Once the assembly, through a majority vote of its members comes to a decision the friends should readily obey it."[66] 'Abdu'l-Bahá explained: "It is incumbent upon every one not to take any step without consulting the Spiritual Assembly, and all must assuredly obey with heart and soul its bidding, and be submissive unto it, that things may be properly ordered and well arranged."[67] "So great is the importance and so supreme is the authority of these assemblies that once 'Abdu'l-Bahá after having himself and in his own handwriting corrected the translation made into Arabic of the Ishráqát (the Effulgences) by Sheikh Faraj, a Kurdish friend from Cairo, directed him in a Tablet to submit the above-named translation to the Spiritual Assembly of Cairo, that he may seek from them before publication their approval and consent."[68] The Universal House of Justice has provided the following specific guidance on the relationship of believers to Local Spiritual Assemblies: "The friends are called upon to give their wholehearted support and cooperation to the Local Spiritual Assembly, first by voting for the membership and then by energetically pursuing its plans and programs, by turning to it in time of trouble or difficulty, by praying for its success and taking delight in its rise to influence and honor. This great prize, this gift of God within each community must be cherished, nurtured, loved, assisted, obeyed and prayed for."[69]

Obedience to, and support of, Assemblies rests on the "profound conviction of the *authority* from God," given to His Manifestation Bahá'u'lláh, passed on to 'Abdu'l-Bahá, and by Him, to the Guardian and the Universal House of Justice; such authority "flows out through the assemblies and creates order based on obedience—once a Bahá'í has this, nothing can shake him."[70] The Covenant summons believers to not only obey the institutions of Bahá'u'lláh's Order, but to love and support them. In a letter on his behalf, Shoghi Effendi stated that without "the spirit of real love" by Bahá'ís for the Faith's institutions, the Cause can never attract "large numbers of people."[71] "It is very unfortunate that some of the believers do not seem to grasp the fact that the administrative order, the Local and National Assemblies, are the pattern for the future, however inadequate they may sometimes seem. We must *obey* and *support* these bodies, for this is the Bahá'í law. Until we learn to do this we cannot make real progress."[72] "The difficulties, and the evidences of immaturity . . . seem to be an inevitable phase in the growth of our Administration, which is so much more perfect than the believers called upon to create it! There are bound to be many misunderstandings, and some small abuses, in erecting a system which is so different from the ways men are used to. But we must not attach undue importance to these things, but look upon them as a mother looks upon the mistakes of her children, realizing that with maturity will come the capacity to handle situations better and with more sound judgement."[73] A deep understanding of the Covenant and of the distinctly spiritual origin and nature of the Administrative Order forms the foundation of believers' love, trust, and support for the Faith's institutions.

E. The Individual's Expression of Criticism through the Channels of the Administrative Order

The Covenant also has implications for how believers may offer criticism through the channels of the Administrative Order. The Bahá'í Writings identify two forms of criticism: "constructive criticism"[74] and "destructive criticism."[75] At "the very root of the Cause lies the principle of the undoubted right of the individual to self-expression, his freedom to declare his conscience and set forth his views."[76] "It is not only the right, but the vital responsibility of every loyal and intelligent member of the Community to offer fully and frankly, but with due respect and consideration to the authority of the Assembly, any suggestion, recommendation or criticism he conscientiously feels he should in order to improve and remedy certain existing conditions or trends in his local Community . . . ."[77] This is the essence of constructive criticism.

In contrast to constructive criticism, which aids the community, destructive criticism renders a disservice. All "criticisms and discussions of a negative character which may result in undermining the authority of the Assembly as a body should be strictly avoided."[78] Such negative criticism, which includes "continually challenging and criticizing the decisions" of Assemblies,[79] "stunts the . . . development of the community,"[80] "prevents the rapid growth of the Faith and repels those who are yet outside the community."[81] The Writings emphasize: "Vicious criticism is indeed a calamity," the root of which is "lack of faith in the system of Bahá'u'lláh" and failure to follow the "Bahá'í laws in voting, in electing, in serving, and in abiding by Assembly decisions."[82]

"The Administrative Order provides channels for expression of criticism"[83] and the "voicing of . . . grievances or disagreements."[84] "Bahá'ís are 'fully entitled to address criticisms to their Assemblies' and offer their recommendations."[85] In addition to sharing one's concerns with a Local or National Spiritual Assembly, one may also confide in a Counsellor or Auxiliary Board member.[86] Further, "one of the principal functions of the Nineteen Day Feast is to provide a forum for 'open and constructive criticism and deliberation regarding the state of affairs within the local Bahá'í community'. . . ."[87] It should be noted, however, that "complaints about the actions of an individual member of an Assembly should be made directly and confidentially to the Assembly itself, not made to other individuals or . . . raised at a Nineteen Day Feast."[88] Therefore, there exists a "clear distinction between, on the one hand, the prohibition of backbiting, which would include adverse comments about individuals or institutions made to other individuals privately or publicly, and, on the other hand, the encouragement to unburden oneself of one's concerns" to the institutions of the Administrative Order.[89]

"When Bahá'ís have addressed their criticisms, suggestions and advice to their Assemblies, including their views 'about policies or individual members of elected bodies,' they must 'whole-heartedly accept the advice or decision of the Assembly.'"[90] "All Bahá'ís are fallible human beings, each one has his own insights, enthusiasms and degree of wisdom and understanding. Differences of viewpoint could cause the community to fragment into a thousand pieces, if it were not cemented together by the strong bond of the Covenant, and if the friends were not willing to subordinate their own ideas to the considered decisions that issue from the divinely ordained process of consultation and, at the same time, exercise the utmost forbearance towards their fellow believers, their individual characteristics and their shortcomings."[91]

Because the "the path of unity is the only path that can lead to the civilization envisioned by Bahá'u'lláh,"[92] believers are enjoined to support the decisions of Assemblies, even if they personally disagree with such decisions. 'Abdu'l-Bahá has given the assurance that an incorrect decision will eventually be corrected if unity exists: "as it is in unity the truth will be revealed and the wrong made right."[93] Even "if an assembly makes an ill-advised decision it must be upheld in order to preserve the unity of the community. Appeal can be made from the Local Assembly's decision to the National Assembly . . . . But the principle of authority invested in our elected bodies must be upheld."[94] Therefore, while divers views and contributions are welcome during the consultative process, once an Assembly makes a decision, it would be inconsistent with Bahá'u'lláh's teachings on unity for a believer's personal beliefs to be expressed in dissent and opposition within the community. "A believer can ask the Assembly why they made a certain decision and politely request them to reconsider. But then he must leave it at that, and not go on disrupting local affairs through insisting on his own views. . . . We all have a right to our opinions, we are bound to think differently; but a Bahá'í must accept the majority decision of his Assembly, realizing that acceptance and harmony—even if a mistake has been made—are the really important things, and when we serve the Cause properly, in the Bahá'í way, God will right any wrongs done in the end."[95] "All should be ready and willing to set aside every personal sense of grievance—justified or unjustified— for the good of the Cause, because the people will never embrace it until they see in its Community life mirrored what is so conspicuously lacking in the world: love and unity."[96] Thus, in "terms of the Covenant, dissidence is a moral and intellectual contradiction of the main objective animating the Bahá'í community, namely, the establishment of the unity of humankind."[97]

Study Questions

Answer the following questions based on the above Overview:

CONTENT QUESTIONS

1. What are the "two authoritative centers appointed to which the believers must turn"?

2. "This Administrative Order consists, on the one hand, of a series of _____ councils, universal, secondary and local, in which are vested _____, _____ and _____ powers over the Bahá'í community and, on the other, of _____ and _____ believers appointed for the specific purposes of _____ and _____ the Faith of Bahá'u'lláh under the guidance of the Head of that Faith."

3. Whose writings are authoritative for Bahá'ís? Are oral statements attributed to Bahá'u'lláh authoritative?

4. What is the distinction between the interpretations of 'Abdu'l-Bahá and the Guardian and the interpretations of individual believers?

5. In what ways does the Administrative Order represent a departure from past and existing administrative systems?

6. In 1994, the Universal House of Justice observed that certain "unsavoury characteristics" of American life had come to exert "too great a sway over the manner of management of the Bahá'í community and over the behaviour of portions of its rank and file in relation to the Cause." What "unsavoury characteristics" did the House of Justice identify?

7. What kind of criticism should be strictly avoided? What are the effects of such criticism?

8. What channels does the Administrative Order provide for the voicing of criticism?

9. When a Bahá'í has addressed criticism to an Assembly, how should he respond to the Assembly's decision?

APPLICATION/DISCUSSION QUESTIONS

1. Why is firmness in the Covenant dependent on one's relationship to the Faith's two authoritative centers—the Book with its Interpreter and the Universal House of Justice?

2. How does the concept that the Manifestation of God "is of a higher realm and has a perception far above that of any human being" assist believers to carry out spiritual principles or laws that they may not initially understand?

3. In relating to and interacting with the institutions of the Bahá'í Administrative Order, what are ways a Bahá'í may personally combat the prevalent, societal attitudes of skepticism toward authority?

4. A Bahá'í is concerned that the Nineteen Day Feast in his local Bahá'í community is disorganized and uninspiring, so he wishes to bring the matter to the Local Spiritual Assembly's attention. Give an example of how criticism regarding this issue may be constructively presented to the Assembly. Give a contrasting example of how criticism regarding this issue may be negatively presented to the Assembly. How do the two examples differ in motive, manner, and mode?

Quotations for Reflection

Answer the questions following the quotations below:

1. ". . . one center is the Book with its Interpreter, and the other is the

Universal House of Justice guided by God to decide on whatever is not explicitly revealed in the Book. This pattern of centers and their relationships is apparent at every stage in the unfoldment of the Cause."

(The Universal House of Justice, *Messages from the Universal House of Justice: 1963-1986*, p. 160)

"The Administrative Order conceived by Bahá'u'lláh accomplishes its divinely ordained purpose through a system of institutions, each with its defined sphere of action. The central governing body of the Order is the Universal House of Justice, whose terms of reference are the revealed Word of Bahá'u'lláh together with the interpretations and expositions of 'Abdu'l-Bahá and the Guardian."

(The Universal House of Justice, *The Institution of the Counsellors*, p. 1)

". . . one center is the _____ with its _____, and the other is the _____ _____ ___ _____ guided by God to decide on whatever is not explicitly revealed in the Book."

How has the pattern of centers and their relationships been apparent at every stage in the unfoldment of the Cause?

What are the terms of reference of the Universal House of Justice? Why are the terms of reference of the Universal House of Justice also of significance for individual Bahá'ís?

2. "Most important of all, as with any exploration by Bahá'ís of the beliefs and practices of their Faith, electronic discussion will serve the interests of the Cause and its members only as it is conducted within the framework of the Bahá'í Teachings and the truths they enshrine. To attempt to discuss the Cause of God apart from or with disdain for the authoritative guidance inherent in these Teachings would clearly be a logical contradiction."

(On behalf of the Universal House of Justice, *Issues Related to the Study of the Bahá'í Faith*, # 5)

"Every true believer, if he is to deepen in his understanding of the Cause of Bahá'u'lláh, must needs combine profound faith in the unfailing efficacy of His Message and His Covenant, with the humility of recognizing that no one of this generation can claim to have embraced the vastness of His Cause nor to have comprehended the manifold mysteries and potentialities it contains."

> (The Universal House of Justice, *Messages from the Universal House of Justice: 1963-1986*, p. 57)

Any exploration by Bahá'ís of the beliefs and practices of their Faith serves the interests of the Cause when the discussion is conducted in what manner? Why?

What are the necessary and spiritual preconditions if a believer is to deepen his understanding of the Cause of Bahá'u'lláh? How can one grow in fulfilling these spiritual preconditions?

3. "... only the written text of the Revelation is regarded as authoritative. ... Authoritative interpretation is the exclusive prerogative of 'Abdu'l-Bahá and the Guardian, while infallible legislation is the function of the Universal House of Justice.

". . . There is also an important distinction made in the Faith between authoritative interpretation, as described above, and the interpretation which every believer is fully entitled to voice. Believers are free, indeed are encouraged, to study the Writings for themselves and to express their understanding of them. Such personal interpretations can be most illuminating, but all Bahá'ís, including the one expressing the view, however learned he may be, should realize that it is only a personal view and can never be upheld as a standard for others to accept, nor should disputes ever be permitted to arise over differences in such opinions."

> (On behalf of the Universal House of Justice, *Messages from the Universal House of Justice: 1963-1986*, pp. 517-18)

"It is not surprising that individual Bahá'ís hold and express different and sometimes defective understandings of the Teachings; this is but an evidence of the magnitude of the change that this Revelation is to effect in human consciousness. As believers with various insights into the Teachings converse—with patience, tolerance and open and unbiased minds—a deepening of comprehension should take place. The strident insistence on individual views, however, can lead to contention, which is detrimental not only to the spirit of Bahá'í association and collaboration but to the search for truth itself."

(On behalf of the Universal House of Justice, *Issues Related to the Study of the Bahá'í Faith*, # 10)

What is the distinction between authoritative interpretation and individual interpretation?

What qualities and attitudes should characterize believers' sharing of interpretations and insights about the Teachings? What qualities and attitudes should be avoided?

4. "... if any participant in an email discussion feels that a view put forward appears to contradict or undermine the provisions of the Covenant, he should be free to say so, explaining candidly and courteously why he feels as he does. The person who made the initial statement will then be able to re-evaluate his opinion and, if he still believes it to be valid, he should be able to explain why it is not contrary to either the letter or the spirit of the Covenant. The participants in such a discussion should avoid disputation and, if they are unable to resolve an issue, they should refer the point to the Universal House of Justice since, in accordance with the Will and Testament of 'Abdu'l-Bahá, 'By this body all the difficult problems are to be resolved. ..' and it has the authority to decide upon 'all problems which have caused difference, questions that are obscure, and matters that are not expressly recorded in the Book.' In this way the Covenant can illuminate and temper the discourse and make it fruitful."

(On behalf of the Universal House of Justice, to an individual believer, February 16, 1996)

How should a believer respond to views that appear to contradict or undermine the provisions of the Covenant?

197

What is the role of the Universal House of Justice in resolving conflicts between believers? Before believers approach the Universal House of Justice, are there other available resources that may assist in resolving such conflicts?

5. "Our present generation, mainly due to the corruptions that have been identified with organizations, seem to stand against any institution. Religion as an institution is denounced. Government as an institution is denounced. Even marriage as an institution is denounced. We Bahá'ís should not be blinded by such prevalent notions. If such were the case, all the divine Manifestations would not have invariably appointed someone to succeed Them. Undoubtedly, corruptions did enter those institutions, but these corruptions were not due to the very nature of the institutions but to the lack of proper directions as to their powers and nature of their perpetuation. What Bahá'u'lláh has done is not to eliminate all institutions in the Cause but to provide the necessary safeguards that would eliminate corruptions that caused the fall of previous institutions. What those safeguards are is most interesting to study and find out and also most essential to know."

> (On behalf of Shoghi Effendi, quoted in the Universal House of Justice, *Individual Rights and Freedoms in the World Order of Bahá'u'lláh*, p. 11)

"Also relevant to effecting unity is the attitude of the friends, whether serving on any Assembly or not, towards the exercise of authority in the Bahá'í community. People generally tend to be suspicious of those in authority. The reason is not difficult to understand, since human history is replete with examples of the disastrous misuse of authority and power. A reversal of this tendency is not easily achievable, but the Bahá'í friends must be freed of suspicion towards their institutions if the wheels of progress are to turn with uninterrupted speed. A rigorous discipline of thought and action on the part of both the friends and the National Assembly will succeed in meeting this challenge . . . ."

> (The Universal House of Justice, to the National Spiritual Assembly of the Bahá'ís of the United States, May 19, 1994, *Rights & Responsibilities*, p. 38)

"What Bahá'u'lláh has done is not to eliminate all _____ in the Cause but to provide the necessary safeguards that would eliminate _____ that caused the fall of previous institutions." What are these safeguards?

Bahá'ís must strive to be free of what attitude in relation to the exercise of authority within the Bahá'í community?

What are examples of statements that illustrate a believer's support, rather than suspicion, of an Assembly?

6. "The Guardian believes that a great deal of the difficulties from which the believers in . . . feel themselves to be suffering are caused by their neither correctly understanding nor putting into practice the administration. They seem—many of them—to be prone to continually challenging and criticizing the decisions of their Assemblies. If the Bahá'ís undermine the very bodies which are, however immaturely, seeking to co-ordinate Bahá'í activities and administer Bahá'í affairs, if they continually criticize their acts and challenge or belittle their decisions, they not only prevent any real rapid progress in the Faith's development from taking place, but they repel outsiders who quite rightly may ask how we ever expect to unite the whole world when we are so disunited among ourselves!

"There is only one remedy for this: to study the administration, to obey the Assemblies, and each believer seek to perfect his own character as a Bahá'í. We can never exert the influence over others which we can exert over ourselves. If we are better, if we show love, patience, and understanding of the weaknesses of others; if we seek to never criticize but rather encourage, others will do likewise, and we can really help the Cause through our example and spiritual strength."

(On behalf of Shoghi Effendi, *Rights & Responsibilities*, pp. 58-59)

"If Bahá'í individuals deliberately ignore the principles embedded in the Order which Bahá'u'lláh Himself has established to remedy divisiveness in the human family, the Cause for which so much has been sacrificed will surely be set back in its mission to rescue world society from complete disintegration. May not the existence of the Covenant be invoked again and again, so that such repetition may preserve the needed perspective? For, in this age, the Cause of Bahá'u'lláh has been protected against the baneful effects of the misuse of the process of criticism; this has been done by the institution of the Covenant and by the provision of a universal administrative system which incorporates within itself the mechanisms for drawing out the constructive ideas of individuals and using them for the benefit of the entire system."

> (The Universal House of Justice, *Individual Rights and Freedoms in the World Order of Bahá'u'lláh*, p. 16)

> *What are the effects of continually challenging and criticizing the decisions of Assemblies? What is the remedy?*

> *How has the Cause of Bahá'u'lláh been protected against the harmful effects of the misuse of criticism?*

Illustrations

The following illustration explores some of the undesirable societal attitudes that Bahá'ís should strive to avoid in relation to institutions. Within the Bahá'í community, have you witnessed (in others or yourself) any of these attitudes?

". . . what I see to be a very dangerous and pressing mental test to the Bahá'ís in the western countries as well as other parts of the world—is that the believers in these countries live in a society which has developed certain attitudes about social organizations and institutions.

"These attitudes are firstly that people are suspicious and distrustful of their government and its bureaucracy. . . .

"The great mental test we face as believers is the test that we may, unconsciously and inadvertently, transfer those attitudes from the larger society which is manifestly in decline into the Bahá'í administrative system. . . .

". . . we are challenged to detach ourselves, to emancipate ourselves from the prevailing and, indeed, not just prevailing but rapidly increasing sense of suspicion, of distrust and disfavor which characterizes the attitudes of people in our society toward their institutions and avoid such attitudes coming into the relationship of the believers to the Bahá'í institutions.

"They are not the same. They are radically different. This is a system ordained by Bahá'u'lláh, by the Manifestation of God. . . . It has a system to it which enables it to purify itself of any adverse attitude and behavior. It stands quite different from the way of the world. If we bring the way of the world into the Bahá'í Administrative Order, all we will do is temporarily disrupt it. All we will do is irreparably damage our own personal spiritual development.

"We need to develop new attitudes. We need to develop a far deeper understanding of the Covenants of Bahá'u'lláh and 'Abdu'l-Bahá. It is not enough to sign the card to say, 'I believe there is a Covenant. There are these people around with a variety of titles. Whatever they are I accept them. Fine, that's it.' This is not enough, friends.

"We will be swept away because there are dangerous forces in our society. There are insidious influences. We have to protect ourselves now, and our protection is the deepening in the Covenant. . . .

"We need also in dealing with this test, the test of acquiring a new attitude toward our social organizations and institutions, we need to rethink what is criticism. . . . There are passages in the Writings which refer to criticism as being an appropriate measure, an appropriate element of Bahá'í consultative and community practice, and nobody is disagreeing with that. But what we also have in our Writings are references to the extremely dangerous character of what the Guardian refers to as 'vicious and negative' criticism.

"'Criticism and discussions of a negative character, which may result in undermining the authority of the Assembly as a body, should be strictly avoided.'. . .

"We look towards a constructive, developmental Bahá'í community which doesn't pretend it is immune from any means of further development and refinement of its practices and conduct but which is free from what the Guardian refers to as criticism of a negative nature which has the effect of undermining the authority of the Assembly. . . .

"So one of the elements of acquiring the new attitude toward social organizations is deepening in the Covenant, a second one is that of rethinking the nature of criticism because it is a constructive element of Bahá'í consultation, and the third and final element that I mention is quite revolutionary. It is a statement where Shoghi Effendi was asked to define what were the parameters for the Cause in bringing in large numbers of people. And he set out four parameters; three of them are obvious and the fourth one is very unusual. He said these were the requirements without which the Cause can never really bring in large numbers of people. He said:

"'Without the spirit of real love for Bahá'u'lláh, for His Faith and its institutions, and the believers for each other.'. . . .

". . . Shoghi Effendi defines as one of the four requirements for bringing in large numbers of people that we develop a sense of love, a sense of real love for the institutions of the Faith. This is radically new in the Bahá'í Dispensation.

"Where do you find individuals who, since we are in the state of Illinois, who will come to you and say, 'I love the Illinois state legislature.' Where do you find somebody who says, 'I love the House of Representatives,' or 'I love the Senate.'. . . . Where do you find people who say, 'I love the executive branch of government; I love the city council; I love our district administration.' This is foreign to western thought. This is inimical. This is radical. . . .

". . . We are in entirely the opposite direction, because our religion tells us that without the spirit of real love for the institutions of the Cause, we cannot bring in large numbers of people.

". . . it is easy to love institutions which one perceives as functioning marvelously well. . . .

"But can you love an institution which is functioning in an incomplete developmental way, which is making mistakes, which is having trouble with its unity, with its activity, with its executive action, which forgets to advise you of important events and the like? This is our challenge. How can we do it without hypocrisy?

"We can do it the same way a parent loves a child. When the child is stumbling, is behaving badly, is filled with some illness, or is grappling with some social grace, the parent loves the child because the parent sees in that child the potential for development. Through love and nurturance, the child will develop and fulfill its potential. Through criticism and a lack of love the child's growth will be stunted; its development will never be realized.

"So it is we are called upon to love our institutions, not in a sense of artificiality, not in a sense of hypocrisy, but in a sense of perfect faith that these are institutions ordained by Bahá'u'lláh with a glorious, magnificent future ahead of them. Through our love, our nurturance, our support, our compassion, our understanding, they will develop. They will evolve.

"It is this kind of love we seek—radically different from the attitude of criticism, suspicion, disorder, corruption which informs the attitude of people in the society around us toward institutions which are in decline and dissolution."

(Peter Khan, "Mental Tests," *The American Bahá'í*, December 31, 1995 (lecture, Wilmette, Illinois, September 23, 1995))

Analysis Questions

Answer the following questions. Suggested answers appear in Appendix A.

1. Which of the following statements regarding the authoritative Writings of the Bahá'í Faith are true? Circle all correct answers.

A. The Writings of Bahá'u'lláh, the Báb, and 'Abdu'l-Bahá are authoritative.

B. The letters of the Guardian and the decisions of the Universal House of Justice are authoritative.

C. Books by Hands of the Cause of God and Bahá'í scholars are authoritative.

D. If approved for publication, the writings of any Bahá'í are authoritative.

2. In reference to the Guardian, 'Abdu'l-Bahá wrote in His Will and Testament: "He is the Interpreter of the Word of God...." 'Abdu'l-Bahá also stated: "To none is given the right to put forth his own opinion or express his particular conviction." Which one of the following choices

best describes how the above-quoted statements may be understood?

    A. Individual believers cannot have personal opinions or convictions about the Word of God.

    B. Individual believers cannot share their personal opinions and understandings with others.

    C. Only Assemblies may interpret the Word of God.

    D. Individuals may not authoritatively interpret the Word of God like the Guardian; however, they may share their personal understandings as long as they do not impose them upon others.

3. Which of the following statements accurately describe the manner in which criticism should be expressed within the Bahá'í community? Circle all correct answers.

    A. It would be proper to address criticisms about a community's functioning to a Spiritual Assembly—Local or National.

    B. It would be proper to share complaints about an Assembly member at the Nineteen Day Feast.

    C. It would be proper to address criticisms about a community's functioning to an Auxiliary Board member.

    D. It would be proper to share complaints about the Assembly with other community members.

Memorization and Presentation Exercises

A. Memorizing the Sacred and Authoritative Writings

Commit to memory the following quotations (or two of your choosing from this chapter):

"Blessed is the man that hath acknowledged his belief in God and in His signs, and recognized that 'He shall not be asked of His doings'. Such a recognition hath been made by God the ornament of every belief and its very foundation. . . .

"Whoso hath not recognized this sublime and fundamental verity, and hath failed to attain this most exalted station, the winds of doubt will agitate him, and the sayings of the infidels will distract his soul. He that hath acknowledged this principle will be endowed with the most perfect constancy."

(Bahá'u'lláh, *The Kitáb-i-Aqdas*, parags. 161, 163)

". . .Vicious criticism is indeed a calamity. But its root is lack of faith in the system of Bahá'u'lláh, i.e., the Administrative Order—and lack of obedience to Him—for He has forbidden it!"

(On behalf of Shoghi Effendi, *Lights of Guidance*, p. 92)

B. Presenting the Themes of the Covenant

Prepare a brief presentation on the theme of the individual and the Covenant.

In your explanation, include discussion of:

1. the two authoritative centers and the Administrative Order;
2. the individual's relationship to the Faith's authoritative Writings;
3. the individual's relationship to the institutions of the Administrative Order; and
4. the individual's expression of criticism through the channels of the Administrative Order.

Share your presentation with a partner or group.

APPENDIX
ANSWERS
TO ANALYSIS QUESTIONS

CHAPTER 1

1. The suggested answer is "C." The Covenant of Bahá'u'lláh was "made clearly and explicitly in writing."[1] Previous Manifestations of God have revealed Lesser Covenants, but these Covenants have been "shrouded in mystery."[2] Answers "A," "B," and "D" are incorrect because they are inconsistent with the above references.

2. The suggested answers are "A," "B," and "C." The Universal House of Justice has explained that the "Covenant of Bahá'u'lláh embodies the spirit, instrumentality and method to attain" the goal of the oneness of humankind, and 'Abdu'l-Bahá was "the incorruptible medium for applying the Word to practical measures for the raising up of a new civilization."[3] Answer "D" is incorrect in light of the above reference.

3. The suggested answer is "D." The Covenant is "the ultimate guarantee that the Faith will remain true to its divine origin throughout the centuries."[4] This group of believers is attempting to add, without any apparent authority in the Bahá'í Writings, another branch to the Administrative Order. The Covenant "protects the Cause from individuals who, through the assertion of their own wills, would try to force God's Cause into the paths of their own preference."[5] Answer "C" is a good answer as such a claim would eventually affect the unity of the Faith; however, the immediate issue is whether the Faith's integrity—its faithfulness to its original teachings—is ensured through the Covenant. Therefore, "D" is the best answer. Answers "A" and "B" are incorrect because they find no support in the Bahá'í Writings.

CHAPTER 2

1. The suggested answer is "D." In *God Passes By*, Shoghi Effendi

explained: "This same Covenant He [Bahá'u'lláh] had anticipated in His Kitáb-i-Aqdas . . . and had incorporated it in a special document which He designated as 'the Book of My Covenant[]'. . . ."[6] Answer "D," unlike the others, illustrates the distinction between the fact that the Kitáb-i-Aqdas alluded to the Covenant without explicitly naming 'Abdu'l-Bahá and the Kitáb-i-'Ahd's explicit establishment of the Covenant.

2. The suggested answers are "B" and "D." 'Abdu'l-Bahá is the authorized Interpreter of Bahá'u'lláh's Word, and by turning toward the authorized Interpreter, the unity of the Faith can be maintained. "To ward off such dissensions as these and prevent any person from creating a division or sect the Blessed Perfection, Bahá'u'lláh, appointed a central authoritative Personage, declaring Him to be the expounder of the Book. This implies that the people in general do not understand the meanings of the Book, but this appointed One does understand."[7] Further, to "ensure unity and agreement He [Bahá'u'lláh] has entered into a Covenant with all the people of the world, . . . so that no one may interpret or explain the religion of God according to his own view or opinion and thus create a sect founded upon his individual understanding of the divine Words."[8] Answers "A" and "C" are incorrect because they are inconsistent with the above references.

3. The suggested answers are "A" and "C." As Bahá'u'lláh made clear in reference to 'Abdu'l-Bahá: "Whoso turneth towards Him hath turned towards God, and whoso turneth away from Him hath turned away from My Beauty, hath repudiated My Proof, and transgressed against Me."[9] 'Abdu'l-Bahá similarly confirmed that "whosoever obeys the Center of the Covenant appointed by Bahá'u'lláh has obeyed Bahá'u'lláh, and whosoever disobeys Him has disobeyed Bahá'u'lláh."[10] Finally, "[w]hatever is written or said" by 'Abdu'l-Bahá "is conformable to the truth and under the protection of the Blessed Beauty. He is infallible."[11] Answers "B" and "D" are incorrect because they are inconsistent with the above references.

CHAPTER 3
1. The suggested answers are "B" and "C." In the Kitáb-i-'Ahd, Bahá'u'lláh conferred upon Mírzá Muḥammad-'Alí a rank second only to 'Abdu'l-Bahá. However, after Bahá'u'lláh's passing, Mírzá

Muḥammad-'Alí deviated from the Covenant, thereby forfeiting his station. Bahá'u'lláh had said in reference to Mírzá Muḥammad-'Alí: "He, verily, is but one of My servants . . . Should he for a moment pass out from under the shadow of the Cause, he surely shall be brought to naught."[12] In His Will and Testament, 'Abdu'l-Bahá wrote: "I am thus constrained to write these lines for the protection of the Cause of God, the preservation of His Law, the safeguarding of His Word and the safety of His Teachings."[13] Answers "A" and "D" are incorrect as they lack historical support and are inconsistent with 'Abdu'l-Bahá's role as the perfect Exemplar of the Teachings of Bahá'u'lláh.

2. The suggested answers are "A," "C," and "D." Bahá'u'lláh declared that Mírzá Muḥammad-'Alí "is but one of My servants . . . Should he for a moment pass out from under the shadow of the Cause, he surely shall be brought to naught."[14] This implies that Mírzá Muḥammad-'Alí, like all other servants of God, had free will by which he could choose to be firm in, or to deviate from, the Covenant. History has borne out the truth of answers "C" and "D." Answer "B" is incorrect in light of the above-quoted verse from Bahá'u'lláh.

3. The suggested answers are "A," "B," and "D." Answers "A" and "D" find support in the clear provisions of the Covenant, and the truth of "B" has been borne out by history. Answer "C" is incorrect because it lacks historical support.

CHAPTER 4
1. The suggested answer is "C." This answer best describes the succession of authority in the Bahá'í Faith. Shoghi Effendi observed: "They [Bahá'u'lláh and 'Abdu'l-Bahá] have . . ., in unequivocal and emphatic language, appointed those twin institutions of the House of Justice and of the Guardianship as their chosen Successors . . . ."[15] Moreover, as discussed in Chapter 2, Bahá'u'lláh was succeeded by 'Abdu'l-Bahá. Answer "B" fails to take into account the principle that the Administrative Order's twin pillars—the Guardianship and the Universal House of Justice—succeeded Bahá'u'lláh and 'Abdu'l-Bahá. Answer "A" is incorrect because Bahá'u'lláh was succeeded by 'Abdu'l-Bahá, not the

Administrative Order. Answer "D" is incorrect because the Guardianship is one of the twin pillars of the Administrative Order.

2. The suggested answers are "A," "C," and "D." In His Will and Testament, 'Abdu'l-Bahá declared that the Guardian is "the Interpreter of the Word of God."[16] Moreover, among the Guardian's responsibilities were applying the Faith's principles, promulgating its laws, administering its affairs, and coordinating its activities.[17] Answer "B" is incorrect because it is the Universal House of Justice that has the "power to enact laws that are not expressly recorded in the Book."[18]

3. The suggested answers are "B" and "D." Shoghi Effendi was "essentially human."[19] Nevertheless, "the Guardian of the Cause of God, as well as the Universal House of Justice . . ., are both under the care and protection of the Abhá Beauty, under the shelter and unerring guidance of the Exalted One . . . . Whatsoever they decide is of God. Whoso obeyeth him not, neither obeyeth them, hath not obeyed God . . . ."[20] "He is assured the guidance of both Bahá'u'lláh and the Báb, as the Will and Testament of 'Abdu'l-Bahá clearly reveals."[21] "The interpretations written by the beloved Guardian . . . are equally binding as the Text itself."[22] Answers "A" and "C" are incorrect because they are not fully consistent with these truths.

CHAPTER 5

1. The suggested answers are "B," "C," and "D." Answer "B" is correct because it is a historical fact. Answer "C" is correct because the Will and Testament of 'Abdu'l-Bahá had provided that the Hands of the Cause were to "elect from their own number nine persons" who "must give their assent to the choice of the one whom the Guardian of the Cause of God hath chosen as his successor."[23] Answer "D" is correct because there was no one Shoghi Effendi could have appointed as his successor in accordance with the Will and Testament of 'Abdu'l-Bahá, given that Shoghi Effendi did not have any children and there were no remaining Aghsán in the Cause. Answer "A" is incorrect because, arguably, an appointment could not have taken place after Shoghi Effendi's passing inasmuch as the Guardian was required to appoint "in his own life-time"

(not after his passing) "him that shall become his successor."[24] Moreover, because a majority of nine elected Hands had to "give their assent to the choice of the one whom the Guardian of the Cause of God hath chosen as his successor,"[25] there would have been no guarantee that the Hands would have approved the Guardian's choice.

2. The suggested answers are "B" and "D." Answer "B" is correct because Shoghi Effendi referred to the institution of the Hands of the Cause, along with the National Spiritual Assemblies, as occupying "with the Universal House of Justice, next to the Institution of the Guardianship, foremost rank in the divinely ordained administrative hierarchy of the World Order of Bahá'u'lláh."[26] Further, Shoghi Effendi had declared that the Hands of the Cause were "the Chief Stewards of Bahá'u'lláh's embryonic World Commonwealth."[27] Answer "D" is correct because the Hands assumed leadership of the Faith with the unanimous support of the twenty-six National Spiritual Assemblies then in existence in the Bahá'í world.[28] Answer "A" is incorrect because Shoghi Effendi had not explicitly appointed the body of the Hands as his successor. Answer "C" is incorrect because the Hands had "had no certainty of divine guidance such as is incontrovertibly assured to the Guardian and to the Universal House of Justice."[29]

3. The suggested answers are "A," "B," "C," and "D." These answers summarize the requirements of succession set forth in the Will and Testament of 'Abdu'l-Bahá. *See* Chapter 5, section A of the Overview.

CHAPTER 6

1. The suggested answers are "A," "B," and "D." The Universal House of Justice has been "invested by Bahá'u'lláh with the authority to legislate whatsoever has not been explicitly and outwardly recorded in His holy Writ."[30] 'Abdu'l-Bahá wrote: "It is incumbent upon these members (of the Universal House of Justice) to . . . deliberate upon all problems which have caused difference, questions that are obscure and matters that are not expressly recorded in the Book . . . and bear upon daily transactions . . . ."[31] Moreover, Shoghi Effendi explained that "the International House of Justice . . . will guide, organize and unify the affairs of the Movement

throughout the world."[32] Answer "C" is incorrect because "the Guardian of the Faith has been made the Interpreter of the Word of God and . . . the Universal House of Justice has been invested with the function of legislating on matters not expressly revealed in the teachings."[33] "[T]he Universal House of Justice will not engage in interpreting the Holy Writings."[34]

2. The suggested answers are "A" and "B." "[A] three-stage election has been provided by 'Abdu'l-Bahá for the formation of the International House of Justice, and . . . it is explicitly provided in His Will and Testament that the 'Secondary House of Justice (*i.e.*, National Assemblies) must elect the members of the Universal One[]' . . . ."[35] Answer "C" is incorrect because Shoghi Effendi explicitly stated that "the establishment of the Supreme House of Justice is in no way dependent upon the adoption of the Bahá'í Faith by the mass of the peoples of the world . . . ."[36] Answer "D" is likewise incorrect because there is nothing in the Writings mandating that the Guardian call the election of the Universal House of Justice. In fact, 'Abdu'l-Bahá declared: "At whatever time all the beloved of God in each country appoint their delegates, and these in turn elect their representatives, and these representatives elect a body, that body shall be regarded as the Supreme House of Justice."[37]

3. The suggested answers are "B" and "C." "The Guardian had given the Bahá'í world explicit and detailed plans covering the period until Riḍván 1963, the end of the Ten Year Crusade"; however, from "that point onward, unless the Faith were to be endangered, further divine guidance was essential."[38] Moreover, it was urgent that the Universal House of Justice be elected because the Guardian had died without being able to appoint a successor, and this "presented an obscure question not covered by the explicit Holy Text," which question only the Universal House of Justice could pronounce upon.[39] Answer "A" is incorrect because the Guardian had never stated that 1963 was the only year the Universal House of Justice could be elected. In fact, 'Abdu'l-Bahá had contemplated the formation of the Universal House of Justice in His own lifetime and had commanded the cousin of the Báb "to arrange for the election of the Universal House of Justice should the threats against the Master

materialize."[40] Although answer "D" sets forth a true statement, the answer is incorrect because there was no requirement in the Bahá'í Writings that the Universal House of Justice only be elected on the one hundredth anniversary of the Declaration of Bahá'u'lláh.

CHAPTER 7

1. The suggested answers are "A," "C," and "D." "Future Guardians are clearly envisaged and referred to in the Writings, but there is nowhere any promise or guarantee that the line of Guardians would endure forever; on the contrary there are clear indications that the line could be broken."[41] The Kitáb-i-Aqdas anticipates a break in the line of Guardians, as it states that after "the Dawning-place of Revelation," the authority regarding endowments "shall pass to the Aghsán, and after them to the House of Justice—should it be established in the world by then."[42] Answer "B" is incorrect because it is inconsistent with the above.

2. The suggested answers are "A" and "D." The Bahá'í Writings envisaged the Guardian and the Universal House of Justice functioning together. For example, the Guardian was to be the "sacred head and the distinguished member for life" of the Universal House of Justice.[43] Moreover, Shoghi Effendi declared that the Guardianship and the Universal House of Justice were "inseparable institutions."[44] Inseparability, however, does not mean simultaneous functioning, as the Guardian functioned in the absence of the Universal House of Justice for thirty-six years, and now the Universal House of Justice must function in the absence of a living Guardian. For this reason, answers "B" and "C" are incorrect.

3. The suggested answers are "A," "B," and "D." "First, . . . there are a number of functions and objects which the Guardianship shares with the Universal House of Justice and which the House of Justice must continue to pursue. Secondly, there are other functions of the Guardianship which, in the absence of a Guardian, devolve upon the Universal House of Justice, for example, the Headship of the Faith, the responsibility for directing the work of the Institution of the Hands of the Cause of God and of ensuring the continuing discharge of the functions of protection and propagation vested in that Institution, and the right to administer the Ḥuqúqu'lláh.

213

Thirdly, there are those prerogatives and duties which lie exclusively within the sphere of the Guardian himself and, therefore, in the absence of a Guardian, are inoperative except insofar as the monumental work already performed by Shoghi Effendi continues to be of enduring benefit to the Faith. Such a function is that of authoritative interpretation of the Teachings."[45] Answer "C" is incorrect in light of the above passage.

CHAPTER 8

1. The suggested answer is "D." "[T]he body of the House of Justice is under the protection and unerring guidance of God: this is called conferred infallibility."[46] Answer "A" is incorrect because the infallibility of the Universal House of Justice is not "essential infallibility," which is "peculiar to the supreme Manifestation."[47] Answers "B" and "C" are incorrect because the individual members of the House of Justice are not infallible.[48]

2. The suggested answers are "B," "C," and "D." Like the Guardian, the Universal House of Justice "wants to be provided with facts when called upon to render a decision, and like him it may well change its decision when new facts emerge."[49] "If that House of Justice shall decide unanimously, or by a majority, upon any question not mentioned in the Book, that decision and command will be guarded from mistake."[50] Answer "A" is incorrect because the Universal House of Justice "is not omniscient."[51]

3. The suggested answers are "A," "B," and "D." "Whatever will be its decision, by majority vote, shall be the real truth, inasmuch as that House is under the protection, unerring guidance and care of the one true Lord. He shall guard it from error and will protect it under the wing of His sanctity and infallibility."[52] "If that House of Justice shall decide unanimously, or by a majority, upon any question not mentioned in the Book, that decision and command will be guarded from mistake."[53] The laws of the Kitáb-i-Aqdas are "to be implemented gradually in accordance with the guidance given by God through those infallible Institutions which lie at the heart of the Covenant. Indeed, one of those Institutions, the Universal House of Justice, has been given by Bahá'u'lláh the task not

only of applying the laws but of supplementing them and of making laws on all matters not explicitly covered in the Sacred Text."[54] Answer "C" is incorrect because interpretation is outside of the sphere of jurisdiction of the Universal House of Justice: "[T]he Guardian of the Faith has been made the Interpreter of the Word and . . . the Universal House of Justice has been invested with the function of legislating on matters not expressly revealed in the teachings. . . . Neither can, nor will ever, infringe upon the sacred and prescribed domain of the other."[55]

CHAPTER 9

1. The suggested answer is "C." As the Universal House of Justice has explained: "When a person declares his acceptance of Bahá'u'lláh as a Manifestation of God he becomes a party to the Covenant and accepts the totality of His Revelation. If he then turns round and attacks Bahá'u'lláh or the central Institution of the Faith he violates the Covenant."[56] Answers "A," "B," and "D" are incorrect in light of the following passages: "People who have withdrawn from the Cause because they no longer feel that they can support its Teachings and Institutions sincerely, are not Covenant-breakers—they are non-Bahá'ís and should just be treated as such."[57] "In general, . . . a person who has withdrawn from the Faith is regarded as being among the generality of humankind with whom the Bahá'ís are enjoined to associate 'in joy and fragrance'."[58] "A believer failing in his duties in living the Bahá'í life would be a breaker of God's Eternal Covenant, in the general sense of becoming heedless in following the way of God, not in the sense of being a Covenant-breaker of Bahá'u'lláh's Lesser Covenant deserving to be identified and declared as such and to be shunned by the friends."[59]

2. The suggested answers are "B," "C," and "D." "The believers are commanded to shun Covenant-breakers . . . ."[60] Moreover, believers are "strictly forbidden" from having "personal contact or entering into correspondence" with Covenant-breakers.[61] Also, "the friends are warned, in the strongest terms, of the danger of reading" the literature of Covenant-breakers.[62] Answer "A" is incorrect because it is inconsistent with the Bahá'í Writings, such as the following passages: "The Master and Bahá'u'lláh have taught us that associating with these souls is not likely

to heal them at all, but on the contrary exposes one to grave danger of contagion. The history of the Faith has proved this over and over again. The only way we can prove to such people that they are wrong is to censure their conduct; if we sympathise with them we only fortify their perversity and waywardness."[63] "Strive ye then with all your heart to treat compassionately all humankind—except for those who have some selfish, private motive, or some disease of the soul."[64]

3. The suggested answer is "C." The Universal House of Justice has instructed that the "friends should . . . ignore any materials produced by Covenant-breakers which they may receive unsolicited by email or happen on while exploring the World Wide Web."[65] Answers "A," "B," and "D" are incorrect because they are inconsistent with the above instruction.

CHAPTER 10
1. The suggested answers are "A" and "B." The "Writings of the Báb and Bahá'u'lláh, those of 'Abdu'l-Bahá, the letters of the Guardian and the decisions of the Universal House of Justice . . . are authoritative . . . ."[66] "[W]ritings by Bahá'ís . . . have no authority at all apart from their own internal reasonableness."[67] Answers "C" and "D" are incorrect because they are inconsistent with the above passages.

2. The suggested answer is "D." As the Universal House of Justice has explained: "A clear distinction is made in our Faith between authoritative interpretation and the interpretation or understanding that each individual arrives at for himself from his study of its teachings. While the former is confined to the Guardian, the latter, according to the guidance given to us by the Guardian himself, should by no means be suppressed. . . . The friends must therefore learn to . . . express their own views without pressing them on their fellow Bahá'ís."[68] Answers "A," "B," and "C" are incorrect because they are inconsistent with these principles.

3. The suggested answers are "A" and "C." Bahá'ís are "fully entitled to address criticisms to their assemblies."[69] One may also share concerns with an Auxiliary Board member.[70] However, "complaints about the actions of an individual member of an Assembly should be made directly

and confidentially to the Assembly itself, not made to other individuals or even raised at a Nineteen Day Feast."[71] The "prohibition of backbiting" includes "adverse comments about . . . institutions made to other individuals privately or publicly."[72] Answers "B" and "D" are incorrect in light of these principles.

REFERENCES

Full bibliographic information as to the following references appears in the Bibliography.

INTRODUCTION

1. 'Abdu'l-Bahá, *The Promulgation of Universal Peace*, p. 381; 'Abdu'l-Bahá, *The Covenant*, # 13 ("Today, the most important affair is firmness in the Covenant . . . .").

2. On behalf of the Universal House of Justice, *Issues Related to the Study of the Bahá'í Faith*, # 9.

3. The Universal House of Justice, *The Institution of the Counsellors*, p. 26.

4. 'Abdu'l-Bahá, quoted in Shoghi Effendi, *God Passes By*, p. 239.

5. On behalf of Shoghi Effendi, *The Light of Divine Guidance*, vol. 2, p. 83.

6. On behalf of Shoghi Effendi, *The Importance of Deepening our Knowledge and Understanding of the Faith*, # 151.

7. The Universal House of Justice, *The Holy Year*, p. 35.

8. 'Abdu'l-Bahá, quoted in Shoghi Effendi, *God Passes By*, p. 238; *see* 'Abdu'l-Bahá, *Tablets of the Divine Plan*, p. 51 ("It is evident that the axis of the oneness of the world of humanity is the power of the Covenant and nothing else."); the Universal House of Justice, *The Institution of the Counsellors*, p. 26 ("The pivot of the oneness of humankind is the power of the Covenant . . . .").

9. Shoghi Effendi, *Citadel of Faith*, p. 89.

10. *Selections from the Writings of 'Abdu'l-Bahá*, p. 211.

11. Shoghi Effendi, *Bahá'í Administration*, p. 192.

12. Shoghi Effendi, *Citadel of Faith*, p. 5.

13. 'Abdu'l-Bahá, quoted in Shoghi Effendi, *The World Order of Bahá'u'lláh*, p. 136.

14. Shoghi Effendi, *Letters from the Guardian to Australia and New Zealand: 1923-1957*, p. 76; *see id.*, p. 93; Shoghi Effendi, *Citadel of Faith*, p. 76.

15. On behalf of Shoghi Effendi, *Japan Will Turn Ablaze*, p. 68.

16. On behalf of Shoghi Effendi, *The Importance of Deepening our Knowledge and Understanding of the Faith*, # 150.

17. The Universal House of Justice, *A Wider Horizon*, p. 48.

18. *See* the Universal House of Justice, *The Holy Year*, p. 38; *see* on behalf of Shoghi Effendi, *Unfolding Destiny*, p. 235 ("Also he feels it would be good

219

to have some course on the Covenant, the force that binds and strengthens the Bahá'í community and holds it together, when so many man-made institutions are disintegrating and going on the rocks of discord and lack of faith.").

19. The Universal House of Justice, *The Four Year Plan*, p. 68.

20. *See* Shoghi Effendi, *God Passes By*, p. 28.

21. *See Selections from the Writings of 'Abdu'l-Bahá*, p. 223.

22. The Universal House of Justice, quoted in *The Covenant: Its Meaning and Origin and Our Attitude Toward It*, p. 39.

23. *Cf. The Proofs of Bahá'u'lláh's Mission.*

24. On behalf of Shoghi Effendi, *Lights of Guidance*, p. 544.

25. *See* on behalf of Shoghi Effendi, *Lights of Guidance*, p. 310; on behalf of Shoghi Effendi, *Directives from the Guardian*, p. 30 ("If a person can accept Bahá'u'lláh's function, it should not present any difficulty to them to also accept what He has ordained in a Divinely guided individual in matters pertaining to the Faith."); on behalf of Shoghi Effendi, *The Importance of Deepening our Knowledge and Understanding of the Faith*, # 150 ("But once a Bahá'í has the profound conviction of the *authority* from God, vested in the Prophet, passed on to the Master, and by Him, to the Guardians, and which flows out through the assemblies and creates order based on obedience—once a Bahá'í has this, nothing can shake him.") (emphasis in original).

26. *Tablets of Bahá'u'lláh*, pp. 219-23.

27. Shoghi Effendi, *The World Order of Bahá'u'lláh*, pp. 97-157.

28. *See* the Universal House of Justice, *Messages from the Universal House of Justice: 1963-1986*, pp. 50-58, 83-90, 156-61. These three letters have also been separately published in the booklet entitled *The Guardianship and the Universal House of Justice*.

29. Bahá'u'lláh, quoted in Shoghi Effendi, *God Passes By*, p. 238.

30. *See* Shoghi Effendi, *God Passes By*, p. 238.

31. Shoghi Effendi, *God Passes By*, p. 325.

32. Shoghi Effendi, *The World Order of Bahá'u'lláh*, p. 144.

33. On behalf of Shoghi Effendi, *The Light of Divine Guidance*, vol. 1, p. 65.

34. *See* on behalf of Shoghi Effendi, *The Light of Divine Guidance*, vol. 1, p. 65; *id.*, pp. 156-57 ("He was also very glad to see that the believers are studying the Covenant of the Master. For in the Master's Will and Testament are enshrined the principles underlying the World Order, and unless the believers fully grasp the greatness, functions, and purpose of the institutions outlined in that Testament (and elaborated by the Guardian in his book 'The

Dispensation of Bahá'u'lláh') they will not be able to properly function as Bahá'ís individually or collectively."); on behalf of Shoghi Effendi, *The Importance of Deepening our Knowledge and Understanding of the Faith*, # 129 ("The Guardian would advise that in their studies of the Will and Testament the young believers should use the 'Dispensation', which will undoubtedly help them considerably to grasp the full implications of that sacred and historic Document which he has described as the 'Charter of the New World Order'.").

35. Rúḥíyyih Rabbaní, *The Priceless Pearl*, p. 213.

36. The Universal House of Justice, *Messages from the Universal House of Justice: 1963-1986*, p. 238; *see id.*, p. 229 ("WITH GRATEFUL JOYOUS HEARTS ANNOUNCE ENTIRE BAHÁ'Í WORLD ADOPTION PROFOUNDLY SIGNIFICANT STEP IN UNFOLDMENT MISSION SUPREME ORGAN BAHÁ'Í WORLD COMMONWEALTH THROUGH FORMULATION CONSTITUTION UNIVERSAL HOUSE JUSTICE. AFTER OFFERING HUMBLE PRAYERS GRATITUDE ON DAY COVENANT AT THREE SACRED THRESHOLDS BAHJÍ HAIFA MEMBERS GATHERED COUNCIL CHAMBER PRECINCTS HOUSE BLESSED MASTER APPENDED THEIR SIGNATURES FIXED SEAL ON INSTRUMENT ENVISAGED WRITINGS BELOVED GUARDIAN HAILED BY HIM AS MOST GREAT LAW FAITH BAHÁ'U'LLÁH.").

37. *Cf.* on behalf of the Universal House of Justice, *Issues Related to the Study of the Bahá'í Faith*, # 8 ("The issues raised seem to resolve themselves into two points: the first being whether or not the Universal House of Justice has the authority to make authoritative interpretations; the second is whether anyone has the right to challenge the authority or actions of the Universal House of Justice. When these issues are approached with an understanding of the unity underlying all the Teachings, clarification results. . . . The above points have both been covered in three letters written by the Universal House of Justice on 9 March 1965, 27 May 1966 and 7 December 1969. Unfortunately it seems that many of the friends have not studied these letters deeply or understood their implications.").

38. The Universal House of Justice, *Messages from the Universal House of Justice: 1963-1986*, p. 57.

39. *See* Shoghi Effendi, *Bahá'í Administration*, p. 62 ("And as we make an effort to demonstrate that love to the world may we also clear our minds of any lingering trace of unhappy misunderstandings that might obscure our clear conception of the exact purpose and methods of this new world order, so challenging and complex, yet so consummate and wise. . . . We must trust to time, and the guidance of God's Universal House of Justice, to obtain a clearer and fuller understanding of its provisions and implications."); *e.g.*, on behalf of Shoghi Effendi, *Lights of Guidance*, p. 182 ("The contents of

the Will of the Master is far too much for the present generation to comprehend. It needs at least a century of actual working before the treasures of wisdom hidden in it can be revealed.").

40. The Universal House of Justice, *Messages from the Universal House of Justice: 1963-1986*, p. 50.
41. On behalf of the Universal House of Justice, *Issues Related to the Study of the Bahá'í Faith*, # 8.
42. On behalf of the Universal House of Justice, *Issues Related to the Study of the Bahá'í Faith*, # 8.
43. The Universal House of Justice, *Messages from the Universal House of Justice: 1963-1986*, p. 87.
44. The Universal House of Justice, *The Holy Year*, p. 32.

CHAPTER 1
THE COVENANT OF BAHÁ'U'LLÁH:
SIGNIFICANCE, MEANING, AND PURPOSES

1. On behalf of Shoghi Effendi, *The Light of Divine Guidance*, vol. 2, p. 86.
2. 'Abdu'l-Bahá, *Bahá'í World Faith*, p. 357.
3. *Selections from the Writings of 'Abdu'l-Bahá*, p. 210.
4. *Tablets of Abdul-Baha Abbas*, vol. 1, p. 83.
5. The Universal House of Justice, *The Four Year Plan*, p. 68.
6. 'Abdu'l-Bahá, *Tablets of the Divine Plan*, pp. 51-52.
7. The Universal House of Justice, quoted in *The Covenant*, Introduction.
8. For instance, there is the "Eternal Covenant." *See* on behalf of the Universal House of Justice, quoted in *The Covenant: Its Meaning and Origin and Our Attitude Toward It*, p. 74 ("A believer failing in his duties in living the Bahá'í life would be a breaker of God's Eternal Covenant, in the general sense of becoming heedless in following the way of God, not in the sense of being a Covenant-breaker of Bahá'u'lláh's Lesser Covenant deserving to be identified and declared as such and to be shunned by the friends."); *e.g.*, Bahá'u'lláh, *The Kitáb-i-Aqdas*, parag. 2 ("They that have violated the Covenant of God by breaking His commandments, and have turned back on their heels, these have erred grievously in the sight of God, the All-Possessing, the Most High."); *id.*, parag. 149 ("Recite ye the verses of God every morn and eventide. Whoso faileth to recite them hath not been faithful to the Covenant of God and His Testament . . . ."); *Selections from the Writings of 'Abdu'l-Bahá*, p. 71 ("Should any one of you enter a city, he should become a centre of attraction by reason of his sincerity, his faithfulness and love, his honesty and fidelity, his truthfulness and loving-kind-

ness towards all the peoples of the world, so that the people of that city may cry out and say: 'This man is unquestionably a Bahá'í, for his manners, his behaviour, his conduct, his morals, his nature, and disposition reflect the attributes of the Bahá'ís.' Not until ye attain this station can ye be said to have been faithful to the Covenant and Testament of God. For He hath, through irrefutable Texts, entered into a binding Covenant with us all, requiring us to act in accordance with His sacred instructions and counsels.").

Reference is also made in the Bahá'í Writings to the "Most Great Covenant." *See* Shoghi Effendi, *The World Order of Bahá'u'lláh*, p. 192 ("'The sovereigns of the world,' writes 'Abdu'l-Bahá . . ., 'must conclude a binding treaty, and establish a covenant, the provisions of which shall be sound, inviolable and definite. They must proclaim it to all the world, and obtain for it the sanction of all the human race . . . All the forces of humanity must be mobilized to insure the stability and permanence of this Most Great Covenant . . . The fundamental principle underlying this solemn Pact should be so fixed that if any government later violate any one of its provisions, all the governments on earth should arise to reduce it to utter submission, nay the human race as a whole should resolve, with every power at its disposal, to destroy that government.'").

Yet another Covenant is the "Everlasting Covenant." *See* Shoghi Effendi, *The Promised Day is Come*, p. 123 ("Then will the coming of age of the entire human race be proclaimed and celebrated by all the peoples and nations of the earth. Then will the banner of the Most Great Peace be hoisted. Then will the worldwide sovereignty of Bahá'u'lláh—the Establisher of the Kingdom of the Father foretold by the Son, and anticipated by the Prophets of God before Him and after Him—be recognized, acclaimed, and firmly established. Then will a world civilization be born, flourish, and perpetuate itself, a civilization with a fullness of life such as the world has never seen nor can as yet conceive. Then will the Everlasting Covenant be fulfilled in its completeness."); *see also* on behalf of Shoghi Effendi, *Lights of Guidance*, p. 181 ("The Most Great Covenant is different from the Everlasting Covenant.").

9. The Universal House of Justice, quoted in *The Covenant*, Introduction; *see* Shoghi Effendi, *The World Order of Bahá'u'lláh*, p. 137 (". . . that general Covenant which, as inculcated by the Bahá'í teaching, God Himself invariably establishes with mankind when He inaugurates a new Dispensation.").

10. *Selections from the Writings of the Báb*, p. 87; *see Selections from the Writings of 'Abdu'l-Bahá*, p. 207 ("And it is a basic principle of the Law of God that in every Prophetic Mission, He entereth into a Covenant with all believers—a Covenant that endureth until the end of that Mission, until the promised day when the Personage stipulated at the outset of the Mission is made manifest. Consider Moses, He Who conversed with God. Verily, upon Mount Sinai, Moses entered into a Covenant regarding the Messiah, with all those

souls who would live in the day of the Messiah. And those souls, although they appeared many centuries after Moses, were nevertheless—so far as the Covenant, which is outside time, was concerned—present there with Moses.").

11. 'Abdu'l-Bahá, *Bahá'í World Faith*, p. 358.

12. Bahá'u'lláh, *The Kitáb-i-Aqdas*, parag. 37 ("We pray God that He may graciously assist him to retract and repudiate such claim. Should he repent, God will, no doubt, forgive him. If, however, he persisteth in his error, God will, assuredly, send down one who will deal mercilessly with him. Terrible, indeed, is God in punishing! Whosoever interpreteth this verse otherwise than its obvious meaning is deprived of the Spirit of God and of His mercy which encompasseth all created things."); *see* Bahá'u'lláh, quoted in Shoghi Effendi, *The World Order of Bahá'u'lláh*, p. 132 ("Should a man appear . . . ere the lapse of a full thousand years—each year consisting of twelve months according to the Qur'án, and of nineteen months of nineteen days each, according to the Bayán—and if such a man reveal to your eyes all the signs of God, unhesitatingly reject him!"); 'Abdu'l-Bahá, *The Covenant*, # 13 ("[T]he Promised One of Bahá'u'lláh will appear after one thousand or thousands of years."); *Selections from the Writings of 'Abdu'l-Bahá*, pp. 67-68 ("We have noted what thou didst write to Jináb-i-Ibn-Abhar, and thy question regarding the verse: 'Whoso layeth claim to a Revelation direct from God, ere the expiration of a full thousand years, such a man is assuredly a lying impostor.'[¶] The meaning of this is that any individual who, before the expiry of a full thousand years—years known and clearly established by common usage and requiring no interpretation—should lay claim to a Revelation direct from God, even though he should reveal certain signs, that man is assuredly false and an impostor. . . . [¶] The substance is, that prior to the completion of a thousand years, no individual may presume to breathe a word. All must consider themselves to be of the order of subjects, submissive and obedient to the commandments of God and the laws of the House of Justice. Should any deviate by so much as a needle's point from the decrees of the Universal House of Justice, or falter in his compliance therewith, then is he of the outcast and rejected."); Shoghi Effendi, *God Passes By*, p. 214 ("In this Charter of the future world civilization [the Kitáb-i-Aqdas] its Author . . . rules out the possibility of the appearance of another Manifestation ere the lapse of at least one thousand years."); Shoghi Effendi, *The World Order of Bahá'u'lláh*, p. 143 ("With the ascension of Bahá'u'lláh the Day-Star of Divine guidance . . . had finally sunk below the horizon of 'Akká, never to rise again ere the complete revolution of one thousand years."); *cf.* 'Abdu'l-Bahá, quoted in the Universal House of Justice, *Messages from the Universal House of Justice: 1963-1986*, p. 52 ("My purpose is this, that ere the expiration of a thousand years, no one has the right to utter a single word, even to claim the station of Guardianship.").

13. The Universal House of Justice, *The Kitáb-i-Aqdas*, Introduction, p. 8; *The*

Kitáb-i-Aqdas, Note # 62; *cf.* on behalf of the Universal House of Justice, to an individual believer, December 23, 2004 ("Regarding the Notes section that appears in the English language edition of 'The Kitáb-i-Aqdas: The Most Holy Book', the compilers of the notes were appointed by the House of Justice, and the results of their work were accepted by it. Further credit may be found in the Introduction to 'The Kitáb-i-Aqdas'.").

14. *The Kitáb-i-Aqdas*, Note # 62; *see* Shoghi Effendi, *God Passes By*, p. 100 ("A Revelation . . . inaugurating an era of at least a thousand years' duration . . . was, as already noted, born amidst the darkness of a subterranean dungeon in Ṭihrán—an abominable pit that had once served as a reservoir of water for one of the public baths of the city.").

15. The Universal House of Justice, quoted in *The Covenant*, Introduction.

16. The Universal House of Justice, *Developing Distinctive Bahá'í Communities*, 5.1.

17. Shoghi Effendi, *God Passes By*, p. 27.

18. Shoghi Effendi, *God Passes By*, p. 28; *see* on behalf of Shoghi Effendi, quoted in the Universal House of Justice, *Individual Rights and Freedoms in the World Order of Bahá'u'lláh*, p. 11 ("Our present generation, mainly due to the corruptions that have been identified with organizations, seem to stand against any institution. . . . We Bahá'ís should not be blinded by such prevalent notions. If such were the case, all the divine Manifestations would not have invariably appointed someone to succeed Them. Undoubtedly, corruptions did enter those institutions, but these corruptions were not due to the very nature of the institutions but to the lack of proper directions as to their powers and nature of their perpetuation.").

19. On behalf of Shoghi Effendi, *Lights of Guidance*, p. 163; *see id.*, p. 493 ("First concerning the statement of Jesus Christ 'Thou art Peter and upon this rock etc.'; this saying of Jesus establishes beyond any doubt the primacy of Peter and also the principle of succession, but is not explicit enough regarding the nature and functioning of the Church itself."); *cf.* Matthew 16:18 ("And I say also unto thee, That thou art Peter, and upon this rock I will build my church; and the gates of hell shall not prevail against it.").

20. *See* Shoghi Effendi, *The World Order of Bahá'u'lláh*, p. 21.

21. Shoghi Effendi, *The World Order of Bahá'u'lláh*, p. 20; 'Abdu'l-Bahá, *The Promulgation of Universal Peace*, p. 386 ("[T]he Bahá'í dispensation is distinguished from all others in this fact, the purpose of Bahá'u'lláh being that no one could arise to cause differences and disunion. After the departure of Christ various sects and denominations arose, each one claiming to be the true channel of Christianity, but none of them possessed a written authority from Christ; none could produce proof from Him; yet all claimed His sanction and approval.").

22. Shoghi Effendi, *The World Order of Bahá'u'lláh*, p. 21.

23. *See* Shoghi Effendi, *The World Order of Bahá'u'lláh*, p. 145 (". . . the Imám 'Alí, the cousin and legitimate successor of the Prophet . . . ."); *see also* Adib Taherzadeh, *The Covenant of Bahá'u'lláh*, p. 99 ("Having completed the rites of pilgrimage to Mecca in the last year of His life, Muḥammad, on His way back to Medina, ordered the large concourse of His followers to stop at a place known as Ghadír-i-Khumm. In that vast plain a number of saddles were stacked up, making an improvised pulpit from which Muḥammad delivered an important address to the congregation. There, He is reported to have taken 'Alí by the hand and said, 'Whoever considers Me as his Lord, then 'Alí is also his Lord.'").

24. Shoghi Effendi, *The World Order of Bahá'u'lláh*, p. 21.

25. *Cf.* on behalf of Shoghi Effendi, *Lights of Guidance*, p. 163 ("The real reason why Christ did not make some explicit statement regarding His succession is not known, and cannot be known. For how can we, poor humans, claim to unravel the mysteries of God's mind and purpose, and to grasp the inscrutable dispensations of His providence. The utmost we can do is to give some explanations, but these must necessarily fail to give the fundamental reason to the problem we seek to solve.").

26. *See* Shoghi Effendi, *The World Order of Bahá'u'lláh*, pp. 20-21 ("None, I feel, will question the fact that the fundamental reason why the unity of the Church of Christ was irretrievably shattered, and its influence was in the course of time undermined, was that the Edifice which the Fathers of the Church reared after the passing of His First Apostle was an Edifice that rested in nowise upon the explicit directions of Christ Himself. The authority and features of their administration were wholly inferred, and indirectly derived, with more or less justification, from certain vague and fragmentary references which they found scattered amongst His utterances as recorded in the Gospel. Not one of the sacraments of the Church; not one of the rites and ceremonies which the Christian Fathers have elaborately devised and ostentatiously observed; not one of the elements of the severe discipline they rigorously imposed upon the primitive Christians; none of these reposed on the direct authority of Christ, or emanated from His specific utterances. Not one of these did Christ conceive, none did He specifically invest with sufficient authority to either interpret His Word, or to add to what He had not specifically enjoined. . . . In the Muḥammadan Revelation, however, although His Faith as compared with that of Christ was, so far as the administration of His Dispensation is concerned, more complete and more specific in its provisions, yet in the matter of succession, it gave no written, no binding and conclusive instructions to those whose mission was to propagate His Cause. For the text of the Qur'án, the ordinances of which regarding prayer, fasting, marriage, divorce, inheritance, pilgrimage, and the like, have after

the revolution of thirteen hundred years remained intact and operative, gives no definite guidance regarding the Law of Succession, the source of all the dissensions, the controversies, and schisms which have dismembered and discredited Islám.").

27. The Universal House of Justice, quoted in *The Power of the Covenant*, Part Two, pp. 4-5.

28. *Will and Testament of 'Abdu'l-Bahá*, p. 3.

29. *Selections from the Writings of 'Abdu'l-Bahá*, p. 211; *see* 'Abdu'l-Bahá, *Star of the West*, vol. XII, no. 14, p. 227 ("In former cycles no distinct Covenant was made in writing by the Supreme Pen; no distinct personage was appointed to be the Standard differentiating falsehood from truth, so that whatsoever he said was to stand as truth and that which he repudiated was to be known as falsehood.").

30. Shoghi Effendi, *The World Order of Bahá'u'lláh*, pp. 21-22; *see* 'Abdu'l-Bahá, quoted in Shoghi Effendi, *God Passes By*, p. 239 (". . . 'the almighty Covenant, the like of which the sacred Dispensations of the past have never witnessed' and 'one of the distinctive features of this most mighty cycle.'"); Shoghi Effendi, *The World Order of Bahá'u'lláh*, p. 145 ("Nowhere in the sacred scriptures of any of the world's religious systems, nor even in the writings of the Inaugurator of the Bábí Dispensation, do we find any provisions establishing a covenant or providing for an administrative order that can compare in scope and authority with those that lie at the very basis of the Bahá'í Dispensation."); *see also* the Universal House of Justice, *Messages from the Universal House of Justice: 1963-1986*, p. 15 ("The two unique features which distinguish it [the Covenant of Bahá'u'lláh] from all religious covenants of the past are unchanged and operative. The revealed Word, in its original purity, amplified by the divinely guided interpretations of 'Abdu'l-Bahá and Shoghi Effendi, remains immutable, unadulterated by any man-made creeds or dogmas, unwarrantable inferences or unauthorized interpretations. The channel of divine guidance, providing flexibility in all the affairs of mankind, remains open through that Institution which was founded by Bahá'u'lláh and endowed by Him with supreme authority and unfailing guidance, and of which the Master wrote: 'Unto this body all things must be referred.'").

31. The Universal House of Justice, *The Holy Year*, p. 38.

32. Bahá'u'lláh, quoted in Shoghi Effendi, *The World Order of Bahá'u'lláh*, p. 163; *see* Shoghi Effendi, *The World Order of Bahá'u'lláh*, pp. 42-43 ("The principle of the Oneness of Mankind—the pivot round which all the teachings of Bahá'u'lláh revolve—is no mere outburst of ignorant emotionalism or an expression of vague and pious hope. . . . It does not constitute merely the enunciation of an ideal, but stands inseparably associated with an institution adequate to embody its truth, demonstrate its validity, and

perpetuate its influence. It implies an organic change in the structure of present-day society, a change such as the world has not yet experienced."); the Universal House of Justice, *A Wider Horizon*, p. 7 ("From the beginning of His stupendous mission, Bahá'u'lláh urged upon the attention of nations the necessity of ordering human affairs in such a way as to bring into being a world unified in all the essential aspects of its life.").

33. The Universal House of Justice, *The Holy Year*, p. 35 (". . . a Covenant intended by its divine Author to unite the races and nations of the earth.").

34. The Universal House of Justice, *The Holy Year*, p. 39.

35. The Universal House of Justice, *The Holy Year*, p. 39.

36. The Universal House of Justice, quoted in *The Covenant*, Introduction.

37. Shoghi Effendi, *The World Order of Bahá'u'lláh*, p. 144.

38. The Universal House of Justice, quoted in *The Covenant: Its Meaning and Origin and Our Attitude Toward It*, p. 39.

39. On behalf of the Universal House of Justice, *The Covenant*, # 19.

40. The Universal House of Justice, *The Institution of the Counsellors*, p. 26.

41. The Universal House of Justice, *The Holy Year*, p. 32.

42. *See* Shoghi Effendi, *God Passes By*, pp. 244-45 ("Above all the Covenant that was to perpetuate the influence of that Faith, insure its integrity, safeguard it from schism, and stimulate its world-wide expansion, had been fixed on an inviolable basis."); *id.*, p. 158 (". . . the Covenant designed to preserve its unity and perpetuate its influence . . . ."); *id.*, p. 223 ("The Covenant designed to safeguard the unity and integrity of its world-embracing system had been irrevocably bequeathed to posterity."); *The Constitution of the Universal House of Justice*, pp. 3-4 ("To direct and canalize the forces released by His Revelation He instituted His Covenant, whose power has preserved the integrity of His Faith, maintained its unity and stimulated its world-wide expansion throughout the successive ministries of 'Abdu'l-Bahá and Shoghi Effendi."); *see also* Shoghi Effendi, *The World Order of Bahá'u'lláh*, p. 148 ("Their [the Guardianship and the Universal House of Justice's] common, their fundamental object is to insure the continuity of that divinely-appointed authority which flows from the Source of our Faith, to safeguard the unity of its followers and to maintain the integrity and flexibility of its teachings.").

43. The Universal House of Justice, quoted in *The Covenant: Its Meaning and Origin and Our Attitude Toward It*, p. 52.

44. On behalf of the Universal House of Justice, to an individual believer, February 16, 1996; *see* 'Abdu'l-Bahá, *The Promulgation of Universal Peace*, p. 456 ("To ensure unity and agreement He has entered into a Covenant with all the people of the world, including the interpreter and

explainer of His teachings, so that no one may interpret or explain the religion of God according to his own view or opinion and thus create a sect founded upon his individual understanding of the divine Words."); *Selections from the Writings of 'Abdu'l-Bahá*, p. 215 ("Do not disrupt Bahá'í unity, and know that this unity cannot be maintained save through faith in the Covenant of God.").

45. 'Abdu'l-Bahá, *Bahá'í World Faith*, pp. 357-58; *see* 'Abdu'l-Bahá, *Star of the West*, vol. V, no. 15, p. 233 ("[W]e must all turn our faces to the appointed Center in order that the Bahá'í Unity might be preserved; otherwise in one year the Bahá'ís would be divided into a thousand sects.").

46. The Universal House of Justice, *The Holy Year*, p. 39.

47. *See* Shoghi Effendi, *This Decisive Hour*, p. 66 ("That such a secession, however, whether effected by those who apostatize their faith or preach heretical doctrines, should have failed, after the lapse of a century, to split in twain the entire body of the adherents of the Faith, or to create a grave, a permanent and irremediable breach in its organic structure, is a fact too eloquent for even a casual observer of the internal processes of its Administrative Order to either deny or ignore."); *see also* Chapter 9, p. 159 & n.7.

48. On behalf of the Universal House of Justice, to an individual believer, February 16, 1996.

49. On behalf of the Universal House of Justice, *Issues Related to the Study of the Bahá'í Faith*, # 7; *see id.*, # 6 ("Authority . . . to ensure . . . the integrity of the Word of God . . . is conferred upon the Administrative Order to which the Covenant has given birth.").

50. Shoghi Effendi, *God Passes By*, p. 245; *see id.*, p. 314.

51. The Universal House of Justice, *The Holy Year*, p. 36.

52. "The Completion of the Bahá'í World Crusade: 1953-1963," *The Bahá'í World*, vol. XIII, pp. 460-61; *The Ministry of the Custodians: 1957-1963*, p. 13.

53. The Universal House of Justice, *A Wider Horizon*, p. 55.

54. The Universal House of Justice, *The Holy Year*, p. 26.

55. *The Constitution of the Universal House of Justice*, p. 3.

56. *The Constitution of the Universal House of Justice*, p. 4.

57. The Universal House of Justice, *The Holy Year*, p. 39.

CHAPTER 2
'ABDU'L-BAHÁ: THE CENTER OF THE COVENANT

1. The Universal House of Justice, quoted in *The Power of the Covenant*, Part Two, pp. 4-5.

2. Shoghi Effendi, *God Passes By*, p. 238.

3. Shoghi Effendi, *God Passes By*, p. 238.

4. *See The Kitáb-i-Aqdas*, Note # 66.

5. *See* Shoghi Effendi, *God Passes By*, p. 239.

6. Bahá'u'lláh, *Bahá'í World Faith*, pp. 204-07; *see* Shoghi Effendi, *God Passes By*, pp. 177, 242; Shoghi Effendi, *The World Order of Bahá'u'lláh*, pp. 134-35; Adib Taherzadeh, *The Revelation of Bahá'u'lláh*, vol. 2, p. 388.

7. Bahá'u'lláh, quoted in Shoghi Effendi, *The World Order of Bahá'u'lláh*, p. 135.

8. Shoghi Effendi, *God Passes By*, p. 242 (quoting Bahá'u'lláh).

9. *See* Shoghi Effendi, *God Passes By*, p. 238; *see also* Shoghi Effendi, *The Promised Day Is Come*, p. 25 ("In the Kitáb-i-Aqdas (The Most Holy Book), that priceless treasury enshrining for all time the brightest emanations of the mind of Bahá'u'lláh, the Charter of His World Order, the chief repository of His laws, the Harbinger of His Covenant . . . .").

10. Shoghi Effendi, *God Passes By*, p. 214.

11. Bahá'u'lláh, *The Kitáb-i-Aqdas*, parag. 121.

12. Bahá'u'lláh, *The Kitáb-i-Aqdas*, parag. 174.

13. *The Kitáb-i-Aqdas*, Note # 145.

14. *See* Shoghi Effendi, *God Passes By*, p. 242 ("On Him ['Abdu'l-Bahá] . . ., the Author of the Kitáb-i-Aqdas, in a celebrated passage, subsequently elucidated in the 'Book of My Covenant,' had bestowed the function of interpreting His Holy Writ, proclaiming Him, at the same time, to be the One 'Whom God hath purposed, Who hath branched from this Ancient Root.'"); *The Kitáb-i-Aqdas*, Note # 145.

15. *The Kitáb-i-Aqdas*, Note # 184; *see* Shoghi Effendi, *God Passes By*, p. 213 (". . . the function of interpretation which it [the Kitáb-i-Aqdas] confers upon His Successor . . . .").

16. Shoghi Effendi, *The World Order of Bahá'u'lláh*, p. 136 (quoting 'Abdu'l-Bahá).

17. 'Abdu'l-Bahá, *Bahá'í World Faith*, pp. 358-59.

18. Shoghi Effendi, *God Passes By*, p. 177.

19. Shoghi Effendi, *God Passes By*, p. 239.

20. The Universal House of Justice, *The Holy Year*, p. 32.

21. Shoghi Effendi, *God Passes By*, p. 238.

22. Shoghi Effendi, *God Passes By*, p. 238.

23. *Tablets of Bahá'u'lláh*, pp. 221-22.

24. *See The Kitáb-i-Aqdas*, Note # 66.

25. On behalf of Shoghi Effendi, *The Light of Divine Guidance*, vol. 1, p. 62 ("The term 'afnán' means literally small branch, and refers to the relatives of the Báb, both men and women. As the Báb's only son died while in infancy, the former had no direct descendants. The 'afnán' are, therefore, all indirectly related to the Báb.").

26. *The Kitáb-i-Aqdas*, Note # 66.

27. *See* Bahá'u'lláh, *Prayers and Meditations*, p. 34; Shoghi Effendi, *God Passes By*, p. 188.

28. *See* Shoghi Effendi, *God Passes By*, p. 240.

29. On the occasion of His visit to Beirut, 'Abdu'l-Bahá had been addressed as the "Most Mighty Branch" in a letter dictated by Bahá'u'lláh: "Praise be to Him Who hath honored the Land of Bá (Beirut) through the presence of Him round Whom all names revolve. All the atoms of the earth have announced unto all created things that from behind the gate of the Prison-city there hath appeared and above its horizon there hath shone forth the Orb of the beauty of the great, the Most Mighty Branch of God—His ancient and immutable Mystery—proceeding on its way to another land. Sorrow, thereby, hath enveloped this Prison-city, whilst another land rejoiceth . . ." Bahá'u'lláh, quoted in Shoghi Effendi, *The World Order of Bahá'u'lláh*, p. 136; *see* Bahá'u'lláh, *Star of the West*, vol. VIII, no. 14, p. 185 (addressing Tablet to "my Greatest Branch"); *see also* H.M. Balyuzi, *Bahá'u'lláh: The King of Glory*, p. 378.

Likewise, Bahá'u'lláh referred to 'Abdu'l-Bahá as the "Most Great Branch" in *Epistle to the Son of the Wolf*: "Our late brother Mírzá Muḥammad-Ḥasan's daughter . . . who had been betrothed to the Most Great Branch ('Abdu'l-Bahá) was taken by the sister of this Wronged One from Núr to her own house, and from there sent unto another place." Bahá'u'lláh, *Epistle to the Son of the Wolf*, p. 170. When 'Abdu'l-Bahá was a child in Ṭihrán, S̲h̲ahr-Bánú was betrothed to Him. She was the daughter of Mírzá Muḥammad-Ḥasan, an older half-brother of Bahá'u'lláh. *See* H.M. Balyuzi, *Bahá'u'lláh: The King of Glory*, pp. 342-44; Adib Taherzadeh, *The Revelation of Bahá'u'lláh*, vol. 2, p. 205.

Additionally, there are accounts of oral statements of Bahá'u'lláh referring to 'Abdu'l-Bahá as the "Most Great Branch." *E.g.*, H.M. Balyuzi, *'Abdu'l-Bahá: The Centre of the Covenant of Bahá'u'lláh*, p. 44; H.M. Balyuzi, *Bahá'u'lláh: The King of Glory*, p. 417; Munírih K̲h̲ánum, *Munírih K̲h̲ánum: Memoirs and Letters*, p. 49; Adib Taherzadeh, *The Covenant of Bahá'u'lláh*, pp. 138-39.

'Abdu'l-Bahá also elucidated the meaning of "the Branch." *See* 'Abdu'l-Bahá, *Star of the West*, vol. VIII, no. 14, p. 186 ("But if any soul asks concerning the station of this servant the answer is—'Abdu'l-Bahá. If he inquires after the meaning of The Branch, the answer is—'Abdu'l-Bahá. If he desires to know the significance of the verse regarding The Branch, the answer is—'Abdu'l-Bahá. If he insists upon the explanation of the meaning of 'The Branch extended from the Ancient Root,' the answer is—'Abdu'l-Bahá.").

30. *E.g.*, Nabíl-i-A'zam, *The Dawn-Breakers*, pp. 100, 159, 440, 441, 586, 591, 616, 650; Adib Taherzadeh, *The Child of the Covenant*, p. 132; Adib Taherzadeh, *The Revelation of Bahá'u'lláh*, vol. 2, p. 199; Adib Taherzadeh, *The Revelation of Bahá'u'lláh*, vol. 3, p. 122. That 'Abdu'l-Bahá was recognized as the "Most Great Branch" is even confirmed by statements of His enemies—Mírzá Muḥammad-'Alí and Mírzá Badí'u'lláh. *See* Mirza Badi ullah, *An Epistle to the Bahá'í World*, pp. 13-14.

31. *See* Adib Taherzadeh, *The Child of the Covenant*, pp. 147-48; H.M. Balyuzi, *Bahá'u'lláh: The King of Glory*, p. 420.

32. The Universal House of Justice, *Messages from the Universal House of Justice: 1963-1986*, p. 160; *see* Adib Taherzadeh, *The Covenant of Bahá'u'lláh*, p. 141 ("It is known that 'Alí-Muḥammad Varqá, the renowned Apostle of Bahá'u'lláh, asked Him about the identity of the person alluded to in the above verses [from the Kitáb-i-Aqdas]. In a Tablet addressed to Varqá, Bahá'u'lláh indicated that the intended person was the Most Great Branch, and after Him the Greater Branch."); Jináb-i-Fáḍil-i-Mázandaráni, *Asráru'l-Áthár*, vol. 5, pp. 297-99 (quoting above-referenced Tablet addressed to Varqá).

33. The Universal House of Justice, *The Holy Year*, p. 39 ("Bahá'u'lláh, in the Book of His Covenant, confirmed the appointment of His Son 'Abdu'l-Bahá as the interpreter of His Word and the Center of His Covenant.").

34. *See* Shoghi Effendi, *God Passes By*, pp. 246, 405.

35. Shoghi Effendi, *God Passes By*, p. 314; Shoghi Effendi, *The World Order of Bahá'u'lláh*, p. 143 ("'Abdu'l-Bahá . . . incarnates an institution for which we can find no parallel whatsoever in any of the world's recognized religious systems . . . ."); *id.*, p. 131 (". . . One Who, not only in the Dispensation of Bahá'u'lláh but in the entire field of religious history, fulfills a unique function.").

36. The Universal House of Justice, *The Kitáb-i-Aqdas*, Introduction, p. 3; *see* Shoghi Effendi, *God Passes By*, p. 243 ("He had been elevated to the high office of Center of Bahá'u'lláh's Covenant, and been made the successor of the Manifestation of God Himself . . . .").

37. The Universal House of Justice, *The Holy Year*, p. 25.

38. 'Abdu'l-Bahá, *The Promulgation of Universal Peace*, pp. 455-56.

39. 'Abdu'l-Bahá, *The Compilation of Compilations*, vol. I, p. 128; *see* 'Abdu'l-Bahá, *The Covenant*, # 13 ("In case of differences, 'Abdu'l-Bahá must be consulted. All must revolve around his good pleasure."); *Selections from the Writings of 'Abdu'l-Bahá*, p. 195 ("[I]f on some point or other a difference ariseth among two conflicting groups, let them refer to the Centre of the Covenant for a solution to the problem.").

40. 'Abdu'l-Bahá, *The Promulgation of Universal Peace*, p. 386.

41. 'Abdu'l-Bahá, *The Promulgation of Universal Peace*, p. 323.

42. The Universal House of Justice, *The Holy Year*, p. 33.

43. The Universal House of Justice, *The Holy Year*, p. 39.

44. Shoghi Effendi, *The World Order of Bahá'u'lláh*, p. 127.

45. 'Abdu'l-Bahá, quoted in Shoghi Effendi, *The World Order of Bahá'u'lláh*, p. 138; *see* 'Abdu'l-Bahá, quoted in Udo Schaefer *et al.*, *Making the Crooked Straight*, p. 197 ("'Abdu'l-Bahá is the interpreter of the Book and not the enactor of laws not revealed in the Book.").

46. 'Abdu'l-Bahá, *The Promulgation of Universal Peace*, p. 382.

47. On behalf of the Universal House of Justice, *Messages from the Universal House of Justice: 1963-1986*, p. 518.

48. On behalf of the Universal House of Justice, *Messages from the Universal House of Justice: 1963-1986*, p. 518; *see* the Universal House of Justice, *The Kitáb-i-Aqdas*, Introduction, p. 3 ("The twenty-nine years of 'Abdu'l-Bahá's ministry endowed the Bahá'í world with a luminous body of commentary that opens multiple vistas of understanding on His Father's purpose.").

49. *See* Shoghi Effendi, *The Promised Day is Come*, p. 14.

50. *See* Shoghi Effendi, *The World Order of Bahá'u'lláh*, p. 144.

51. The Universal House of Justice, *The Holy Year*, p. 39.

52. *Selections from the Writings of 'Abdu'l-Bahá*, p. 246.

53. Reported words of 'Abdu'l-Bahá, quoted in May Maxwell, *An Early Pilgrimage*, p. 42.

54. *See Will and Testament of 'Abdu'l-Bahá*, p. 10 ("This wronged servant has spent his days and nights in promoting the Cause and urging the peoples to service. He rested not a moment, till the fame of the Cause of God was noised abroad in the world and the celestial strains from the Abhá Kingdom roused the East and the West. The beloved of God must also follow the same example. This is the secret of faithfulness, this is the requirement of servitude to the Threshold of Bahá!"); *see also* Shoghi Effendi, *Bahá'í Admin-*

istration, p. 125 ("It was He, our beloved 'Abdu'l-Bahá, our true and shining Exemplar, who with infinite tact and patience, whether in His public utterances or in private converse, adapted the presentation of the fundamentals of the Cause to the varying capacities and the spiritual receptiveness of His hearers."); Shoghi Effendi, *The Importance of Deepening our Knowledge and Understanding of the Faith*, # 73 ("The Bahá'í youth must be taught how to teach the Cause of God. . . . They must become thoroughly familiar with the language used and the example set by 'Abdu'l-Bahá in His public addresses throughout the West."); on behalf of Shoghi Effendi, *The Gift of Teaching*, # 105 ("We should teach as the Master taught. He was the perfect Exemplar of the Teachings. He proclaimed the universal truths, and, through love and wise demonstration of the universal verities of the Faith, attracted the hearts and the minds.").

55. *Selections from the Writings of 'Abdu'l-Bahá*, p. 245.

56. The Universal House of Justice, *A Wider Horizon*, p. 49.

57. On behalf of Shoghi Effendi, *Family Life*, # 69; *see* 'Abdu'l-Bahá, quoted in on behalf of the Universal House of Justice, to an individual believer, April 2, 1985 ("The friends of God and the handmaids of the All-Merciful should know that in every movement of 'Abdu'l-Bahá, in every word He uttereth, there lieth a great wisdom.").

58. *See* Shoghi Effendi, *God Passes By*, p. 245.

59. Bahá'u'lláh, quoted in Shoghi Effendi, *The World Order of Bahá'u'lláh*, p. 135.

60. Bahá'u'lláh, quoted in Shoghi Effendi, *The World Order of Bahá'u'lláh*, p. 135.

61. Bahá'u'lláh, quoted in Shoghi Effendi, *The World Order of Bahá'u'lláh*, p. 135.

62. 'Abdu'l-Bahá, *Bahá'í World Faith*, p. 358.

63. *Selections from the Writings of 'Abdu'l-Bahá*, p. 209.

64. 'Abdu'l-Bahá, quoted in Shoghi Effendi, *The World Order of Bahá'u'lláh*, p. 138.

65. *Selections from the Writings of 'Abdu'l-Bahá*, p. 214.

66. 'Abdu'l-Bahá, *Star of the West*, vol. XII, no. 14, p. 227.

67. Shoghi Effendi, *God Passes By*, p. 245 ("The continuity of that unerring guidance vouchsafed to it since its birth was now assured."); *id.*, p. 299 (". . . it began, after His ascension, under the unerring guidance, and as a result of the unfailing solicitude, of a wise, a vigilant and loving Master . . . ."); *id.*, p. 315 (". . . the prophecies which the unerring pen of the appointed Center of Bahá'u'lláh's Covenant has recorded."); *id.*, p. 325 ("The creative energies unleashed by the Originator of the Law of God in this age

gave birth, through their impact upon the mind of Him Who had been chosen as its unerring Expounder . . . ."); *id.*, p. 389 (". . . the testimony from the unerring pen of the Center of Bahá'u'lláh's Covenant . . . ."); Shoghi Effendi, *The Advent of Divine Justice*, p. 90 (". . . ordained for it by the unerring pen of 'Abdu'l-Bahá."); Shoghi Effendi, *Citadel of Faith*, p. 127 (". . . forecast by 'Abdu'l-Bahá's unerring pen . . . ."); Shoghi Effendi, *This Decisive Hour*, p. 123 (". . . those epoch-making Tablets wherein the unerring pen of their Master has traced the course of their Mission . . . ."); Shoghi Effendi, *Messages to the Bahá'í World*, p. 103 (". . . we may well ponder the portentous prophecies uttered well-nigh fourscore years ago, by the Author of our Faith, as well as the dire predictions made by Him Who is the unerring Interpreter of His teachings . . . ."); *id.*, p. 127 (". . . invested by the unerring Pen of the Center of His Covenant . . . ."); Shoghi Effendi, *The World Order of Bahá'u'lláh*, p. 134 (". . . the unerring Interpreter of His Word . . . .").

68. The Universal House of Justice, *A Wider Horizon*, p. 49.

69. On behalf of the Universal House of Justice, quoted in *The Covenant: Its Meaning and Origin and Our Attitude Toward It*, p. 30; *see* on behalf of Shoghi Effendi, quoted in on behalf of the Universal House of Justice, to an individual believer, April 27, 1995 ("Whatever the Master has said is based on the teachings of Bahá'u'lláh. He was the perfect Interpreter, had lived with Him all His life; therefore what He says has the same standing, even if a text of Bahá'u'lláh is not available. . . ."); on behalf of Shoghi Effendi, *Lights of Guidance*, pp. 486-87 ("Shoghi Effendi wishes to emphasize that what is truly authoritative are the words of the Master. In all such cases we should try and find out what He has said and abide by His words, even though they seem in conflict with the findings of modern scholars. If He does not say anything on the subject, then the individual is free to accept, or refute what scholars . . . say. Through the discussion of these (statements by scholars), the truth will ultimately be found, but at no time should their decision be considered as final.").

70. 'Abdu'l-Bahá, *The Promulgation of Universal Peace*, p. 386.

71. 'Abdu'l-Bahá, *Bahá'í World Faith*, p. 358.

72. Shoghi Effendi, *The World Order of Bahá'u'lláh*, p. 139.

73. Shoghi Effendi, *The World Order of Bahá'u'lláh*, p. 139.

74. On behalf of Shoghi Effendi, *Unfolding Destiny*, p. 440.

75. Shoghi Effendi, *God Passes By*, p. 242; *see* Shoghi Effendi, *The World Order of Bahá'u'lláh*, p. 139 ("He ['Abdu'l-Bahá] . . . does not inherently possess that indefinable yet all-pervading reality the exclusive possession of which is the hallmark of Prophethood . . . .").

76. Shoghi Effendi, *The World Order of Bahá'u'lláh*, p. 139.

77. Shoghi Effendi, *The World Order of Bahá'u'lláh*, p. 131.
78. Shoghi Effendi, *The World Order of Bahá'u'lláh*, p. 132.
79. Shoghi Effendi, *The World Order of Bahá'u'lláh*, p. 132.
80. 'Abdu'l-Bahá, quoted in Shoghi Effendi, *The World Order of Bahá'u'lláh*, p. 133.
81. Shoghi Effendi, *The World Order of Bahá'u'lláh*, p. 133.
82. Shoghi Effendi, *The World Order of Bahá'u'lláh*, p. 133.
83. Shoghi Effendi, *The World Order of Bahá'u'lláh*, p. 134.

CHAPTER 3
THE REBELLION AND EXCOMMUNICATION OF MÍRZÁ MUHAMMAD-'ALÍ

1. Shoghi Effendi, *God Passes By*, p. 245.
2. Shoghi Effendi, *God Passes By*, pp. 245-46.
3. *See* Shoghi Effendi, *God Passes By*, p. 246.
4. Shoghi Effendi, *God Passes By*, p. 246.
5. Shoghi Effendi, *God Passes By*, p. 246.
6. Shoghi Effendi, *God Passes By*, p. 246.
7. Shoghi Effendi, *God Passes By*, p. 246.
8. Shoghi Effendi, *God Passes By*, pp. 246-47.
9. *See* Shoghi Effendi, *God Passes By*, p. 248.
10. *See* Shoghi Effendi, *God Passes By*, p. 248.
11. Shoghi Effendi, *God Passes By*, pp. 248-49.
12. *Tablets of Bahá'u'lláh*, p. 222; *see* Shoghi Effendi, *God Passes By*, p. 246.
13. *See* Adib Taherzadeh, *The Covenant of Bahá'u'lláh*, pp. 126-27.
14. *See* Shoghi Effendi, *God Passes By*, pp. 249, 251.
15. Bahá'u'lláh, quoted in Shoghi Effendi, *God Passes By*, p. 251; *see Will and Testament of 'Abdu'l-Bahá*, p. 6; *see also* H.M. Balyuzi, *Bahá'u'lláh: The King of Glory*, p. 417 ("Bahá'u'lláh oftentimes warned the believers to remain steadfast and loyal to the Covenant. Once, Hájí Mírzá Habíbu'lláh tells us, He pointed to Mírzá Muhammad-'Alí, Mírzá Díyá'u'lláh and Mírzá Badí'u'lláh and said: 'Should one of our Aghsán ever for a moment pass out from the shadow of the Cause he shall cease to be of any consequence.'").
16. Bahá'u'lláh, quoted in Shoghi Effendi, *God Passes By*, p. 251.
17. *Will and Testament of 'Abdu'l-Bahá*, p. 5.

18. *Will and Testament of 'Abdu'l-Bahá*, pp. 6-7.

19. *Will and Testament of 'Abdu'l-Bahá*, p. 9.

20. Shoghi Effendi, *God Passes By*, p. 320.

21. *Will and Testament of 'Abdu'l-Bahá*, pp. 5-6.

22. *Will and Testament of 'Abdu'l-Bahá*, p. 25.

23. Shoghi Effendi, *God Passes By*, p. 320.

24. Shoghi Effendi, *This Decisive Hour*, p. 19.

25. Shoghi Effendi, *This Decisive Hour*, p. 19.

26. Shoghi Effendi, *This Decisive Hour*, p. 19.

27. *See* Bahá'u'lláh, quoted in Shoghi Effendi, *God Passes By*, p. 251.

28. *See* Shoghi Effendi, *God Passes By*, p. 328.

CHAPTER 4
SHOGHI EFFENDI: THE GUARDIAN OF THE CAUSE OF GOD

1. Shoghi Effendi, *God Passes By*, p. 328; *cf.* the Universal House of Justice, quoted in *The Power of the Covenant*, Part Two, pp. 22-23 ("'Abdu'l-Bahá's Will was written in three parts at three different times in His life. All three parts are in His handwriting and are signed by Him. All three, comprising twelve pages in all, were in an envelope under lock and key in His safe when He died. The face of the envelope was addressed to Shoghi Effendi in the Master's handwriting and signed by Him. On the back it bears three more signatures of 'Abdu'l-Bahá across the flap where it was stuck down.").

2. *Will and Testament of 'Abdu'l-Bahá*, pp. 5-9.

3. Shoghi Effendi, *God Passes By*, p. 325.

4. *See* Shoghi Effendi, *The World Order of Bahá'u'lláh*, p. 147.

5. Shoghi Effendi, *This Decisive Hour*, p. 122; *see* Shoghi Effendi, *The World Order of Bahá'u'lláh*, p. 144.

6. The Báb, quoted in Shoghi Effendi, *The World Order of Bahá'u'lláh*, pp. 146-47.

7. Bahá'u'lláh, *The Kitáb-i-Aqdas*, parag. 181.

8. Shoghi Effendi, *The World Order of Bahá'u'lláh*, p. 19; *see id.*, pp. 3-4.

9. Shoghi Effendi, *God Passes By*, p. 325.

10. Shoghi Effendi, *God Passes By*, p. 268.

11. Shoghi Effendi, *God Passes By*, p. xv.

12. Shoghi Effendi, *God Passes By*, p. 326.

13. Shoghi Effendi, *The World Order of Bahá'u'lláh*, p. 145.

14. *See* Shoghi Effendi, *The World Order of Bahá'u'lláh*, p. 145 ("Does the

text of either the Gospel or the Qur'án confer sufficient authority upon those leaders and councils that have claimed the right and assumed the function of interpreting the provisions of their sacred scriptures and of administering the affairs of their respective communities? Could Peter, the admitted chief of the Apostles, or the Imám 'Alí, the cousin and legitimate successor of the Prophet, produce in support of the primacy with which both had been invested written and explicit affirmations from Christ and Muḥammad that could have silenced those who either among their contemporaries or in a later age have repudiated their authority and, by their action, precipitated the schisms that persist until the present day? Where, we may confidently ask, in the recorded sayings of Jesus Christ, whether in the matter of succession or in the provision of a set of specific laws and clearly defined administrative ordinances, as distinguished from purely spiritual principles, can we find anything approaching the detailed injunctions, laws and warnings that abound in the authenticated utterances of both Bahá'u'lláh and 'Abdu'l-Bahá?").

15. Shoghi Effendi, *The World Order of Bahá'u'lláh*, pp. 145-46; *see id.*, pp. 21-22 ("Both in the administrative provisions of the Bahá'í Dispensation, and in the matter of succession, as embodied in the twin institutions of the House of Justice and of the Guardianship, the followers of Bahá'u'lláh can summon to their aid such irrefutable evidences of Divine Guidance that none can resist, that none can belittle or ignore. Therein lies the distinguishing feature of the Bahá'í Revelation. Therein lies the strength of the unity of the Faith, of the validity of a Revelation that claims not to destroy or belittle previous Revelations, but to connect, unify, and fulfill them.").

16. *See* on behalf of the Universal House of Justice, *Issues Related to the Study of the Bahá'í Faith*, # 6.

17. Shoghi Effendi, *The World Order of Bahá'u'lláh*, p. 147; on behalf of the Universal House of Justice, *Lights of Guidance*, p. 312.

18. The Universal House of Justice, quoted in *The Covenant: Its Meaning and Origin and Our Attitude Toward It*, p. 37.

19. *See* Chapter 6.

20. Shoghi Effendi, *The World Order of Bahá'u'lláh*, p. 147; *see* Shoghi Effendi, *God Passes By*, p. 214 ("In this Charter of the future world civilization its Author . . . anticipates by implication the institution of Guardianship . . . ."). In the Kitáb-i-Aqdas, Bahá'u'lláh declared: "Endowments dedicated to charity revert to God, the Revealer of Signs. None hath the right to dispose of them without leave from Him Who is the Dawning-place of Revelation. After Him, this authority shall pass to the Aghsán, and after them to the House of Justice—should it be established in the world by then . . . ." Bahá'u'lláh, *The Kitáb-i-Aqdas*, parag. 42. Thus, endowments revert to God, and no one has the right to dispose of them without the permission of "the Dawning-place of Revelation." After Him, "this authority

238

shall pass to the Aghsán . . . ." "Aghsán" is an Arabic word meaning "branches." *The Kitáb-i-Aqdas*, Note # 66. "This term is used by Bahá'u'lláh to designate His male descendants." *Id.* "This passage of the Aqdas, therefore, anticipates the succession of chosen Aghsán and thus the institution of the Guardianship . . . ." *Id.*

Another reference in the Kitáb-i-Aqdas anticipating by implication the institution of the Guardianship is in relation to Ḥuqúqu'lláh (the Right of God). The law of Ḥuqúqu'lláh is "ordained in the Kitáb-i-Aqdas without provision being made for who is to receive it; in His Will and Testament 'Abdu'l-Bahá fills this gap by stating 'It is to be offered through the guardian of the Cause of God. . . .'" The Universal House of Justice, quoted in *The Covenant: Its Meaning and Origin and Our Attitude Toward It*, p. 37 n.9.

Finally, the institution of the Guardianship was anticipated by 'Abdu'l-Bahá in His lifetime. *See* Shoghi Effendi, *The World Order of Bahá'u'lláh*, p. 150 ("It should be borne in mind that the institution of the Guardianship has been anticipated by 'Abdu'l-Bahá in an allusion He made in a Tablet addressed, long before His own ascension, to three of His friends in Persia. To their question as to whether there would be any person to whom all the Bahá'ís would be called upon to turn after His ascension He made the following reply: 'As to the question ye have asked me, know verily that this is a well-guarded secret. It is even as a gem concealed within its shell. That it will be revealed is predestined. The time will come when its light will appear, when its evidences will be made manifest, and its secrets unraveled.'").

21. *See* Shoghi Effendi, *God Passes By*, p. 328; the Universal House of Justice, *Messages from the Universal House of Justice: 1963-1986*, p. 160.

22. The Universal House of Justice, *Messages from the Universal House of Justice: 1963-1986*, p. 160.

23. *See* Shoghi Effendi, *God Passes By*, p. 328.

24. Shoghi Effendi, *The World Order of Bahá'u'lláh*, pp. 19-20.

25. The Universal House of Justice, quoted in *The Covenant: Its Meaning and Origin and Our Attitude Toward It*, p. 37.

26. *The Kitáb-i-Aqdas*, Note # 66; *cf.* Rúḥíyyih Rabbaní, *The Priceless Pearl*, pp. 1-3 (discussing 'Abdu'l-Bahá's allusions to His successor).

27. On behalf of the Universal House of Justice, *The Covenant*, # 24.

28. *Will and Testament of 'Abdu'l-Bahá*, p. 11. The terms 'Abdu'l-Bahá used in appointing Shoghi Effendi as His successor parallel Bahá'u'lláh's words in relation to 'Abdu'l-Bahá. *See Tablets of Bahá'u'lláh*, p. 221 ("It is incumbent upon the Aghsán, the Afnán and My Kindred to turn, one and all, their faces towards the Most Mighty Branch.").

29. *See* Adib Taherzadeh, *The Child of the Covenant*, pp. 265-66.

30. *Will and Testament of 'Abdu'l-Bahá*, p. 11; *see id.*, p. 3 (". . . that primal

branch of the Divine and Sacred Lote-Tree, grown out, blest, tender, verdant and flourishing from the Twin Holy Trees . . . ."; ". . . the blest and sacred bough that hath branched out from the Twin Holy Trees.").

31. *See The Kitáb-i-Aqdas*, Note # 128.

32. *Will and Testament of 'Abdu'l-Bahá*, p. 11.

33. Shoghi Effendi, *The World Order of Bahá'u'lláh*, p. 151.

34. On behalf of the Universal House of Justice, *Messages from the Universal House of Justice: 1963-1986*, p. 646.

35. On behalf of the Universal House of Justice, *Messages from the Universal House of Justice: 1963-1986*, p. 646.

36. From a transcript of a letter written on behalf of Shoghi Effendi, November 20, 1941, quoted in Ian Semple, "Interpretation and the Guardianship" (lecture, Haifa, Israel, February 18, 1984 and lecture, Wilmette, Illinois, September 6, 2001).

37. On behalf of Shoghi Effendi, *Lights of Guidance*, p. 238; *e.g.*, on behalf of Shoghi Effendi, *Dawn of a New Day*, p. 200 ("The words 'Be thou as a flame of fire to My enemies and a river of life eternal to My loved ones' should not be taken in their literal sense. Bahá'u'lláh's advice is that again we should flee from the enemies of God, and instead seek the fellowship of His lovers."); on behalf of Shoghi Effendi, *Lights of Guidance*, pp. 538-39 ("What Bahá'u'lláh means by the faculty of sight and hearing is the physical faculty, not a spiritual abstraction. He means that we have been given eyes and ears to appreciate what goes on in this world, by Almighty God; in other words, we can read the Teachings and listen to the Message of the Prophet. This is to be taken literally."); on behalf of Shoghi Effendi, *High Endeavours*, p. 71 ("As there is nothing specific about Joseph Smith in the teachings, the Guardian has no statement to make on his position or about the accuracy of any statement in the Book of Mormon regarding American history or its peoples.").

38. *Will and Testament of 'Abdu'l-Bahá*, p. 14.

39. Shoghi Effendi, *The World Order of Bahá'u'lláh*, p. 150.

40. On behalf of the Universal House of Justice, *Issues Related to the Study of the Bahá'í Faith*, # 8.

41. Shoghi Effendi, *The World Order of Bahá'u'lláh*, p. 148.

42. Shoghi Effendi, *The World Order of Bahá'u'lláh*, p. 148.

43. On behalf of the Universal House of Justice, to an individual believer, January 20, 1998.

44. *Will and Testament of 'Abdu'l-Bahá*, p. 11.

45. On behalf of Shoghi Effendi, *Lights of Guidance*, p. 314.

46. *The Kitáb-i-Aqdas*, Note # 130.

47. On behalf of Shoghi Effendi, *Lights of Guidance*, p. 314.

48. On behalf of Shoghi Effendi, *Directives from the Guardian*, p. 30.

49. On behalf of the Universal House of Justice, *Lights of Guidance*, p. 312.

50. On behalf of the Universal House of Justice, to an individual believer, July 25, 1974.

51. On behalf of the Universal House of Justice, to an individual believer, January 20, 1998.

52. On behalf of Shoghi Effendi, *Unfolding Destiny*, p. 449.

53. From a transcript of a letter written on behalf of Shoghi Effendi, November 20, 1941, quoted in Ian Semple, "Interpretation and the Guardianship" (lecture, Haifa, Israel, February 18, 1984 and lecture, Wilmette, Illinois, September 6, 2001).

54. Shoghi Effendi, *The World Order of Bahá'u'lláh*, p. 151.

55. Shoghi Effendi, *The World Order of Bahá'u'lláh*, p. 151.

56. Shoghi Effendi, *The World Order of Bahá'u'lláh*, p. 151.

57. Shoghi Effendi, *The World Order of Bahá'u'lláh*, p. 151.

58. *See* Shoghi Effendi, *The World Order of Bahá'u'lláh*, p. 151; *cf.* on behalf of Shoghi Effendi, *Lights of Guidance*, p. 459 ("We pray to God, or to Bahá'u'lláh, as we please. But if in our thoughts we desire to turn to the Guardian first and then address our prayer, there is no objection, as long as we always bear in mind he is only the Guardian, and do not confuse his station with that of the Prophet or even of the Master.").

59. From a transcript of a letter written on behalf of Shoghi Effendi, November 20, 1941, quoted in Ian Semple, "Interpretation and the Guardianship" (lecture, Haifa, Israel, February 18, 1984 and lecture, Wilmette, Illinois, September 6, 2001).

60. *Will and Testament of 'Abdu'l-Bahá*, pp. 11-12.

61. *Will and Testament of 'Abdu'l-Bahá*, p. 11.

62. The Universal House of Justice, *Messages from the Universal House of Justice: 1963-1986*, p. 56.

63. On behalf of Shoghi Effendi, quoted in on behalf of the Universal House of Justice, *Lights of Guidance*, p. 312; *see* on behalf of Shoghi Effendi, *Directives from the Guardian*, p. 30 ("When he [the Guardian] feels that a certain thing is essential for the protection of the Cause, even if it is something that affects a person personally, he must be obeyed, but when he gives advice, such as that he gave you in a previous letter about your future, it is not binding; you are free to follow it or not as you please.").

The following references address the issue of the authority of letters written on behalf of the Guardian. *See* Shoghi Effendi, *Principles of Bahá'í Administration*, p. 101 ("Whatever letters are sent in my behalf from Haifa are all read and approved by me before mailing. There is no exception whatever to this rule."); on behalf of Shoghi Effendi, *Lights of Guidance*, p. 314 ("Instructions sent on behalf of the Guardian are binding, as are the words of the Guardian; although of course, they are not the Guardian's words."); on behalf of Shoghi Effendi, *Unfolding Destiny*, p. 260 ("Although the secretaries of the Guardian convey his thoughts and instructions and these messages are authoritative, their words are in no sense the same as his, their style certainly not the same, and their authority less, for they use their own terms and not his exact words in conveying his messages.").

CHAPTER 5
THE PASSING OF SHOGHI EFFENDI AND THE MINISTRY OF THE HANDS OF THE CAUSE OF GOD

1. *Will and Testament of 'Abdu'l-Bahá*, p. 11.

2. *Will and Testament of 'Abdu'l-Bahá*, p. 11.

3. *Will and Testament of 'Abdu'l-Bahá*, p. 12.

4. *Will and Testament of 'Abdu'l-Bahá*, p. 12.

5. *Will and Testament of 'Abdu'l-Bahá*, p. 12.

6. *Will and Testament of 'Abdu'l-Bahá*, p. 11.

7. *Will and Testament of 'Abdu'l-Bahá*, p. 12.

8. *Will and Testament of 'Abdu'l-Bahá*, p. 12.

9. *Will and Testament of 'Abdu'l-Bahá*, p. 12.

10. *The Ministry of the Custodians: 1957-1963*, pp. 27-29.

11. The Universal House of Justice, *Messages from the Universal House of Justice: 1963-1986*, p. 6.

12. The Universal House of Justice, *Messages from the Universal House of Justice: 1963-1986*, p. 51.

13. The Universal House of Justice, *The Institution of the Counsellors*, p. 5; Shoghi Effendi, *The World Order of Bahá'u'lláh*, p. 147.

14. *See The Kitáb-i-Aqdas*, Note # 183; Barron Harper, *Lights of Fortitude*, pp. 1-18.

15. *See The Kitáb-i-Aqdas*, Note # 183.

16. The Universal House of Justice, *The Institution of the Counsellors*, p. 5.

17. *See Will and Testament of 'Abdu'l-Bahá*, pp. 12-13; Shoghi Effendi, *God Passes By*, p. 328.

18. *See The Kitáb-i-Aqdas*, Note # 183.

19. *Will and Testament of 'Abdu'l-Bahá*, p. 13.

20. *Will and Testament of 'Abdu'l-Bahá*, p. 12.

21. See *The Ministry of the Custodians: 1957-1963*, pp. xxii-xxiv.

22. See *The Ministry of the Custodians: 1957-1963*, pp. xxii-xxiv.

23. Shoghi Effendi, *Messages to the Bahá'í World*, p. 58.

24. Shoghi Effendi, *Messages to the Bahá'í World*, p. 122.

25. Shoghi Effendi, *Messages to the Bahá'í World*, p. 123.

26. Shoghi Effendi, *Messages to the Bahá'í World*, p. 123.

27. On behalf of Shoghi Effendi, *Directives from the Guardian*, p. 31 ("The rank and position of the Hands of the Cause are superior to the position of the National Assemblies. In writing concerning the Hands, therefore, when there is reference to the Institutions of the Faith, after the Guardian should be mentioned the Hands, and then the National Bodies. . .").

28. Shoghi Effendi, *Messages to the Bahá'í World*, p. 127.

29. Shoghi Effendi, *Messages to the Bahá'í World*, p. 127.

30. Shoghi Effendi, *Messages to the Bahá'í World*, p. 127.

31. See *The Ministry of the Custodians: 1957-1963*, p. 30.

32. The Universal House of Justice, *Messages from the Universal House of Justice: 1963-1986*, p. 51; see *The Ministry of the Custodians: 1957-1963*, pp. 41-50.

33. See *The Ministry of the Custodians: 1957-1963*, pp. 122, 166.

34. The Universal House of Justice, *Messages from the Universal House of Justice: 1963-1986*, p. 51.

35. *The Ministry of the Custodians: 1957-1963*, p. 13.

36. *The Ministry of the Custodians: 1957-1963*, pp. 28-30.

37. *The Ministry of the Custodians: 1957-1963*, p. 29.

38. *The Ministry of the Custodians: 1957-1963*, pp. 35-36.

39. *The Ministry of the Custodians: 1957-1963*, pp. 16, 196-97; Barron Harper, *Lights of Fortitude*, p. 303.

40. See *Will and Testament of 'Abdu'l-Bahá*, p. 12.

41. See *Will and Testament of 'Abdu'l-Bahá*, p. 12.

42. See *Will and Testament of 'Abdu'l-Bahá*, p. 12. As for the Will and Testament's requirement that Shoghi Effendi appoint his "first-born" or another "branch," Remey argued that any believer can be a "branch." However, this argument overlooked the fact that in the Will and Testament (and in other Writings of Bahá'u'lláh and 'Abdu'l-Bahá), the Arabic term translated as "branch" ("Ghuṣn"; plural is "Aghṣán") was used to refer exclu-

sively to Bahá'u'lláh's male descendants; the term did not apply to any other category of people. *See* Research Department of the Universal House of Justice, memorandum dated July 5, 2000 ("There are three words used in the Writings, which have been translated as 'branch' in English. They are S͟hák͟hih, G͟huṣn, and Far'. The first, S͟hák͟hih, is Persian and it has been used by 'Abdu'l-Bahá in connection with believers and their relationship to the Tree of the Cause. . . . The second word, G͟huṣn, is Arabic and has been used in the Bahá'í Writings exclusively to denote the male descendants of Bahá'u'lláh and 'Abdu'l-Bahá. . . . As to the third word, Far', this word has been used by 'Abdu'l-Bahá in 'Some Answered Questions' in relation to 'Alí and Joshua. This is an Arabic word and it is used in a broad sense to indicate the relationship of members of both the Ag͟hṣán and the Afnán families.").

That the term "branches" or "Ag͟hṣán" is distinct from references to believers generally is evident from the uses of the term in the Will and Testament of 'Abdu'l-Bahá and in other authoritative Writings. *See Will and Testament of 'Abdu'l-Bahá*, p. 11 ("O my loving friends! After the passing away of this wronged one, it is incumbent upon the Ag͟hṣán (Branches), the Afnán (Twigs) of the Sacred Lote-Tree, the Hands (pillars) of the Cause of God and the loved ones of the Abhá Beauty to turn unto Shoghi Effendi . . . as he is the sign of God, the chosen branch, the Guardian of the Cause of God, he unto whom all the Ag͟hṣán, the Afnán, the Hands of the Cause of God and His loved ones must turn."); *Tablets of Bahá'u'lláh*, p. 221 ("The Will of the divine Testator is this: It is incumbent upon the Ag͟hṣán, the Afnán and My Kindred to turn, one and all, their faces towards the Most Mighty Branch."); *id.*, p. 222 ("It is enjoined upon everyone to manifest love towards the Ag͟hṣán, but God hath not granted them any right to the property of others. [¶] O ye My Ag͟hṣán, My Afnán and My Kindred! We exhort you to fear God, to perform praiseworthy deeds and to do that which is meet and seemly and serveth to exalt your station. . . . It is incumbent upon everyone to show courtesy to, and have regard for the Ag͟hṣán, that thereby the Cause of God may be glorified and His Word exalted."); *Selections from the Writings of 'Abdu'l-Bahá*, p. 214 ("And in the Book of the Covenant He explicitly saith that the object of this verse 'Who hath branched from this Ancient Root' is the Most Mighty Branch. And He commandeth all the Ag͟hṣán, the Afnán, the kindred and the Bahá'ís to turn toward Him.").

The specialized meaning of the term "branch" is even revealed by Shoghi Effendi's translation into English of 'Abdu'l-Bahá's Will and Testament, which declared that the Guardian must choose as his successor either his "first-born" or "another branch." *Will and Testament of 'Abdu'l-Bahá*, p. 12. The word "another" implies that the "first-born" is a "branch" and that the term has a particularized meaning.

43. *See Will and Testament of 'Abdu'l-Bahá*, p. 12.

44. *The Ministry of the Custodians: 1957-1963*, pp. 205, 232; *Mason Remey and Those Who Followed Him*, November 29, 2001; *cf.* Shoghi Effendi, *Messages to the Bahá'í World*, pp. 7-8.

45. *See* Shoghi Effendi, *Messages to the Bahá'í World*, pp. 7-8.

46. *The Ministry of the Custodians: 1957-1963*, p. 232; *The Power of the Covenant*, Part Two, p. 25.

47. *E.g.*, on behalf of Shoghi Effendi, *Directives from the Guardian*, p. 72 ("At present there are women on the International Council, and this will continue as long as it exists, but when the International House of Justice is elected, there will only be men on it, as this is the law of the *Aqdas*.").

48. *Will and Testament of 'Abdu'l-Bahá*, p. 14 ("[T]hese secondary Houses of Justice must elect the members of the Universal one.").

49. *See The Ministry of the Custodians: 1957-1963*, pp. 234-35.

50. 'Abdu'l-Bahá, *The Promulgation of Universal Peace*, p. 456.

51. 'Abdu'l-Bahá, quoted in the Universal House of Justice, *Messages from the Universal House of Justice: 1963-1986*, p. 52.

52. *See The Ministry of the Custodians: 1957-1963*, pp. 35-36.

53. *See The Ministry of the Custodians: 1957-1963*, p. 16.

54. *The Ministry of the Custodians: 1957-1963*, p. 223 ("ENTIRE BODY HANDS OBEDIENT PROVISIONS WILL TESTAMENT CENTRE COVENANT COMMUNICATIONS BELOVED GUARDIAN ENJOINING THEM PROTECT HOLY CAUSE ATTACKS ENEMIES WITHIN WITHOUT ANNOUNCE BAHA'I WORLD MASON REMEY COVENANT BREAKER EXPELLED FAITH . . . ."); *see id.*, pp. 208, 223-24.

55. *See* Mason Remey, quoted in on behalf of the Universal House of Justice, to an individual believer, June 4, 1997.

56. *See* Mason Remey, quoted in on behalf of the Universal House of Justice, to an individual believer, June 4, 1997.

57. On behalf of Shoghi Effendi, quoted in Udo Schaefer *et al.*, *Making the Crooked Straight*, p. 185 n.218.

58. *Will and Testament of 'Abdu'l-Bahá*, p. 12.

59. *Will and Testament of 'Abdu'l-Bahá*, p. 13.

60. *See* Mason Remey, quoted in on behalf of the Universal House of Justice, to an individual believer, June 4, 1997.

61. *Will and Testament of 'Abdu'l-Bahá*, p. 12.

62. *See The Ministry of the Custodians: 1957-1963*, p. 223.

63. *See* the Universal House of Justice, *Messages from the Universal House of*

Justice: 1963-1986, p. 271.

64. *See Mason Remey and Those Who Followed Him*, November 29, 2001.

65. *See* the Universal House of Justice, *Messages from the Universal House of Justice: 1963-1986*, p. 271.

66. The Universal House of Justice, *Messages from the Universal House of Justice: 1963-1986*, p. 52.

67. *See* Charlotte M. Linfoot, "First International Convention," *The Bahá'í World*, vol. XIV, p. 427.

68. The Universal House of Justice, *Messages from the Universal House of Justice: 1963-1986*, p. 6.

CHAPTER 6
THE UNIVERSAL HOUSE OF JUSTICE:
SIGNIFICANCE, ORIGIN, AUTHORITY, AND ELECTION

1. On behalf of the Universal House of Justice, *Issues Related to the Study of the Bahá'í Faith*, # 6.

2. Shoghi Effendi, *God Passes By*, p. 326; *see* Shoghi Effendi, *The World Order of Bahá'u'lláh*, p. 154 (". . . the specific provisions requiring its democratic election by the representatives of the faithful . . . .).

3. *Tablets of Bahá'u'lláh*, p. 125.

4. *Will and Testament of 'Abdu'l-Bahá*, p. 14.

5. Shoghi Effendi, *The Compilation of Compilations*, vol. I, p. 328.

6. Shoghi Effendi, *Messages to the Bahá'í World*, p. 149.

7. Shoghi Effendi, *The Advent of Divine Justice*, p. 22.

8. Shoghi Effendi, *The World Order of Bahá'u'lláh*, p. 89.

9. Shoghi Effendi, *God Passes By*, p. 214.

10. *Tablets of Bahá'u'lláh*, p. 68.

11. *Tablets of Bahá'u'lláh*, pp. 128-29.

12. 'Abdu'l-Bahá, *The Promulgation of Universal Peace*, p. 455.

13. *Selections from the Writings of 'Abdu'l-Bahá*, p. 215.

14. *Selections from the Writings of 'Abdu'l-Bahá*, p. 215.

15. 'Abdu'l-Bahá, *The Covenant*, # 13.

16. Shoghi Effendi, *The Compilation of Compilations*, vol. I, p. 329.

17. *Will and Testament of 'Abdu'l-Bahá*, p. 19; *see* 'Abdu'l-Bahá, quoted in the Universal House of Justice, *Messages from the Universal House of Justice: 1963-1986*, pp. 52-53 ("The Most Holy Book is the Book to which all peoples shall refer, and in it the Laws of God have been revealed. Laws not

mentioned in the Book should be referred to the decision of the Universal House of Justice.").

18. Bahá'u'lláh, *The Kitáb-i-Aqdas*, Q&A 49; *see id.*, Q&A 50 ("QUESTION: *Concerning the legitimacy or otherwise of marrying one's relatives.* ANSWER: These matters likewise rest with the Trustees of the House of Justice.").

19. Shoghi Effendi, *The World Order of Bahá'u'lláh*, p. 23; Shoghi Effendi, *God Passes By*, pp. 218-19 ("To the trustees of the House of Justice He assigns the duty of legislating on matters not expressly provided in His writings, and promises that God will 'inspire them with whatsoever He willeth.'"); *see Tablets of Bahá'u'lláh*, p. 27 ("All matters of State should be referred to the House of Justice, but acts of worship must be observed according to that which God hath revealed in His Book."); *e.g.*, the Universal House of Justice, to an individual believer, February 21, 1964 ("We greatly admire your deep feelings of love and devotion for the beloved Guardian, and we are grateful for your suggestion of a befitting passage for the salutation and praise of Shoghi Effendi. [¶] However, since 'acts of worship must be observed according to that which God hath revealed in His Book', the Universal House of Justice does not feel it proper to prescribe any particular portion of the Writings which could be used by the friends for this purpose. We must therefore leave it to the individual believer to select for himself from time to time those passages which best express his feelings of love, respect and gratitude for the labours of the beloved Guardian.").

20. 'Abdu'l-Bahá, quoted in the Universal House of Justice, *Messages from the Universal House of Justice: 1963-1986*, p. 85; *cf.* on behalf of the Universal House of Justice, *Messages from the Universal House of Justice: 1963-1986*, p. 518 ("[T]he attitude to legislation is different in the Bahá'í Faith. The human tendency in past Dispensations has been to want every question answered and to arrive at a binding decision affecting every small detail of belief or practice. The tendency in the Bahá'í Dispensation, from the time of Bahá'u'lláh Himself, has been to clarify the governing principles, to make binding pronouncements on details which are considered essential, but to leave a wide area to the conscience of the individual.").

21. On behalf of Shoghi Effendi, *Lights of Guidance*, p. 342.

22. Shoghi Effendi, *The World Order of Bahá'u'lláh*, p. 23.

23. *Will and Testament of 'Abdu'l-Bahá*, p. 20.

24. Shoghi Effendi, *The World Order of Bahá'u'lláh*, p. 23.

25. *Will and Testament of 'Abdu'l-Bahá*, p. 20; *e.g.*, the Universal House of Justice, to all National Spiritual Assemblies, April 4, 2001 ("The International Teaching Centre has sought elucidation of issues concerning the attitude of Bahá'ís and Bahá'í institutions towards those who have with-

drawn from the Faith. In response, we have provided the following comments . . . .").

26. Shoghi Effendi, *Bahá'í Administration*, p. 47.

27. On behalf of the Universal House of Justice, to an individual believer, August 27, 1998.

28. On behalf of the Universal House of Justice, *Messages from the Universal House of Justice: 1963-1986*, p. 646.

29. The Universal House of Justice, *Messages from the Universal House of Justice: 1963-1986*, p. 56.

30. On behalf of the Universal House of Justice, *Messages from the Universal House of Justice: 1963-1986*, p. 646.

31. On behalf of the Universal House of Justice, *Messages from the Universal House of Justice: 1963-1986*, p. 518.

32. On behalf of the Universal House of Justice, *Messages from the Universal House of Justice: 1963-1986*, p. 646.

33. On behalf of the Universal House of Justice, *Lights of Guidance*, pp. 319-20.

34. On behalf of the Universal House of Justice, *Lights of Guidance*, p. 312 (quoting Shoghi Effendi, *The World Order of Bahá'u'lláh*, p. 148).

35. Shoghi Effendi, *The World Order of Bahá'u'lláh*, p. 148.

36. Shoghi Effendi, *The World Order of Bahá'u'lláh*, p. 20; *see id.*, p. 145 (". . . the body designed to . . . apply His legislative ordinances.").

37. *Will and Testament of 'Abdu'l-Bahá*, p. 14.

38. *Will and Testament of 'Abdu'l-Bahá*, p. 20.

39. On behalf of the Universal House of Justice, *Issues Related to the Study of the Bahá'í Faith*, # 7.

40. *See* on behalf of the Universal House of Justice, *Issues Related to the Study of the Bahá'í Faith*, # 8.

41. On behalf of the Universal House of Justice, *Issues Related to the Study of the Bahá'í Faith*, # 7.

42. On behalf of the Universal House of Justice, *Issues Related to the Study of the Bahá'í Faith*, # 7.

43. *See* Shoghi Effendi, *Citadel of Faith*, p. 90.

44. Shoghi Effendi, *The Compilation of Compilations*, vol. I, p. 329.

45. Shoghi Effendi, *Bahá'í Administration*, p. 39.

46. On behalf of the Universal House of Justice, *Messages from the Universal House of Justice: 1963-1986*, p. 646.

47. Shoghi Effendi, *Bahá'í Administration*, p. 62; *see Tablets of Bahá'u'lláh*, p. 89 ("It is incumbent upon the ministers of the House of Justice to promote

the Lesser Peace so that the people of the earth may be relieved from the burden of exorbitant expenditures.").

48. Shoghi Effendi, *The World Order of Bahá'u'lláh*, p. 7.

49. *Will and Testament of 'Abdu'l-Bahá*, p. 14.

50. 'Abdu'l-Bahá, quoted in the Universal House of Justice, *Messages from the Universal House of Justice: 1963-1986*, p. 53.

51. Shoghi Effendi, *Bahá'í Administration*, p. 84; *see* Shoghi Effendi, *The World Order of Bahá'u'lláh*, p. 7 ("For upon the National Houses of Justice of the East and the West devolves the task, in conformity with the explicit provisions of the Will, of electing directly the members of the International House of Justice."); *see also* Shoghi Effendi, *Bahá'í Administration*, pp. 84-85 ("Should the appointing of the delegates be made a part of the functions of local Spiritual Assemblies, who are already elected bodies, the principle of a four-stage election would be introduced which would be at variance with the provisions explicitly laid down in the Master's Tablet. On the other hand, were the local Spiritual Assemblies, the number of whose members is strictly confined to nine, to elect directly the members of the National Spiritual Assembly—thus maintaining the principle of a three-stage election—all Bahá'í localities, which must necessarily differ in numerical strength, would then have to share equally in the election of the National Spiritual Assembly—a practice which would be contrary to fairness and justice.").

52. *See* 'Abdu'l-Bahá, quoted in the Universal House of Justice, *Messages from the Universal House of Justice: 1963-1986*, p. 53.

53. Shoghi Effendi, *The World Order of Bahá'u'lláh*, p. 7.

54. Shoghi Effendi, *The World Order of Bahá'u'lláh*, p. 17.

55. The Universal House of Justice, *Messages from the Universal House of Justice: 1963-1986*, p. 53.

56. *See* Rúḥíyyih Rabbání, *The Priceless Pearl*, pp. 247-48; Adib Taherzadeh, *The Covenant of Bahá'u'lláh*, pp. 292-93.

57. Shoghi Effendi, *Bahá'í Administration*, p. 41.

58. On behalf of Shoghi Effendi, *Messages of Shoghi Effendi to the Indian Subcontinent: 1923-1957*, p. 210; *see* Shoghi Effendi, *The World Order of Bahá'u'lláh*, p. 7.

59. Shoghi Effendi, *The Compilation of Compilations*, vol. I, p. 328; *see* Shoghi Effendi, *Citadel of Faith*, p. 6 ("During this Formative Age of the Faith, and in the course of present and succeeding epochs, the last and crowning stage in the erection of the framework of the Administrative Order of the Faith of Bahá'u'lláh—the election of the Universal House of Justice—will have been completed . . . ."); Shoghi Effendi, *The World Order of Bahá'u'lláh*, p.

48 ("Ours, dearly-beloved co-workers, is the paramount duty to continue, with undimmed vision and unabated zeal, to assist in the final erection of that Edifice the foundations of which Bahá'u'lláh has laid in our hearts, to derive added hope and strength from the general trend of recent events, however dark their immediate effects, and to pray with unremitting fervor that He may hasten the approach of the realization of that Wondrous Vision which constitutes the brightest emanation of His Mind and the fairest fruit of the fairest civilization the world has yet seen. [¶] Might not the hundredth anniversary of the Declaration of the Faith of Bahá'u'lláh mark the inauguration of so vast an era in human history?"); *see also* Shoghi Effendi, *God Passes By*, pp. 330, 332-33 ("Conscious of the necessity of constructing, as a first step, a broad and solid base upon which the pillars of that mighty structure could subsequently be raised; fully aware that upon these pillars, when firmly established, the dome, the final unit crowning the entire edifice, must eventually rest . . ., the pioneer builders of a divinely-conceived Order undertook, in complete unison, and despite the great diversity in their outlook, customs and languages, the double task of establishing and of consolidating their local councils, elected by the rank and file of the believers, and designed to direct, coordinate and extend the activities of the followers of a far-flung Faith. . . . Having established the structure of their local Assemblies—the base of the edifice which the Architect of the Administrative Order of the Faith of Bahá'u'lláh had directed them to erect—His disciples, in both the East and the West, unhesitatingly embarked on the next and more difficult stage, of their high enterprise. In countries where the local Bahá'í communities had sufficiently advanced in number and in influence measures were taken for the initiation of National Assemblies, the pivots round which all national undertakings must revolve. Designated by 'Abdu'l-Bahá in His Will as the 'Secondary Houses of Justice,' they constitute the electoral bodies in the formation of the International House of Justice, and are empowered to direct, unify, coordinate and stimulate the activities of individuals as well as local Assemblies within their jurisdiction. Resting on the broad base of organized local communities, themselves pillars sustaining the institution which must be regarded as the apex of the Bahá'í Administrative Order, these Assemblies are elected, according to the principle of proportional representation, by delegates representative of Bahá'í local communities assembled at Convention during the period of the Riḍván Festival . . . .").

60. *See* David Hofman, *A Commentary on the Will and Testament of 'Abdu'l-Bahá*, p. 25 ("The National House of Justice, or 'secondary' House as it is termed in the Will, is 'Abdu'l-Bahá's own contribution to the institutions of the world order. The Universal and Local Houses were designed by Bahá'u'lláh, but it is the Master who institutes [in His Will and Testament] the intermediary or secondary body.").

61. *The Ministry of the Custodians: 1957-1963*, p. 13.

62. *The Bahá'í Faith 1844-1963 Information Statistical & Comparative*, pp. 22-24.

63. *The Bahá'í Faith 1844-1963 Information Statistical & Comparative*, pp. 45, 47-54.

64. In a cable issued in 1951, Shoghi Effendi announced the "formation of first International Bahá'í Council, forerunner of supreme administrative institution destined to emerge in fullness of time within precincts beneath shadow of World Spiritual Center of Faith already established in twin cities of 'Akká and Haifa." Shoghi Effendi, *Messages to the Bahá'í World*, p. 7. He envisioned that the formation of the International Bahá'í Council was "destined to culminate in emergence of Universal House of Justice." *Id.*, p. 20. Shoghi Effendi also referred to the evolution of the appointed International Bahá'í Council into an "officially recognized Bahá'í Court," "its transformation into duly elected body," and "its efflorescence into Universal House of Justice." *Id.*, pp. 7-8; *see id.*, pp. 13, 152; Shoghi Effendi, *Citadel of Faith*, pp. 94-95.

After its appointment in 1951, the International Bahá'í Council performed important services for the Faith. *See* "The International Bahá'í Council," *The Bahá'í World*, vol. XIII, pp. 395-401. Following Shoghi Effendi's passing in 1957, the International Bahá'í Council continued to carry out duties at the Bahá'í World Center under the direction of the Hands of the Cause. In 1959, the Hands of the Cause called for the election of the International Bahá'í Council during Riḍván 1961. *The Ministry of the Custodians: 1957-1963*, p. 168. The Hands declared that the "embryonic institution established . . . by the beloved Guardian will thus enter its final stage preceding the election of the Universal House of Justice." *Id.* The Hands of the Cause further explained that every effort would be made "to establish a Bahá'í Court in the Holy Land prior to the date set" for the election of the International Bahá'í Council; however, they emphasized that "the Guardian himself clearly indicated this goal, due to the strong trend towards the secularization of Religious Courts in this part of the world, might not be achieved." *Id.*, pp. 168-69. Because of this trend toward secularization, it was ultimately not possible to establish an "officially recognized Bahá'í Court" prior to the election of the Universal House of Justice; nevertheless, the final stage preceding the election of the Universal House of Justice—namely, the election of the International Bahá'í Council—was successfully carried out in 1961. *See id.*, p. 282; *cf.* the Universal House of Justice, *Messages from the Universal House of Justice: 1963-1986*, p. 83 ("You query the timing of the election of the Universal House of Justice in view of the Guardian's statement: '. . . given favorable circumstances, under which the Bahá'ís of Persia and of the adjoining countries under Soviet rule, may be enabled to elect their national representatives . . . the only remaining obstacle in the way of the definite formation of the International House of Justice will have been removed.' On 19th April 1947 the Guardian, in a letter written on his behalf by his secretary, replied to the inquiry of an individual believer about this passage: 'At the time he referred to Russia there were Bahá'ís there, now the Community has practically ceased to exist; therefore the formation of the International House of Justice cannot depend on a Russian National Spiritual Assembly. But other strong National Spiritual Assemblies will have to be built up before it can be established.'").

65. The Universal House of Justice, *Messages from the Universal House of Justice: 1963-1986*, p. 50.

66. The Universal House of Justice, *Messages from the Universal House of Justice: 1963-1986*, pp. 50-51.

67. The Universal House of Justice, *Messages from the Universal House of Justice: 1963-1986*, p. 51.

68. The Universal House of Justice, *Messages from the Universal House of Justice: 1963-1986*, p. 51.

69. *See Will and Testament of 'Abdu'l-Bahá*, p. 14.

70. 'Abdu'l-Bahá, quoted in the Universal House of Justice, *Messages from the Universal House of Justice: 1963-1986*, p. 53 (emphasis added).

71. *See The Constitution of the Universal House of Justice*, p. 11 ("An election of the Universal House of Justice shall be held once every five years unless otherwise decided by the Universal House of Justice . . . .").

72. Shoghi Effendi, *The Compilation of Compilations*, vol. I, p. 333.

CHAPTER 7
THE TWIN INSTITUTIONS OF THE GUARDIANSHIP
AND THE UNIVERSAL HOUSE OF JUSTICE

1. *Cf.* on behalf of the Universal House of Justice, *Lights of Guidance*, p. 311 ("Regarding your first question, it is important that when considering the references to the Guardianship in the writings of the Faith, and especially when striving to understand how these references apply at the present time, you should realize that the word 'guardianship' is used with various meanings in different contexts. In certain contexts it indicates the office and function of the Guardian himself, in others it refers to the line of Guardians, in still others it bears a more extended meaning embracing the Guardian, and his attendant institutions.").

2. Shoghi Effendi, *The World Order of Bahá'u'lláh*, pp. 18, 19-20, 148, 157; Shoghi Effendi, *This Decisive Hour*, p. 46; Shoghi Effendi, *Messages to the Bahá'í World*, p. 19.

3. Shoghi Effendi, *The World Order of Bahá'u'lláh*, pp. 147, 148.

4. The Universal House of Justice, *Messages from the Universal House of Justice: 1963-1986*, p. 156.

5. Shoghi Effendi, *The World Order of Bahá'u'lláh*, p. 148.

6. The Universal House of Justice, *Messages from the Universal House of Justice: 1963-1986*, p. 156.

7. *Will and Testament of 'Abdu'l-Bahá*, p. 11; *cf.* on behalf of Shoghi Effendi, *The Light of Divine Guidance*, vol. 2, p. 82 ("[O]ne of the reasons God has given us the institution of Guardianship is to prevent men from crystallizing the Cause of God into a rigid system.").

8. Shoghi Effendi, *The World Order of Bahá'u'lláh*, p. 150.

9. Shoghi Effendi, *The World Order of Bahá'u'lláh*, p. 148.

10. *Will and Testament of 'Abdu'l-Bahá*, p. 14.

11. *See* Shoghi Effendi, *The World Order of Bahá'u'lláh*, pp. 148, 150.

12. The Universal House of Justice, *Messages from the Universal House of Justice: 1963-1986*, p. 158.

13. The Universal House of Justice, *Messages from the Universal House of Justice: 1963-1986*, p. 158.

14. Bahá'u'lláh, *The Kitáb-i-Aqdas*, parag. 42.

15. Bahá'u'lláh, *The Kitáb-i-Aqdas*, parag. 42; *cf.* Bahá'u'lláh, *Lights of Guidance*, p. 322 ("May My praise, salutations, and greetings rest upon the stars of the heaven of Thy knowledge—the Hands of Thy Cause—they who circled round Thy Will, spoke not save after Thy leave, and clung not save unto Thy hem."); Bahá'u'lláh, quoted in Nader Saiedi, *Logos and Civilization*, p. 277 ("He hath constructed the house of His Cause by His pervasive will upon the foundation of eloquent speech and the pillar of wisdom, and He hath created for it protectors and defenders who shall preserve it from the faithless and the perverse and those who speak out of ignorance. They are the ones who shall not overstep what God hath revealed in the Book nor shall they speak except by His leave on the Day of Return. I testify that they are the hands of His Cause amongst mankind and the lamps of His guidance between heaven and earth.") (provisional translation).

16. Bahá'u'lláh, *The Kitáb-i-Aqdas,* parag. 42 (emphasis added).

17. The Universal House of Justice, *Messages from the Universal House of Justice: 1963-1986*, p. 159.

18. The Universal House of Justice, *Messages from the Universal House of Justice: 1963-1986*, p. 15; *see id.*, p. 89; the Universal House of Justice, *Wellspring of Guidance*, p. 11.

19. The Universal House of Justice, *Messages from the Universal House of Justice: 1963-1986*, p. 158.

20. Bahá'u'lláh, quoted in the Universal House of Justice, *Messages from the*

Universal House of Justice: 1963-1986, p. 159.

21. 'Abdu'l-Bahá, quoted in the Universal House of Justice, *Messages from the Universal House of Justice: 1963-1986*, p. 159.

22. 'Abdu'l-Bahá, quoted in the Universal House of Justice, *Messages from the Universal House of Justice: 1963-1986*, p. 159.

23. *Selections from the Writings of 'Abdu'l-Bahá*, p. 210.

24. The Universal House of Justice, *Messages from the Universal House of Justice: 1963-1986*, pp. 88-89.

25. The Universal House of Justice, *Messages from the Universal House of Justice: 1963-1986*, p. 159.

26. Shoghi Effendi, *The World Order of Bahá'u'lláh*, p. 148; Shoghi Effendi, *Citadel of Faith*, p. 76 (". . . the inseparable institutions of the Guardianship and of the Universal House of Justice . . . .").

27. Shoghi Effendi, *The World Order of Bahá'u'lláh*, p. 148.

28. Shoghi Effendi, *The World Order of Bahá'u'lláh*, p. 148.

29. The Universal House of Justice, *Messages from the Universal House of Justice: 1963-1986*, p. 87.

30. Shoghi Effendi, *The World Order of Bahá'u'lláh*, p. 148.

31. The Universal House of Justice, *Messages from the Universal House of Justice: 1963-1986*, p. 87.

32. The Universal House of Justice, *Messages from the Universal House of Justice: 1963-1986*, p. 87.

33. On behalf of the Universal House of Justice, to an individual believer, April 2, 1985.

34. *See* Chapter 8.

35. *Tablets of Bahá'u'lláh*, p. 68.

36. *Will and Testament of 'Abdu'l-Bahá*, p. 19.

37. 'Abdu'l-Bahá, quoted in the Universal House of Justice, *Messages from the Universal House of Justice: 1963-1986*, pp. 85-86; *see Will and Testament of 'Abdu'l-Bahá*, p. 14 ("And now, concerning the House of Justice which God hath ordained as the source of all good and freed from all error, it must be elected by universal suffrage, that is, by the believers.").

38. Shoghi Effendi, *The World Order of Bahá'u'lláh*, p. 153.

39. The Universal House of Justice, *Messages from the Universal House of Justice: 1963-1986*, p. 157.

40. The Universal House of Justice, *Messages from the Universal House of Justice: 1963-1986*, p. 84.

41. On behalf of the Universal House of Justice, to an individual believer, April 2, 1985.

42. On behalf of the Universal House of Justice, to an individual believer, April 2, 1985.

43. Shoghi Effendi, *The World Order of Bahá'u'lláh*, p. 150.

44. Shoghi Effendi, *The World Order of Bahá'u'lláh*, p. 148; *id.*, p. 8.

45. Shoghi Effendi, *The World Order of Bahá'u'lláh*, p. 150; *see id.*, p. 8 ("It must be also clearly understood by every believer that the institution of Guardianship does not under any circumstances abrogate, or even in the slightest degree detract from, the powers granted to the Universal House of Justice by Bahá'u'lláh in the Kitáb-i-Aqdas, and repeatedly and solemnly confirmed by 'Abdu'l-Bahá in His Will. It does not constitute in any manner a contradiction to the Will and Writings of Bahá'u'lláh, nor does it nullify any of His revealed instructions. It enhances the prestige of that exalted assembly, stabilizes its supreme position, safeguards its unity, assures the continuity of its labors, without presuming in the slightest to infringe upon the inviolability of its clearly-defined sphere of jurisdiction.").

46. Shoghi Effendi, *The World Order of Bahá'u'lláh*, p. 148.

47. On behalf of the Universal House of Justice, *Issues Related to the Study of the Bahá'í Faith*, # 8.

48. The Universal House of Justice, *Messages from the Universal House of Justice: 1963-1986*, p. 161.

49. The responsibility of the Universal House of Justice in this regard is analogous to the Guardian's exercise of certain responsibilities prior to the establishment of the Universal House of Justice. *See* on behalf of Shoghi Effendi, *Japan Will Turn Ablaze*, p. 94 ("The National Assemblies themselves report directly to Haifa—to the Universal House of Justice, when it is established; and until that time, to the Guardian himself.").

50. *See The Constitution of the Universal House of Justice*, p. 4 ("There being no successor to Shoghi Effendi as Guardian of the Cause of God, the Universal House of Justice is the Head of the Faith and its supreme institution, to which all must turn, and on it rests the ultimate responsibility for ensuring the unity and progress of the Cause of God. Further, there devolve upon it the duties of directing and coordinating the work of the Hands of the Cause, of ensuring the continuing discharge of the functions of protection and propagation vested in that institution, and of providing for the receipt and disbursement of the Ḥuqúqu'lláh.").

   The Universal House of Justice "must, in the absence of the Guardian, receive and disburse the Ḥuqúqu'lláh . . . ." The Universal House of Justice, *Messages from the Universal House of Justice: 1963-1986*, p. 90; the Universal House of Justice, *Ḥuqúqu'lláh*, # 101 ("'Abdu'l-Bahá in one of His Tablets has stated: 'Disposition of the Ḥuqúq, wholly or partly, is permissible, but this should be done by permission of the authority in the

Cause to whom all must turn.' The provision in His Will and Testament that the Ḥuqúqu'lláh 'is to be offered through the guardian of the Cause of God. . .' is clearly in accord with this principle. In another Tablet 'Abdu'l-Bahá referred to the Universal House of Justice as 'the authority to whom all must turn' and it is clear that in the absence of the Guardian it is the supreme and central institution of the Cause. Moreover, before 'Abdu'l-Bahá, Bahá'u'lláh had revealed the following: 'There is a prescribed ruling for the Ḥuqúqu'lláh. After the House of Justice hath come into being, the law thereof will be made manifest, in conformity with the Will of God.' In accordance with these explicit texts it is clearly within the jurisdiction of the Universal House of Justice to decide about the receipt and disbursement of Ḥuqúqu'lláh at the present time."); *see* Bahá'u'lláh, *Ḥuqúqu'lláh*, # 20 ("According to that which is revealed in the Most Holy Book, Ḥuqúqu'lláh is fixed at the rate of 19 mithqáls out of every 100 mithqáls worth of gold. . . . Moreover certain rights have been fixed for the House of Justice. However, before its establishment and the appearance of its members, the appropriation of such funds is and will be subject to the approval of Him Who is the Eternal Truth."); on behalf of Shoghi Effendi, *Ḥuqúqu'lláh*, # 80 ("Ḥuqúqu'lláh is paid to the Centre of the Cause.").

51. On behalf of the Universal House of Justice, *Lights of Guidance*, p. 311.

52. The Universal House of Justice, *Messages from the Universal House of Justice: 1963-1986*, p. 89 (quoting Shoghi Effendi, *The World Order of Bahá'u'lláh*, p. 89).

CHAPTER 8
THE INFALLIBILITY OF THE UNIVERSAL HOUSE OF JUSTICE

1. *Tablets of Bahá'u'lláh*, p. 68.

2. *Tablets of Bahá'u'lláh*, p. 27.

3. *Will and Testament of 'Abdu'l-Bahá*, p. 14.

4. *Will and Testament of 'Abdu'l-Bahá*, p. 19.

5. *Will and Testament of 'Abdu'l-Bahá*, p. 11.

6. 'Abdu'l-Bahá, *The Promulgation of Universal Peace*, p. 455.

7. 'Abdu'l-Bahá, *The Promulgation of Universal Peace*, p. 455.

8. 'Abdu'l-Bahá, *Some Answered Questions*, p. 171.

9. 'Abdu'l-Bahá, *Some Answered Questions*, p. 171.

10. 'Abdu'l-Bahá, *Some Answered Questions*, p. 173; *see Tablets of Bahá'u'lláh*, pp. 108-09 ("[T]he Most Great Infallibility is confined to the One Whose station is immeasurably exalted beyond ordinances or prohibitions and is sanctified from errors and omissions. Indeed He is a Light

which is not followed by darkness and a Truth not overtaken by error. Were He to pronounce water to be wine or heaven to be earth or light to be fire, He speaketh the truth and no doubt would there be about it; and unto no one is given the right to question His authority or to say why or wherefore. . . . Were He to pronounce right to be wrong or denial to be belief, He speaketh the truth as bidden by God. This is a station wherein sins or trespasses neither exist nor are mentioned.").

11. 'Abdu'l-Bahá, *Some Answered Questions*, p. 173.

12. 'Abdu'l-Bahá, *Some Answered Questions*, p. 172.

13. 'Abdu'l-Bahá, *Some Answered Questions*, p. 172.

14. 'Abdu'l-Bahá, *Some Answered Questions*, pp. 172-73; *see* on behalf of the Universal House of Justice, quoted in Janet A. Khan and Peter J. Khan, *Advancement of Women: A Bahá'í Perspective*, p. 132 ("A vital distinction between the opinions and perceptions of the individual members of this body and the decision of the Universal House of Justice, is emphasised by 'Abdu'l-Bahá in the statement: 'Let it not be imagined that the House of Justice will take any decision according to its own concepts and opinions. God forbid! The Supreme House of Justice will take decisions and establish laws through the inspiration and confirmation of the Holy Spirit, because it is in the safe-keeping and under the shelter and protection of the Ancient Beauty . . .'").

15. On behalf of Shoghi Effendi, *Unfolding Destiny*, p. 449.

16. *Tablets of Bahá'u'lláh*, p. 149.

17. On behalf of the Universal House of Justice, *Lights of Guidance*, p. 312.

18. On behalf of the Universal House of Justice, *Lights of Guidance*, p. 312; *see* on behalf of the Universal House of Justice, quoted in Udo Schaefer *et al.*, *Making the Crooked Straight*, pp. 181-82 n.212 ("With regard to decisions taken by the Universal House of Justice itself, instructions it issues, and the relationship of these to the information supplied, it is obvious that the nature of a decision or instruction is affected by the information on which it is made.").

19. *See* Shoghi Effendi, *The World Order of Bahá'u'lláh*, p. 100 ("An exact and thorough comprehension of so vast a system, so sublime a revelation, so sacred a trust, is for obvious reasons beyond the reach and ken of our finite minds."); the Universal House of Justice, quoted in *The Covenant: Its Meaning and Origin and Our Attitude Toward It*, p. 51 ("[N]o human being can have a full and correct understanding of the revelation of God . . . ."); the Universal House of Justice, *Messages from the Universal House of Justice: 1963-1986*, p. 87 ("In past dispensations many errors arose because the believers in God's Revelation were overanxious to encompass the Divine Message within the framework of their limited understanding, to define doctrines where definition was beyond their power, to explain mysteries which

only the wisdom and experience of a later age would make comprehensible, to argue that something was true because it appeared desirable and necessary. Such compromises with essential truth, such intellectual pride, we must scrupulously avoid."); on behalf of the Universal House of Justice, *The Compilation of Compilations*, vol. III, p. 258 ("[D]ivine Revelation is infallible and proceeds from an all-encompassing knowledge of the Truth, but when individual Bahá'ís attempt to apply Sacred Texts to any specific problem or situation they do so using their own minds which are of limited understanding."); on behalf of the Universal House of Justice, *Messages from the Universal House of Justice: 1963-1986*, p. 547 ("In considering the whole field of divinely conferred 'infallibility' one must be careful to avoid the literal understanding and petty-mindedness that has so often characterized discussions of this matter in the Christian world. The Manifestation of God (and, to a lesser degree, 'Abdu'l-Bahá and Shoghi Effendi,) has to convey tremendous concepts covering the whole field of human life and activity to people whose present knowledge and degree of understanding are far below His. He must use the limited medium of human language against the limited and often erroneous background of His audience's traditional knowledge and current understanding to raise them to a wholly new level of awareness and behavior. It is a human tendency, against which the Manifestation warns us, to measure His statements against the inaccurate standard of the acquired knowledge of mankind. We tend to take them and place them within one or other of the existing categories of human philosophy or science while, in reality, they transcend these and will, if properly understood, open new and vast horizons to our understanding.").

20. On behalf of Shoghi Effendi, *Lights of Guidance*, p. 312.

21. *Will and Testament of 'Abdu'l-Bahá*, p. 11.

22. 'Abdu'l-Bahá, quoted in the Universal House of Justice, *Messages from the Universal House of Justice: 1963-1986*, p. 53.

23. *Will and Testament of 'Abdu'l-Bahá*, p. 14.

24. *Will and Testament of 'Abdu'l-Bahá*, p. 19.

25. 'Abdu'l-Bahá, *Some Answered Questions*, p. 172.

26. *Will and Testament of 'Abdu'l-Bahá*, p. 11.

27. 'Abdu'l-Bahá, quoted in the Universal House of Justice, *Messages from the Universal House of Justice: 1963-1986*, p. 53.

28. The Universal House of Justice, quoted in *The Covenant: Its Meaning and Origin and Our Attitude Toward It*, p. 39.

29. *See* Shoghi Effendi, *The World Order of Bahá'u'lláh*, p. 148; *see* the Universal House of Justice, *Messages from the Universal House of Justice: 1963-1986*, p. 15 ("The two unique features which distinguish it [the Covenant of Bahá'u'lláh] from all religious covenants of the past are un-

changed and operative. The revealed Word, in its original purity, amplified by the divinely guided interpretations of 'Abdu'l-Bahá and Shoghi Effendi, remains immutable, unadulterated by any man-made creeds or dogmas, unwarrantable inferences or unauthorized interpretations. The channel of divine guidance, providing flexibility in all the affairs of mankind, remains open through that Institution which was founded by Bahá'u'lláh and endowed by Him with supreme authority and unfailing guidance, and of which the Master wrote: 'Unto this body all things must be referred.'").

30. *See* on behalf of the Universal House of Justice, *Messages from the Universal House of Justice: 1963-1986*, p. 448.

31. The Universal House of Justice, quoted in David Hofman, *A Commentary on the Will and Testament of 'Abdu'l-Bahá*, p. 44.

32. *See* the Universal House of Justice, *Messages from the Universal House of Justice: 1963-1986*, p. 51.

33. On behalf of the Universal House of Justice, to an individual believer, February 16, 1996 ("The Administrative Order of Bahá'u'lláh is in the process of growth and unfoldment. . . . As the Bahá'í communities grow, the Universal House of Justice will ensure that this divinely-founded system will unfold in accordance with the unerring guidance of which it is the recipient.").

34. *See* Shoghi Effendi, *The World Order of Bahá'u'lláh*, p. 153.

35. 'Abdu'l-Bahá, quoted in the Universal House of Justice, *Messages from the Universal House of Justice: 1963-1986*, p. 85 (emphasis added).

36. 'Abdu'l-Bahá, quoted in the Universal House of Justice, *Messages from the Universal House of Justice: 1963-1986*, p. 53.

37. On behalf of the Universal House of Justice, to an individual believer, June 14, 1996.

38. The Universal House of Justice, *Messages from the Universal House of Justice: 1963-1986*, p. 161.

39. The Universal House of Justice, *Messages from the Universal House of Justice: 1963-1986*, p. 157; *cf.* on behalf of the Universal House of Justice, to an individual, October 22, 1996 ("As to whether there is a distinction between correspondence from the World Centre that has been signed 'The Universal House of Justice' and that signed on behalf of the Secretariat: In brief, the manner in which each of these letters is prepared depends upon the contents of the letter. Drafts of letters which contain newly formulated policies are consulted upon and approved during a meeting of the House of Justice; correspondence dealing with previously enunciated policies, or with matters of a routine nature, are prepared, as delegated by the House of Justice, by its Secretariat and initialed by at least the majority of the members of the House of Justice before being dispatched. All letters written over the signature of

the Department of the Secretariat are authorized by the Universal House of Justice. [¶] As to whether the materials prepared by the Research Department constitute the authoritative word of the Universal House of Justice on a particular subject . . ., the House of Justice indicates that such materials, though prepared at its direction, represent the views of that Department. While such views are very useful as an aid to resolving perplexities or gaining an enhanced understanding of the Bahá'í Teachings, they should never be taken to be in the same category as the elucidations and clarifications provided by the Universal House of Justice in the exercise of its assigned functions. However, the House of Justice chooses to convey the materials prepared by the Research Department to the friends because it wishes them to be thoughtfully attended to and seriously considered.").

40. *Tablets of Bahá'u'lláh*, p. 27.

41. 'Abdu'l-Bahá, quoted in the Universal House of Justice, *Messages from the Universal House of Justice: 1963-1986*, p. 85.

42. 'Abdu'l-Bahá, quoted in the Universal House of Justice, *Messages from the Universal House of Justice: 1963-1986*, p. 85.

43. *Will and Testament of 'Abdu'l-Bahá*, p. 11.

44. *Will and Testament of 'Abdu'l-Bahá*, p. 26.

45. Shoghi Effendi, *Bahá'í Administration*, p. 62.

46. The Universal House of Justice, quoted in David Hofman, *A Commentary on the Will and Testament of 'Abdu'l-Bahá*, p. 44.

47. On behalf of the Universal House of Justice, *The Covenant*, # 39.

CHAPTER 9
THE PROTECTION OF THE CAUSE OF GOD

1. On behalf of the Universal House of Justice, *The Covenant*, # 19; *see* Shoghi Effendi, *This Decisive Hour*, p. 66 ("[T]he record of its tumultuous history, almost every page of which portrays a fresh crisis, is laden with the description of a new calamity, recounts the tale of a base betrayal, and is stained with the account of unspeakable atrocities . . . .").

2. Shoghi Effendi, *This Decisive Hour*, p. 66.

3. Shoghi Effendi, *God Passes By*, p. 61; *see* Adib Taherzadeh, *The Covenant of Bahá'u'lláh*, *passim*.

4. On behalf of the Universal House of Justice, *The Covenant*, # 19.

5. 'Abdu'l-Bahá, *Bahá'í World Faith*, pp. 357-58.

6. *See* Shoghi Effendi, *This Decisive Hour*, p. 66 ("That such a secession . . ., whether effected by those who apostatize their faith or preach heretical doctrines, should have failed, after the lapse of a century, to split in twain the

entire body of the adherents of the Faith, or to create a grave, a permanent and irremediable breach in its organic structure, is a fact too eloquent for even a casual observer of the internal processes of its Administrative Order to either deny or ignore.").

7. *See* Shoghi Effendi, *The World Order of Bahá'u'lláh*, p. 196; *see* Adib Taherzadeh, *The Covenant of Bahá'u'lláh*, *passim* (detailing numerous failed attempts to create division within the Bahá'í Faith); *Mason Remey and Those Who Followed Him*, November 29, 2001 (describing the fate of those who, since 1960, have unsuccessfully sought to undermine the unity of the Bahá'í Faith). Typically winning over no more than a handful of individuals, attempts to divide the Faith have been unable to attract any serious attention from the millions of Bahá'ís worldwide. Thus, despite efforts to project an image of disunity, those who have tried to create division in the Faith have not been able to demonstrate the existence of any visible and substantial following, particularly one that has survived the test of time. This is in stark contrast to the Bahá'í community whose large number of believers, institutions, activities, and properties are found all over the world and whose size and strength has only increased with the passage of time.

8. Shoghi Effendi, *This Decisive Hour*, p. 66.

9. *Will and Testament of 'Abdu'l-Bahá*, p. 4.

10. *See* the Universal House of Justice, *Messages from the Universal House of Justice: 1963-1986*, p. 86 ("[A]lthough the Hands of the Cause of God have the specific functions of protection and propagation, and are specialized for these functions, it is also the duty of the Universal House of Justice and the Spiritual Assemblies to protect and teach the Cause—indeed teaching is a sacred obligation placed upon every believer by Bahá'u'lláh."); the Universal House of Justice, *The Institution of the Counsellors*, p. 26 ("The pivot of the oneness of humankind is the power of the Covenant, and this power quickens every distinguishing element of Bahá'í life. It is in the context of this unique characteristic of Bahá'u'lláh's Revelation that the institution of the Counsellors approaches its sacred duty to protect the Faith.").

11. *Will and Testament of 'Abdu'l-Bahá*, p. 22.

12. *Will and Testament of 'Abdu'l-Bahá*, p. 19.

13. *Will and Testament of 'Abdu'l-Bahá*, p. 20.

14. On behalf of Shoghi Effendi, *The Light of Divine Guidance*, vol. 2, p. 109.

15. The Universal House of Justice, quoted in *The Covenant: Its Meaning and Origin and Our Attitude Toward It*, p. 74.

16. *See Selections from the Writings of 'Abdu'l-Bahá*, p. 210.

17. *See Selections from the Writings of 'Abdu'l-Bahá*, p. 214.

18. *See* on behalf of Shoghi Effendi, *The Light of Divine Guidance*, vol. 1, p. 135.

19. *Selections from the Writings of 'Abdu'l-Bahá*, pp. 215-16.

20. On behalf of Shoghi Effendi, *Lights of Guidance*, p. 188 (emphasis in original).

21. *Selections from the Writings of 'Abdu'l-Bahá*, p. 214.

22. *See* 'Abdu'l-Bahá, cited in J.E. Esslemont, *Bahá'u'lláh and the New Era*, p. 130.

23. *Will and Testament of 'Abdu'l-Bahá*, p. 12; *see* 'Abdu'l-Bahá, *The Promulgation of Universal Peace*, p. 456 ("There are some people of self-will and desire who do not communicate their intentions to you in clear language. They envelop their meanings in secret statements and insinuations. . . . The purport of my admonition is that certain people will endeavor to influence you in the direction of their own personal views and opinions. Therefore, be upon your guard in order that none may assail the oneness and integrity of Bahá'u'lláh's Cause. Praise be to God! Bahá'u'lláh left nothing unsaid. He explained everything. He left no room for anything further to be said. Yet there are some who for the sake of personal interest and prestige will attempt to sow the seeds of sedition and disloyalty among you.").

24. *See Selections from the Writings of 'Abdu'l-Bahá*, p. 212.

25. On behalf of Shoghi Effendi, *Lights of Guidance*, p. 188.

26. On behalf of Shoghi Effendi, *Messages to Canada*, p. 65.

27. The Universal House of Justice, to all National Spiritual Assemblies, April 4, 2001 ("Sometimes, after a person's withdrawal from the Cause has been accepted, it becomes evident that his statements were insincere and were made merely in order to evade Bahá'í law. . . . An analogous situation arises when a person who is engaged in some activity which he suspects would result in his being declared a Covenant-breaker withdraws from the Faith under the impression that this step would prevent such an outcome. The Universal House of Justice may conclude that the withdrawal provides adequate protection of the community from the individual in question. However, if he persists, following his withdrawal, in trying to undermine the Covenant or joins forces with Covenant-breakers, he may be judged to have broken the Covenant, and the friends would be told to have no association with him. Each such case would be considered in the context of its specific circumstances.").

28. On behalf of Shoghi Effendi, *Directives from the Guardian*, p. 16.

29. On behalf of the Universal House of Justice, quoted in *The Covenant: Its Meaning and Origin and Our Attitude Toward It*, p. 74; *see id.* ("A believer failing in his duties in living the Bahá'í life would be a breaker of God's

Eternal Covenant, in the general sense of becoming heedless in following the way of God . . . .").

30. *See* on behalf of Shoghi Effendi, *Lights of Guidance*, p. 187.

31. *See* on behalf of the Universal House of Justice, to an individual, July 3, 1997 ("In principle, no person can be considered a Covenant-breaker unless he has been so designated by the Head of the Faith. However, it is strongly advised not to associate with those who have fallen under the pernicious influence of groups such as the 'Orthodox Bahá'ís'. They are infected with the spirit of Covenant-breaking, even if they are not all designated as such. Accordingly, the friends should not answer queries from individuals who obviously seek to draw them into the consideration of the spurious claims and logic of the Covenant-breakers.").

32. After 1963, the Hands of the Cause, in their capacity as protectors of the Faith, took action to expel Covenant-breakers and to also reinstate those who had sincerely repented, subject in each instance to the approval of the Universal House of Justice. The Universal House of Justice, *Messages from the Universal House of Justice: 1963-1986*, pp. 16, 247-48. Following the determination by the Universal House of Justice that there was no way for it "to appoint, or to legislate to make it possible to appoint, Hands of the Cause of God," the House of Justice brought into being the institution of the Counsellors "to extend into the future the specific functions of protection and propagation conferred upon the Hands of the Cause of God." *Id.*, p. 44; *The Constitution of the Universal House of Justice*, p. 15. In 1973, the House of Justice established the International Teaching Centre, an institution composed of International Counsellors appointed for five-year terms. The Universal House of Justice, *The Institution of the Counsellors*, p. 7; *see* the Universal House of Justice, *Messages from the Universal House of Justice: 1963-1986*, pp. 246-49. The Hands of the Cause have also been permanent members of the International Teaching Centre since its inception. The Universal House of Justice, *The Institution of the Counsellors*, p. 7. In 1983, the House of Justice devolved increasing responsibility upon the International Teaching Centre, including "the mandate to watch over the security and ensure the protection of the Faith of God." *Id.*, p. 8; the Universal House of Justice, *Messages from the Universal House of Justice: 1963-1986*, p. 578. Today, the International Teaching Centre has the responsibility for deciding whether an individual should be expelled from the Faith, submitting the decision to the Universal House of Justice for its consideration. The Universal House of Justice, *The Institution of the Counsellors*, p. 8.

33. The Universal House of Justice, *The Institution of the Counsellors*, p. 8.

34. The Universal House of Justice, *The Institution of the Counsellors*, p. 8.

35. *Will and Testament of 'Abdu'l-Bahá*, p. 25.

36. 'Abdu'l-Bahá, *Bahá'í World Faith*, p. 430.

37. 'Abdu'l-Bahá, *Bahá'í World Faith*, p. 432.

38. On behalf of Shoghi Effendi, *Directives from the Guardian*, p. 17.

39. The Universal House of Justice, quoted in *The Covenant: Its Meaning and Origin and Our Attitude Toward It*, p. 75.

40. On behalf of Shoghi Effendi, *Lights of Guidance*, pp. 185-86.

41. On behalf of the Universal House of Justice, *Lights of Guidance*, p. 186; *see* on behalf of Shoghi Effendi, *Lights of Guidance*, p. 186 ("With regard to avoiding association with declared Covenant-breakers. Shoghi Effendi says that this does not mean that if one or more of these attends a non-Bahá'í meeting any Bahá'ís present should feel compelled to leave the meeting or to refuse to take part in the meeting, especially if that part has been prearranged. Also if in the course of some business transaction it should become necessary to negotiate with one of these people, in order to clear up the business, that is permissible, provided the association is confined to the matter of the business in hand. It is different if one of these people should come to Bahá'í meeting. Then it would become necessary to ask him in a most tactful and dignified way to leave the meeting as Bahá'ís are forbidden to associate with him.").

As to whether "it is forbidden for the friends to associate with non-Bahá'ís who are in close association with Covenant-Breakers," the Universal House of Justice has written:

> There are no hard and fast rules about such things. Under some conditions the involvement of the non-Bahá'í party may be superficial and harmless, in which case no action should be taken. For example, Bahá'ís have at times used non-Bahá'ís, such as lawyers, to contact Covenant-breakers in certain matters of business.
>
> If, however, the Covenant-breaker is using the non-Bahá'í party to spread his ideas among the friends, the matter should be reported to the Continental Board of Counsellors, and whatever they decide in such cases in consultation with the National Spiritual Assemblies concerned should be unreservedly accepted by the friends.

The Universal House of Justice, *Lights of Guidance*, p. 184. Furthermore,

> . . . if the believers know and meet with people who are acquainted with Covenant Breakers there is no harm in this, for such individuals are not Bahá'ís and have nothing to do with the issues concerned. But those who have left the Cause, knowing all about such matters, and deliberately associate with Cov-

enant Breakers, are well aware of what they do, and we must
not associate with them at all.

On behalf of Shoghi Effendi, *Lights of Guidance*, p. 185.
   Finally, caution must be used in associating with Covenant-breakers'
descendents and families, who may have been infused with the Covenant-
breaking spirit. *See* on behalf of Shoghi Effendi, *The Light of Divine Guidance*, vol. 1, p. 127 ("He noted the report of . . . about her meeting with the
grandchild of Ṣubḥ-i-Azal. He feels that the friends should as much as possible avoid her, as it is very unlikely she has anything but prejudice against
Bahá'u'lláh, in view of her background.").

42. The Universal House of Justice, quoted in *The Covenant: Its Meaning and
   Origin and Our Attitude Toward It*, p. 75.

43. On behalf of Shoghi Effendi, *Principles of Bahá'í Administration*, p. 34.

44. *See The Kitáb-i-Aqdas*, Note # 190 ("Mírzá Yaḥyá . . ., a younger half-
   brother of Bahá'u'lláh . . . arose against Him and opposed His Cause.
   Mírzá Yaḥyá was nominated by the Báb to serve as a figure-head for the
   Bábí community pending the imminent manifestation of the Promised One.
   . . . Mírzá Yaḥyá betrayed the trust of the Báb, claimed to be His succes-
   sor, and intrigued against Bahá'u'lláh, even attempting to have Him mur-
   dered. When Bahá'u'lláh formally declared His Mission to him in
   Adrianople, Mírzá Yaḥyá responded by going to the length of putting for-
   ward his own claim to be the recipient of an independent Revelation. His
   pretensions were eventually rejected by all but a few . . . . He is described by
   Shoghi Effendi as the 'Arch-Breaker of the Covenant of the Bab' (see *God
   Passes By*, chapter X).").

45. *See* Bahá'u'lláh, *The Kitáb-i-Aqdas*, parag. 184 ("Say: O source of per-
   version! . . . Return unto God, humble, submissive and lowly; verily, He
   will put away from thee thy sins, for thy Lord, of a certainty, is the Forgiv-
   ing, the Mighty, the All-Merciful.").

46. On behalf of Shoghi Effendi, *Principles of Bahá'í Administration*, p. 34
   (emphasis in original).

47. *Selections from the Writings of 'Abdu'l-Bahá*, p. 158.

48. On behalf of Shoghi Effendi, *The Light of Divine Guidance*, vol. 1, p. 136.

49. On behalf of Shoghi Effendi, *Lights of Guidance*, p. 184.

50. 'Abdu'l-Bahá, *Star of the West*, vol. V, no. 15, p. 233.

51. The Universal House of Justice, quoted in *The Power of the Covenant*, Part
   Two, p. 9.

52. The Universal House of Justice, quoted in *The Power of the Covenant*, Part
   Two, p. 37.

53. *See* on behalf of Shoghi Effendi, *A Special Measure of Love*, p. 20.

54. *See* 'Abdu'l-Bahá, *Some Answered Questions*, p. 173.

55. On behalf of the Universal House of Justice, *Lights of Guidance*, p. 186.

56. The Universal House of Justice, *The Institution of the Counsellors*, p. 27.

57. The Universal House of Justice, *The Institution of the Counsellors*, p. 27.

58. The Universal House of Justice, quoted in *The Power of the Covenant*, Part Two, p. 44.

59. On behalf of the Universal House of Justice, *Lights of Guidance*, p. 186.

60. On behalf of Shoghi Effendi, *Lights of Guidance*, pp. 190-91.

61. On behalf of the Universal House of Justice, *Lights of Guidance*, p. 190.

62. On behalf of the Universal House of Justice, to an individual, October 7, 1997.

63. On behalf of the Universal House of Justice, to an individual, October 27, 1997.

64. *E.g.*, <<www.bahai.org>>; <<http://reference.bahai.org/en>>.

65. On behalf of the Universal House of Justice, to a National Spiritual Assembly, June 4, 1997.

66. On behalf of the Universal House of Justice, to all National Spiritual Assemblies, April 7, 1999, *The American Bahá'í*, October 16, 1999.

67. On behalf of the Universal House of Justice, to all National Spiritual Assemblies, April 7, 1999, *The American Bahá'í*, October 16, 1999; *cf.* on behalf of the Universal House of Justice, *Issues Related to the Study of the Bahá'í Faith*, # 7, 9, 10.

68. On behalf of the Universal House of Justice, *Issues Related to the Study of the Bahá'í Faith*, # 10.

69. On behalf of the Universal House of Justice, to all National Spiritual Assemblies, April 7, 1999, *The American Bahá'í*, October 16, 1999.

70. On behalf of the Universal House of Justice, *Issues Related to the Study of the Bahá'í Faith*, # 8.

71. On behalf of the Universal House of Justice, *Issues Related to the Study of the Bahá'í Faith*, # 9.

72. On behalf of the Universal House of Justice, to all National Spiritual Assemblies, April 7, 1999, *The American Bahá'í*, October 16, 1999.

73. *Selections from the Writings of 'Abdu'l-Bahá*, p. 80 ("The House of Justice, however, according to the explicit text of the Law of God, is confined to men; this for a wisdom of the Lord God's, which will ere long be made manifest as clearly as the sun at high noon."); 'Abdu'l-Bahá, quoted in Janet A. Khan and Peter J. Khan, *Advancement of Women: A Bahá'í Per-*

spective, pp. 123-24 ("According to the ordinances of the Faith of God, women are the equals of men in all rights save only that of membership on the Universal House of Justice, for as hath been stated in the text of the Book, both the head and the members of the House of Justice are men. However, in all other bodies, such as the Temple Construction Committee, the Teaching Committee, the Spiritual Assembly, and in charitable and scientific associations, women share equally in all rights with men."); on behalf of Shoghi Effendi, *The Compilation of Compilations*, vol. II, p. 369 ("As regards your question concerning the membership of the Universal House of Justice: there is a Tablet from 'Abdu'l-Bahá in which He definitely states that the membership of the Universal House is confined to men, and that the wisdom of it will be fully revealed and appreciated in the future. In the local as well as the national Houses of Justice, however, women have the full right of membership. It is, therefore, only to the International House that they cannot be elected. The Bahá'ís should accept this statement of the Master in a spirit of deep faith, confident that there is a divine guidance and wisdom behind it which will be gradually unfolded to the eyes of the world."); on behalf of Shoghi Effendi, *Directives from the Guardian*, p. 72 ("[W]hen the International House of Justice is elected, there will only be men on it, as this is the law of the *Aqdas*."); on behalf of Shoghi Effendi, *Lights of Guidance*, p. 614 ("As regards the membership of the International House of Justice, 'Abdu'l-Bahá states in a Tablet that it is confined to men, and that the wisdom of it will be revealed as manifest as the sun in the future. In any case the believers should know that, as 'Abdu'l-Bahá Himself has explicitly stated that sexes are equal except in some cases, the exclusion of women from the International House of Justice should not be surprising. From the fact that there is no equality of functions between the sexes one should not, however, infer that either sex is inherently superior or inferior to the other, or that they are unequal in their rights."); on behalf of Shoghi Effendi, quoted in Janet A. Khan and Peter J. Khan, *Advancement of Women: A Bahá'í Perspective*, p. 125 ("The membership of the Universal House of Justice is confined to men. Fixing the number of members, the procedures for election and the term of membership will be known later, as these are not explicitly revealed in the Holy Text."); *The Kitáb-i-Aqdas*, Note # 80 ("It has been elucidated in the writings of 'Abdu'l-Bahá and Shoghi Effendi that, while the membership of the Universal House of Justice is confined to men, both women and men are eligible for election to Secondary and Local Houses of Justice (currently designated as National and Local Spiritual Assemblies)."); *cf.* on behalf of the Universal House of Justice, to an individual believer, June 14, 1996 ("Regarding membership on the Universal House of Justice being restricted to men, you are correct in your understanding that Bahá'u'lláh was explicit about the matter, and consequently it is not within the power of the House of Justice to rule otherwise at this time or at any time in the future.").

74. On behalf of the Universal House of Justice, to all National Spiritual Assemblies, April 7, 1999, *The American Bahá'í*, October 16, 1999.

75. On behalf of the Universal House of Justice, to all National Spiritual Assemblies, April 7, 1999, *The American Bahá'í*, October 16, 1999.

76. On behalf of the Universal House of Justice, to all National Spiritual Assemblies, April 7, 1999, *The American Bahá'í*, October 16, 1999.

77. On behalf of the Universal House of Justice, to an individual, September 24, 1997.

78. On behalf of the Universal House of Justice, *Issues Related to the Study of the Bahá'í Faith*, # 10; *see* on behalf of the Universal House of Justice, to all National Spiritual Assemblies, April 7, 1999, *The American Bahá'í*, October 16, 1999 ("The effect of continued exposure to such insincerity about matters vital to humanity's well-being is spiritually corrosive."); *see also* the Universal House of Justice, to all National Spiritual Assemblies, April 4, 2001 ("There are certain former Bahá'ís whose actions do not necessarily constitute Covenant-breaking, but are seriously destructive. Where such people have shown that they are impervious to explanations or exhortations from the Bahá'í institutions, continued association with them can be burdensome and can exert a spiritually corrosive effect on the faith of believers. In such cases the Head of the Faith may simply advise the Bahá'ís to leave them to their own devices.").

79. On behalf of the Universal House of Justice, to all National Spiritual Assemblies, April 7, 1999, *The American Bahá'í*, October 16, 1999.

80. On behalf of Shoghi Effendi, quoted in on behalf of the Universal House of Justice, to all National Spiritual Assemblies, April 7, 1999, *The American Bahá'í*, October 16, 1999.

81. On behalf of the Universal House of Justice, to all National Spiritual Assemblies, April 7, 1999, *The American Bahá'í*, October 16, 1999.

82. On behalf of Shoghi Effendi, *The Light of Divine Guidance*, vol. 1, p. 134.

83. On behalf of Shoghi Effendi, *The Importance of Deepening our Knowledge and Understanding of the Faith*, # 151.

84. *See* 'Abdu'l-Bahá, *The Compilation of Compilations*, vol. III, p. 254 ("Knowledge is praiseworthy when it is coupled with ethical conduct and virtuous character . . . .").

85. *See Selections from the Writings of 'Abdu'l-Bahá*, p. 259.

86. *See* on behalf of Shoghi Effendi, *Lights of Guidance*, p. 113.

87. *See* on behalf of Shoghi Effendi, *Unfolding Destiny*, p. 454 ("Life is a constant struggle, not only against forces around us, but above all against our own ego.").

88. *Will and Testament of 'Abdu'l-Bahá*, p. 4.

CHAPTER 10
THE INDIVIDUAL AND THE COVENANT

1. The Universal House of Justice, *Messages from the Universal House of Justice: 1963-1986*, p. 160.

2. The Universal House of Justice, *Messages from the Universal House of Justice: 1963-1986*, p. 160.

3. The Universal House of Justice, *Messages from the Universal House of Justice: 1963-1986*, p. 160.

4. 'Abdu'l-Bahá, quoted in Shoghi Effendi, *The World Order of Bahá'u'lláh*, p. 138.

5. *Will and Testament of 'Abdu'l-Bahá*, p. 11.

6. *The Constitution of the Universal House of Justice*, p. 4.

7. The Universal House of Justice, *Messages from the Universal House of Justice: 1963-1986*, p. 160.

8. *The Constitution of the Universal House of Justice*, p. 4.

9. *Will and Testament of 'Abdu'l-Bahá*, p. 19.

10. *Will and Testament of 'Abdu'l-Bahá*, p. 26.

11. Shoghi Effendi, *The Faith of Bahá'u'lláh: A World Religion*, p. 6.

12. *The Constitution of the Universal House of Justice*, p. 8.

13. The Universal House of Justice, *The Institution of the Counsellors*, p. 1.

14. *See* on behalf of the Universal House of Justice, *Issues Related to the Study of the Bahá'í Faith*, # 6.

15. *The Constitution of the Universal House of Justice*, p. 8.

16. The Universal House of Justice, *The Institution of the Counsellors*, p. 1; *see id.* ("This authority is also exercised by Regional Councils, committees and other agencies established by these institutions, to the extent that it is so delegated.").

17. On behalf of Shoghi Effendi, *Messages of Shoghi Effendi to the Indian Subcontinent: 1923-1957*, p. 145.

18. The Universal House of Justice, *Messages from the Universal House of Justice: 1963-1986*, p. 161; *see* on behalf of Shoghi Effendi, *Lights of Guidance*, p. 481 ("When the Master says the Local and National Assemblies are the 'Voice of truth', He means here that they must be obeyed, not that they are infallible.").

19. The Universal House of Justice, *The Institution of the Counsellors*, p. 6.

20. *See* the Universal House of Justice, *The Institution of the Counsellors*, pp. 1-2; *see also* the Universal House of Justice, to the National Spiritual Assembly of the Bahá'ís of the United States, May 19, 1994, *Rights & Responsibili-*

ties, p. 30 ("[A] distinguishing feature of the Administrative Order is the existence of elected institutions, on the one hand, which function corporately with vested legislative, executive and judicial powers, and of appointed, eminent and devoted believers, on the other hand, who function primarily as individuals for the specific purposes of protecting and propagating the Faith under the guidance of the Head of the Faith.").

21. On behalf of the Universal House of Justice, *Issues Related to the Study of the Bahá'í Faith*, # 1.

22. On behalf of the Universal House of Justice, to an individual believer, June 5, 1988.

23. On behalf of Shoghi Effendi, *Lights of Guidance*, pp. 439-40.

24. 'Abdu'l-Bahá, *Lights of Guidance*, p. 439.

25. On behalf of the Universal House of Justice, *Issues Related to the Study of the Bahá'í Faith*, # 1.

26. The Universal House of Justice, *Messages from the Universal House of Justice: 1963-1986*, p. 86.

27. On behalf of Shoghi Effendi, *Messages of Shoghi Effendi to the Indian Subcontinent: 1923-1957*, p. 145.

28. The Universal House of Justice, *The Four Year Plan*, p. 48.

29. On behalf of the Universal House of Justice, *Issues Related to the Study of the Bahá'í Faith*, # 4.

30. *See* 'Abdu'l-Bahá, *Some Answered Questions*, p. 173.

31. *See Gleanings from the Writings of Bahá'u'lláh*, p. 167.

32. On behalf of the Universal House of Justice, *Issues Related to the Study of the Bahá'í Faith*, # 5.

33. On behalf of the Universal House of Justice, *Issues Related to the Study of the Bahá'í Faith*, # 10.

34. The Universal House of Justice, quoted in *The Covenant: Its Meaning and Origin and Our Attitude Toward It*, p. 51.

35. Shoghi Effendi, *The World Order of Bahá'u'lláh*, p. 100.

36. *See* the Universal House of Justice, *Messages from the Universal House of Justice: 1963-1986*, p. 87.

37. *See* on behalf of the Universal House of Justice, *Messages from the Universal House of Justice: 1963-1986*, p. 548.

38. Bahá'u'lláh, *The Kitáb-i-Aqdas*, parag. 162.

39. 'Abdu'l-Bahá, *Some Answered Questions*, p. 173.

40. Bahá'u'lláh, *The Kitáb-i-Aqdas*, parag. 163.

41. Bahá'u'lláh, *The Kitáb-i-Aqdas*, parag. 163; *see Tablets of Bahá'u'lláh*,

p. 51 ("The second Tajallí is to remain steadfast in the Cause of God—exalted be His glory—and to be unswerving in His love. And this can in no wise be attained except through full recognition of Him; and full recognition cannot be obtained save by faith in the blessed words: 'He doeth whatsoever He willeth.' Whoso tenaciously cleaveth unto this sublime word and drinketh deep from the living waters of utterance which are inherent therein, will be imbued with such a constancy that all the books of the world will be powerless to deter him from the Mother Book.").

42. *The Kitáb-i-Aqdas*, Note # 130; *see* the Universal House of Justice, *Lights of Guidance*, pp. 312-13 ("A clear distinction is made in our Faith between authoritative interpretation and the interpretation or understanding that each individual arrives at for himself from his study of its teachings. While the former is confined to the Guardian, the latter, according to the guidance given to us by the Guardian himself, should by no means be suppressed. In fact such individual interpretation is considered the fruit of man's rational power and conducive to a better understanding of the teachings, provided that no disputes or arguments arise among the friends and the individual himself understands and makes it clear that his views are merely his own."); *see also* on behalf of Shoghi Effendi, *Principles of Bahá'í Administration*, pp. 36-37 ("As regards the statement of our own views and explanations of the teachings: Shoghi Effendi believes that we should not restrict the liberty of the individual to express his own views so long as he makes it clear that these views are his own. In fact, such explanations are often helpful and are conductive to a better understanding of the teachings. God has given man a rational power to be used and not killed. [¶] This does not, however, mean that the absolute authority does not remain in the revealed Words. We should try and keep as near to the authority as we can and show that we are faithful to it by quoting from the Words of Bahá'u'lláh in establishing our points. To discard the authority of the revealed Words is heretic and to suppress completely individual interpretation of those Words is also bad. We should try to strike a happy medium between these two extremes.").

43. The Universal House of Justice, *Messages from the Universal House of Justice: 1963-1986*, p. 56; *see* on behalf of Shoghi Effendi, *Lights of Guidance*, p. 314 ("The Will and Testament of Bahá'u'lláh and The Will and Testament of the Master clearly and explicitly indicate that the Interpreter of the Word was the Centre of the Covenant and now is the Guardian. There are no other Interpreters whatsoever and no individual may interpret. This is strictly forbidden."); *id.*, p. 313 ("In view of the fact that guidance in this day, through the bounty of God, and because of the very nature of Bahá'u'lláh's Revelation, has been vouchsafed to man through institutions in *this* world; namely the Guardianship at present; and also in the future, the International House of Justice; individuals are not in a position to interpret the Teachings, and have no justification for claiming special stations.") (emphasis in origi-

271

nal); *id.*, p. 515 ("As regards . . .'s claim to have direct revelations from God; such visions and communications as he may receive cannot, from the standpoint of the Cause, be well considered in the nature of a direct and authoritative revelation from God such as experiences by Divine Prophets and Messengers. There is a fundamental difference between Divine Revelation as vouchsafed by God to His Prophets, and the spiritual experiences and visions which individuals may have. The latter should, under no circumstances, be construed as constituting an infallible source of guidance, even for the person experiencing them."); on behalf of Shoghi Effendi, *The Importance of Deepening our Knowledge and Understanding of the Faith*, # 165 ("The friends need only read the Writings; the answers are all in them; we have no priests in this Faith to interpret or answer for us."); on behalf of the Universal House of Justice, *Issues Related to the Study of the Bahá'í Faith*, # 8 ("Already in *The Dispensation of Bahá'u'lláh* Shoghi Effendi has shown, beyond any doubt, that the function of making authoritative interpretations of the Teachings is confined solely and exclusively to the Guardian. Neither the Universal House of Justice, nor any other institution, person or group of persons can assume that function.").

44. On behalf of the Universal House of Justice, *Issues Related to the Study of the Bahá'í Faith*, # 4.

45. *The Kitáb-i-Aqdas*, Note # 130.

46. The Universal House of Justice, *Lights of Guidance*, p. 313.

47. The Universal House of Justice, *Lights of Guidance*, p. 313.

48. On behalf of the Universal House of Justice, *Issues Related to the Study of the Bahá'í Faith*, # 10.

49. *Tablets of Bahá'u'lláh*, p. 221.

50. On behalf of the Universal House of Justice, *Issues Related to the Study of the Bahá'í Faith*, # 10.

51. The Universal House of Justice, quoted in *The Covenant: Its Meaning and Origin and Our Attitude Toward It*, p. 51.

52. *See* on behalf of the Universal House of Justice, *Issues Related to the Study of the Bahá'í Faith*, # 10.

53. Shoghi Effendi, *The World Order of Bahá'u'lláh*, p. 145.

54. The Universal House of Justice, *Individual Rights and Freedoms in the World Order of Bahá'u'lláh*, pp. 5-6.

55. *See* Shoghi Effendi, *The World Order of Bahá'u'lláh*, p. 18; *see also* on behalf of Shoghi Effendi, *The Compilation of Compilations*, vol. II, p. 59 ("The friends must never mistake the Bahá'í administration for an end in itself. It is merely the instrument of the spirit of the Faith.").

56. *See* the Universal House of Justice, to the National Spiritual Assembly of the

Bahá'ís of the United States, May 19, 1994, *Rights & Responsibilities*, p. 37.

57. *See* the Universal House of Justice, *Reference Supplement*, p. 8.

58. *See* the Universal House of Justice, to the National Spiritual Assembly of the Bahá'ís of the United States, May 19, 1994, *Rights & Responsibilities*, p. 35.

59. The Universal House of Justice, *Individual Rights and Freedoms in the World Order of Bahá'u'lláh*, p. 10.

60. *Tablets of Bahá'u'lláh*, p. 222.

61. The Universal House of Justice, to the National Spiritual Assembly of the Bahá'ís of the United States, May 19, 1994, *Rights & Responsibilities*, p. 36.

62. *See* the Universal House of Justice, to the National Spiritual Assembly of the Bahá'ís of the United States, May 19, 1994, *Rights & Responsibilities*, p. 36.

63. *See* the Universal House of Justice, to the National Spiritual Assembly of the Bahá'ís of the United States, May 19, 1994, *Rights & Responsibilities*, pp. 36-37.

64. The Universal House of Justice, to the National Spiritual Assembly of the Bahá'ís of the United States, May 19, 1994, *Rights & Responsibilities*, p. 37.

65. *See* the Universal House of Justice, *Individual Rights and Freedoms in the World Order of Bahá'u'lláh*, p. 11.

66. On behalf of Shoghi Effendi, *Lights of Guidance*, p. 80.

67. 'Abdu'l-Bahá, quoted in Shoghi Effendi, *God Passes By*, p. 332.

68. Shoghi Effendi, *Bahá'í Administration*, p. 23.

69. The Universal House of Justice, *Messages from the Universal House of Justice: 1963-1986*, p. 265.

70. *See* on behalf of Shoghi Effendi, *The Importance of Deepening our Knowledge and Understanding of the Faith*, # 150 (emphasis in original).

71. On behalf of Shoghi Effendi, *Living the Life*, p. 31.

72. On behalf of Shoghi Effendi, *The Compilation of Compilations*, vol. II, p. 135 (emphasis in original).

73. On behalf of Shoghi Effendi, *Unlocking the Power of Action*, # 31.

74. On behalf of Shoghi Effendi, *Rights & Responsibilities*, p. 58.

75. On behalf of the Universal House of Justice, *Issues Related to the Study of the Bahá'í Faith*, # 7.

76. Shoghi Effendi, *Bahá'í Administration*, p. 63.

77. On behalf of Shoghi Effendi, *Rights & Responsibilities*, p. 58.

78. On behalf of Shoghi Effendi, *Rights & Responsibilities*, p. 58.

79. *See* on behalf of Shoghi Effendi, *Lights of Guidance*, p. 82; on behalf of the Universal House of Justice, *Issues Related to the Study of the Bahá'í Faith*, # 7.

80. The Universal House of Justice, to the National Spiritual Assembly of the Bahá'ís of the United States, May 19, 1994, *Rights & Responsibilities*, p. 46.

81. On behalf of the Universal House of Justice, *Issues Related to the Study of the Bahá'í Faith*, # 7.

82. *See* on behalf of Shoghi Effendi, *Lights of Guidance*, p. 92.

83. The Universal House of Justice, *Individual Rights and Freedoms in the World Order of Bahá'u'lláh*, p. 14.

84. *See* on behalf of the Universal House of Justice, *Issues Related to the Study of the Bahá'í Faith*, # 7.

85. On behalf of the Universal House of Justice, *Issues Related to the Study of the Bahá'í Faith*, # 7 (quoting on behalf of Shoghi Effendi, *Letters from the Guardian to Australia and New Zealand: 1923-1957*, p. 55).

86. On behalf of the Universal House of Justice, *Issues Related to the Study of the Bahá'í Faith*, # 7.

87. On behalf of the Universal House of Justice, *Issues Related to the Study of the Bahá'í Faith*, # 7 (quoting on behalf of Shoghi Effendi, *Stirring of the Spirit*, # 79).

88. On behalf of the Universal House of Justice, *Issues Related to the Study of the Bahá'í Faith*, # 7.

89. *See* on behalf of the Universal House of Justice, *Issues Related to the Study of the Bahá'í Faith*, # 7. Unlike Spiritual Assemblies, which function as "corporate bodies" (i.e., as groups), the members of the institution of the Counsellors (Counsellors and Auxiliary Board members) operate "primarily as individuals." *See* the Universal House of Justice, *Messages from the Universal House of Justice: 1963-1986*, p. 216. Thus, when a believer shares concerns with a member of the institution of the Counsellors, that believer is turning to an institution and not just another individual believer.

90. On behalf of the Universal House of Justice, *Issues Related to the Study of the Bahá'í Faith*, # 7 (quoting on behalf of Shoghi Effendi, *Letters from the Guardian to Australia and New Zealand*, p. 55).

91. On behalf of the Universal House of Justice, *Messages from the Universal House of Justice: 1963-1986*, p. 630.

92. On behalf of the Universal House of Justice, *Issues Related to the Study of the Bahá'í Faith*, # 7.

93. 'Abdu'l-Bahá, *Bahá'í World Faith*, p. 411.

94. On behalf of Shoghi Effendi, *The Light of Divine Guidance*, vol. 1, p. 151.

95. On behalf of Shoghi Effendi, *Local Spiritual Assembly*, p. 27.

96. On behalf of Shoghi Effendi, quoted in on behalf of the Universal House of Justice, *Lights of Guidance*, p. 166.

97. The Universal House of Justice, *Individual Rights and Freedoms in the World Order of Bahá'u'lláh*, p. 16.

APPENDIX: ANSWERS TO ANALYSIS QUESTIONS

1. The Universal House of Justice, quoted in *The Power of the Covenant*, Part Two, pp. 4-5.

2. Shoghi Effendi, *God Passes By*, p. 28.

3. The Universal House of Justice, *The Holy Year*, p. 39.

4. On behalf of the Universal House of Justice, *Issues Related to the Study of the Bahá'í Faith*, # 7.

5. The Universal House of Justice, quoted in *The Covenant: Its Meaning and Origin and Our Attitude Toward It*, p. 52.

6. Shoghi Effendi, *God Passes By*, p. 238.

7. 'Abdu'l-Bahá, *The Promulgation of Universal Peace*, p. 382.

8. 'Abdu'l-Bahá, *The Promulgation of Universal Peace*, p. 456.

9. Bahá'u'lláh, quoted in Shoghi Effendi, *The World Order of Bahá'u'lláh*, p. 135.

10. 'Abdu'l-Bahá, *The Promulgation of Universal Peace*, p. 323.

11. 'Abdu'l-Bahá, *Bahá'í World Faith*, p. 358.

12. Bahá'u'lláh, quoted in Shoghi Effendi, *God Passes By*, p. 251.

13. *Will and Testament of 'Abdu'l-Bahá*, p. 19.

14. Bahá'u'lláh, quoted in Shoghi Effendi, *God Passes By*, p. 251.

15. Shoghi Effendi, *The World Order of Bahá'u'lláh*, pp. 19-20.

16. *Will and Testament of 'Abdu'l-Bahá*, p. 11.

17. *See* Shoghi Effendi, *The World Order of Bahá'u'lláh*, pp. 19-20, 148.

18. *Will and Testament of 'Abdu'l-Bahá*, p. 20.

19. Shoghi Effendi, *The World Order of Bahá'u'lláh*, p. 151.

20. *Will and Testament of 'Abdu'l-Bahá*, p. 11.

21. On behalf of Shoghi Effendi, *Lights of Guidance*, p. 314.

22. The Universal House of Justice, *Messages from the Universal House of Justice: 1963-1986*, p. 56.

23. *Will and Testament of 'Abdu'l-Bahá*, p. 12.

24. *Will and Testament of 'Abdu'l-Bahá*, p. 12.

25. *Will and Testament of 'Abdu'l-Bahá*, p. 12.

26. Shoghi Effendi, *Messages to the Bahá'í World*, p. 123.

27. Shoghi Effendi, *Messages to the Bahá'í World*, p. 127.

28. *The Ministry of the Custodians: 1957-1963*, pp. 41-50.

29. The Universal House of Justice, *Messages from the Universal House of Justice: 1963-1986*, p. 51.

30. Shoghi Effendi, *The World Order of Bahá'u'lláh*, p. 23.

31. *Will and Testament of 'Abdu'l-Bahá*, p. 20.

32. Shoghi Effendi, *Bahá'í Administration*, p. 39.

33. Shoghi Effendi, *The World Order of Bahá'u'lláh*, p. 150.

34. On behalf of the Universal House of Justice, *Messages from the Universal House of Justice: 1963-1986*, p. 646.

35. Shoghi Effendi, *Bahá'í Administration*, p. 84.

36. Shoghi Effendi, *The World Order of Bahá'u'lláh*, p. 7.

37. 'Abdu'l-Bahá, quoted in the Universal House of Justice, *Messages from the Universal House of Justice: 1963-1986*, p. 53.

38. The Universal House of Justice, *Messages from the Universal House of Justice: 1963-1986*, p. 51.

39. *See* the Universal House of Justice, *Messages from the Universal House of Justice: 1963-1986*, p. 50.

40. The Universal House of Justice, *Messages from the Universal House of Justice: 1963-1986*, p. 53.

41. The Universal House of Justice, *Messages from the Universal House of Justice: 1963-1986*, p. 158.

42. Bahá'u'lláh, *The Kitáb-i-Aqdas,* parag. 42.

43. *Will and Testament of 'Abdu'l-Bahá*, p. 14.

44. Shoghi Effendi, *The World Order of Bahá'u'lláh*, p. 148.

45. On behalf of the Universal House of Justice, *Lights of Guidance*, p. 311.

46. 'Abdu'l-Bahá, *Some Answered Questions*, p. 173.

47. 'Abdu'l-Bahá, *Some Answered Questions*, p. 171.

48. *See* 'Abdu'l-Bahá, *Some Answered Questions*, pp. 172-73.

49. On behalf of the Universal House of Justice, *Lights of Guidance*, p. 312.

50. 'Abdu'l-Bahá, *Some Answered Questions*, p. 172.

51. On behalf of the Universal House of Justice, *Lights of Guidance*, p. 312.

52. 'Abdu'l-Bahá, quoted in the Universal House of Justice, *Messages from the Universal House of Justice: 1963-1986*, p. 53.

53. 'Abdu'l-Bahá, *Some Answered Questions*, p. 172.

54. On behalf of the Universal House of Justice, *Messages from the Universal House of Justice: 1963-1986*, p. 448.

55. Shoghi Effendi, *The World Order of Bahá'u'lláh*, p. 150.

56. The Universal House of Justice, quoted in *The Covenant: Its Meaning and Origin and Our Attitude Toward It*, p. 74.

57. On behalf of Shoghi Effendi, *Messages to Canada*, p. 65.

58. The Universal House of Justice, to all National Spiritual Assemblies, April 4, 2001 ("Sometimes, after a person's withdrawal from the Cause has been accepted, it becomes evident that his statements were insincere and were made merely in order to evade Bahá'í law. . . . An analogous situation arises when a person who is engaged in some activity which he suspects would result in his being declared a Covenant-breaker withdraws from the Faith under the impression that this step would prevent such an outcome. The Universal House of Justice may conclude that the withdrawal provides adequate protection of the community from the individual in question. However, if he persists, following his withdrawal, in trying to undermine the Covenant or joins forces with Covenant-breakers, he may be judged to have broken the Covenant, and the friends would be told to have no association with him. Each such case would be considered in the context of its specific circumstances.").

59. On behalf of the Universal House of Justice, quoted in *The Covenant: Its Meaning and Origin and Our Attitude Toward It*, p. 74.

60. The Universal House of Justice, quoted in *The Covenant: Its Meaning and Origin and Our Attitude Toward It*, p. 75.

61. On behalf of the Universal House of Justice, *Lights of Guidance*, p. 186.

62. *See* the Universal House of Justice, quoted in *The Power of the Covenant*, Part Two, p. 39.

63. On behalf of Shoghi Effendi, *Lights of Guidance*, pp. 185-86.

64. *Selections from the Writings of 'Abdu'l-Bahá*, p. 158.

65. On behalf of the Universal House of Justice, to an individual, October 7, 1997.

66. On behalf of the Universal House of Justice, *Issues Related to the Study of the Bahá'í Faith*, # 1.

67. On behalf of the Universal House of Justice, *Issues Related to the Study of the Bahá'í Faith*, # 1.

68. The Universal House of Justice, *Messages from the Universal House of Justice: 1963-1986*, p. 88.

69. On behalf of Shoghi Effendi, *Letters from the Guardian to Australia and New Zealand: 1923-1957*, p. 55.

70. On behalf of the Universal House of Justice, *Issues Related to the Study of the Bahá'í Faith*, # 7.

71. On behalf of the Universal House of Justice, *Issues Related to the Study of the Bahá'í Faith*, # 7.

72. On behalf of the Universal House of Justice, *Issues Related to the Study of the Bahá'í Faith*, # 7.

BIBLIOGRAPHY

Works by the Authoritative Centers of the Faith

Bahá'u'lláh.

———. *Epistle to the Son of the Wolf.* Wilmette, IL: Bahá'í Publishing Trust, 1988.
———. *Gleanings from the Writings of Bahá'u'lláh.* Wilmette, IL: Bahá'í Publishing Trust, 1983.
———. *Kitáb-i-Aqdas: The Most Holy Book.* Haifa: Bahá'í World Centre, 1992.
———. *Prayers and Meditations.* Wilmette, IL: Bahá'í Publishing Trust, 1987.
———. *Tablets of Bahá'u'lláh.* Wilmette, IL: Bahá'í Publishing Trust, 1988.

The Báb.

———. *Selections from the Writings of the Báb.* Haifa: Bahá'í World Centre, 1982.

'Abdu'l-Bahá.

———. *Promulgation of Universal Peace.* 2nd ed. Wilmette, IL: Bahá'í Publishing Trust, 1982.
———. *Selections from the Writings of 'Abdu'l-Bahá.* Haifa: Bahá'í World Centre, 1978.
———. *Some Answered Questions.* Wilmette, IL: Bahá'í Publishing Trust, 1985.
———. *Tablets of Abdul-Baha Abbas.* Vol. I. New York: Bahá'í Publishing Committee, 1930.
———. *Tablets of the Divine Plan.* Wilmette, IL: Bahá'í Publishing Trust, 1993.
———. *Will and Testament of 'Abdu'l-Bahá.* http://reference.bahai.org/en/t/ab/WT/.

Shoghi Effendi.

———. *Advent of Divine Justice.* Wilmette, IL: Bahá'í Publishing Trust, 1984.
———. *Bahá'í Administration.* Wilmette, IL: Bahá'í Publishing Trust, 1968.
———. *Citadel of Faith: Messages to America/1947-1957.* Wilmette, IL: Bahá'í Publishing Trust, 1965.
———. *Dawn of a New Day: Messages to India, 1923-1957.* New Delhi, India: Bahá'í Publishing Trust, [1970].

———. *Directives from the Guardian*. New Delhi, India: Bahá'í Publishing Trust, n.d.

———. *Faith of Bahá'u'lláh: A World Religion*. Wilmette, IL: Bahá'í Publishing Committee, n.d. (reprint from *World Order Magazine*, vol. XIII, no. 7, October 1947).

———. *God Passes By*. Rev. ed. Wilmette, IL: Bahá'í Publishing Trust, 1979.

———. *High Endeavours: Messages to Alaska*. National Spiritual Assembly of the Bahá'ís of Alaska, Inc., 1976.

———. *Letters from the Guardian to Australia and New Zealand: 1923-1957*. Sydney, Australia: National Spiritual Assembly of the Bahá'ís of Australia, Inc., 1971.

———. *Light of Divine Guidance: Messages from the Guardian of the Bahá'í Faith to the Bahá'ís of Germany and Austria*. Vol. I. Hofheim-Langenhain, Germany: Bahá'í-Verlag, 1982.

———. *Light of Divine Guidance: Letters from the Guardian of the Bahá'í Faith to Individual Believers, Groups and Bahá'í Communities in Germany and Austria*. Vol. II. Hofheim-Langenhain, Germany: Bahá'í-Verlag, 1985.

———. *Messages to the Bahá'í World: 1950-57*. Wilmette, IL: Bahá'í Publishing Trust, 1971.

———. *Messages to Canada*. Canada: National Spiritual Assembly of the Bahá'ís of Canada, 1965.

———. *Messages of Shoghi Effendi to the Indian Subcontinent: 1923-1957*. Rev. ed. New Delhi, India: Bahá'í Publishing Trust, 1995.

———. *Promised Day Is Come*. Rev. ed. Wilmette, IL: Bahá'í Publishing Trust, 1980.

———. *This Decisive Hour: Messages from Shoghi Effendi to the North American Bahá'ís, 1932-1946*. Wilmette, IL: Bahá'í Publishing Trust, 2002.

———. *Unfolding Destiny: Messages from the Guardian of the Bahá'í Faith to the Bahá'í Community of the British Isles*. London: Bahá'í Publishing Trust, 1981.

———. *World Order of Bahá'u'lláh: Selected Letters*. 2nd rev. ed. Wilmette, IL: Bahá'í Publishing Trust, 1982.

The Universal House of Justice.

———. *Constitution of the Universal House of Justice*. Haifa: Bahá'í World Centre, 1972.

———. *Four Year Plan: Messages of the Universal House of Justice*. Riviera Beach, FL: Palabra Publications, 1996.

———. *Guardianship and the Universal House of Justice: Selected Messages by or on Behalf of the Universal House of Justice*. Riviera Beach, FL: Palabra Publications, 1996.

————. *Holy Year: 1992-1993.* Riviera Beach, FL: Palabra Publications, 1993.

————. *Individual Rights and Freedoms in the World Order of Bahá'u'lláh: To the Followers of Bahá'u'lláh in the United States of America, A Statement by the Universal House of Justice.* Wilmette, IL: Bahá'í Publishing Trust, 1989.

————. *Institution of the Counsellors: A Document Prepared by the Universal House of Justice.* Bahá'í World Centre, 2001.

————. *Issues Related to the Study of the Bahá'í Faith: Extracts from Letters Written on behalf of the Universal House of Justice.* Wilmette, IL: Bahá'í Publishing Trust, 1999.

————. Letter dated July 25, 1974, on behalf of the Universal House of Justice, to an individual believer.

————. Letter dated March 23, 1975, the Universal House of Justice, to an individual.

————. Letter dated April 2, 1985, on behalf of the Universal House of Justice, to an individual believer.

————. Letter dated June 23, 1987, on behalf of the Universal House of Justice, to an individual believer.

————. Letter dated June 5, 1988, on behalf of the Universal House of Justice, to an individual believer.

————. Letter dated April 27, 1995, on behalf of the Universal House of Justice, to an individual believer.

————. Letter dated February 16, 1996, on behalf of the Universal House of Justice, to an individual believer.

————. Letter dated June 14, 1996, on behalf of the Universal House of Justice, to an individual believer.

————. Letter dated October 22, 1996, on behalf of the Universal House of Justice, to an individual.

————. Letter dated June 4, 1997, on behalf of the Universal House of Justice, to a National Spiritual Assembly.

————. Letter dated June 4, 1997, on behalf of the Universal House of Justice, to an individual believer.

————. Letter dated July 3, 1997, on behalf of the Universal House of Justice, to an individual.

————. Letter dated September 24, 1997, on behalf of the Universal House of Justice, to an individual.

————. Letter dated October 7, 1997, on behalf of the Universal House of Justice, to an individual.

————. Letter dated October 27, 1997, on behalf of the Universal House of Justice, to an individual.

————. Letter dated December 19, 1997, on behalf of the Universal House of Justice, to an individual.

————. Letter dated January 20, 1998, on behalf of the Universal House of Justice,

281

to an individual believer.

———. Letter dated August 27, 1998, on behalf of the Universal House of Justice, to an individual believer.

———. Letter dated April 7, 1999, the Universal House of Justice, to all National Spiritual Assemblies, *The American Bahá'í*, October 16, 1999.

———. Letter dated April 4, 2001, the Universal House of Justice, to all National Spiritual Assemblies.

———. Letter dated December 23, 2004, on behalf of the Universal House of Justice, to an individual believer.

———. *Mason Remey and Those Who Followed Him*, memorandum prepared for the Universal House of Justice, November 29, 2001.

———. Memorandum dated July 5, 2000, Research Department of the Universal House of Justice.

———. *Messages from the Universal House of Justice: 1963-1986, The Third Epoch of the Formative Age*. Wilmette, IL: Bahá'í Publishing Trust, 1996.

———. *Rights & Responsibilities: The Complementary Roles of the Individual and Institutions, Selected Messages by or on behalf of the Universal House of Justice*. Thornhill, Ontario: Bahá'í Canada Publications, 1997.

———. *Wellspring of Guidance: Messages, 1963-1968*. Rev. ed. Wilmette, IL: Bahá'í Publishing Trust, 1976.

———. *A Wider Horizon: Selected Messages of the Universal House of Justice: 1983-1992*. Riviera Beach, FL: Palabra Publications, 1992.

Compilations of Bahá'í Writings.

———. *Bahá'í World Faith: Selected Writings of Bahá'u'lláh and 'Abdu'l-Bahá*. 2nd ed. Wilmette, IL: Bahá'í Publishing Trust, 1956.

———. *Compilation of Compilations*. Vol. I. Maryborough, Victoria, Australia: Bahá'í Publications Australia, 1991.

———. *Compilation of Compilations*. Vol. II. Maryborough, Victoria, Australia: Bahá'í Publications Australia, 1991.

———. *Compilation of Compilations*. Vol. III. Ingleside, NSW, Australia: Bahá'í Publications Australia, 2000.

———. *Covenant: A compilation of extracts from the Bahá'í Writings*. London: Bahá'í Publishing Trust, 1988.

———. *Developing Distinctive Bahá'í Communities: Guidelines for Spiritual Assemblies*. Evanston, IL: National Spiritual Assembly of the Bahá'ís of the United States, 1998.

———. *Family Life*. Oakham, England: Bahá'í Publishing Trust, 1982.

———. *Gift of Teaching*. London: Bahá'í Publishing Trust, 1977.

———. http://reference.bahai.org/en.

———. *Ḥuqúqu'lláh*. Thornhill, Ontario: Bahá'í Canada Publications, 1986.

———. *Importance of Deepening our Knowledge and Understanding of the Faith*.

Thornhill, Ontario: Bahá'í Community of Canada, 1983.

———. *Japan Will Turn Ablaze!* Rev. ed. Bahá'í Publishing Trust of Japan, 1992.

———. *Lights of Guidance: A Bahá'í Reference File.* 3rd rev. ed. New Delhi, India: Bahá'í Publishing Trust, 1994.

———. *Living the Life: A Compilation.* London: Bahá'í Publishing Trust, 1984.

———. *Local Spiritual Assembly: An Institution of the Bahá'í Administrative Order.* Wilmette, IL: Bahá'í Publishing Trust, n.d.

———. *Principles of Bahá'í Administration.* Manchester: Bahá'í Publishing Trust, 1950.

———. *Proofs of Bahá'u'lláh's Mission: Selections from the writings of Bahá'u'lláh, the Báb, 'Abdu'l-Bahá, Shoghi Effendi, and the Universal House of Justice.* 2nd ed. Riviera Beach, FL: Palabra Publications, 1995.

———. *Reference Supplement: Collected Passages on Business, Development and the Bahá'í Funds.* 2nd ed. National Spiritual Assembly of the Bahá'ís of the United States, Office of the Treasurer, 1993.

———. *A Special Measure of Love: The Importance and Nature of the Teaching Work among the Masses: Messages from Shoghi Effendi and the Universal House of Justice.* Wilmette, IL: Bahá'í Publishing Trust, 1974.

———. *Stirring of the Spirit: Celebrating the Institution of the Nineteen Day Feast.* Thornhill, Ontario: Bahá'í Canada Publications, 1990.

———. *Unlocking The Power of Action: A Compilation Prepared by the Research Department of the Universal House of Justice.* National Spiritual Assembly of the Bahá'ís of the United States, 1997.

Other Sources

Afroukhteh, Youness. *Memories of Nine Years in 'Akká.* Oxford: George Ronald, 2003.

Bahá'í Faith 1844-1963 Information Statistical & Comparative. Israel, n.d.

Balyuzi, H.M.

———. *'Abdu'l-Bahá: The Centre of the Covenant of Bahá'u'lláh.* 2nd ed. Oxford: George Ronald, 1987.

———. *Bahá'u'lláh: The King of Glory.* Oxford: George Ronald, 1980.

Brown, Ramona Allen. *Memories of 'Abdu'l-Bahá: Recollections of the Early Days of the Bahá'í Faith in California.* Wilmette, IL: Bahá'í Publishing Trust, 1980.

Chapman, Anita Ioas. *Leroy Ioas: Hand of the Cause of God.* Oxford: George Ronald, 1998.

"The Completion of the Bahá'í World Crusade: 1953-1963." *The Bahá'í World: An International Record.* Vol. XIII, pp. 459-78. Haifa, Israel: The Universal House of Justice, 1980.

Esslemont, J.E. *Bahá'u'lláh and the New Era.* 5th rev. ed. Wilmette, IL: Bahá'í Publishing Trust, 1993.

Harper, Barron. *Lights of Fortitude: Glimpses into the Lives of the Hands of the Cause of God.* Oxford: George Ronald, 1997.

Hofman, David. *A Commentary on the Will and Testament of 'Abdu'l-Bahá.* 4th ed. Oxford: George Ronald, 1989.

"International Bahá'í Council." *The Bahá'í World: An International Record.* Vol. XIII, pp. 395-401. Haifa, Israel: The Universal House of Justice, 1980.

Jináb-i-Fádil-i-Mázandaráni, *Asráru'l-Áthár,* vol. 5. 129 B.E.

Khadem, Riaz. "The Power of Example." In *Zikrullah Khadem: The Itinerant Hand of the Cause of God,* by Javidukht Khadem, pp. 200-13. Wilmette, IL: Bahá'í Publishing Trust, 1990.

Khan, Janet A. and Peter J. Khan. *Advancement of Women: A Bahá'í Perspective.* Wilmette, IL: Bahá'í Publishing Trust, 1998.

Khan, Peter J. "Mental Tests." *The American Bahá'í,* December 31, 1995 (lecture, Wilmette, IL, September 23, 1995).

Linfoot, Charlotte M. "First International Convention." *The Bahá'í World: An International Record.* Vol. XIV, pp. 427-30. Haifa, Israel: The Universal House of Justice, 1974.

Maxwell, May. *An Early Pilgrimage.* Rev. ed. Oxford: George Ronald, 1976.

Ministry of the Custodians: 1957-1963, An Account of the Stewardship of the Hands of the Cause. Haifa: Bahá'í World Centre, 1992.

Mirza Badi ullah, *An Epistle to the Bahai World.* Chicago, IL: Bahai Publishing Society, n.d.

Munírih Khánum, *Munírih Khánum: Memoirs and Letters.* Los Angeles: Kalimát Press, 1986.

Nabíl-i-A'zam, *The Dawn-Breakers: Nabíl's Narrative of the Early Days of the Bahá'í Revelation.* Wilmette, IL: Bahá'í Publishing Trust, 1996.

National Teaching Committee of the National Spiritual Assembly of the Bahá'ís of the United States. *The Covenant: Its Meaning and Origin and Our Attitude Toward It.* National Spiritual Assembly of the Bahá'ís of the United States, 1988.

Power of the Covenant: The Problem of Covenant-Breaking (Part Two). National Spiritual Assembly of the Bahá'ís of Canada, 1987.

Rabbaní, Rúhíyyih. *Priceless Pearl.* London: Bahá'í Publishing Trust, 1969.

Saiedi, Nader. *Logos and Civilization: Spirit, History, and Order in the Writings of Bahá'u'lláh.* Bethesda, MD: University Press of Maryland, 2000.

Sala, Emeric. *The Greenleafs: an eternal union,* Bahá'í News, September 1973.

Schaefer, Udo, *et al. Making the Crooked Straight: A Contribution to Bahá'í Apologetics.* Oxford: George Ronald, 2000.

Semple, Ian.

———. "Infallibility of the Universal House of Justice" (lecture, Haifa, Israel, May 31, 1989).

———. "Interpretation and the Guardianship" (lecture, Haifa, Israel, February 18, 1984 and lecture, Wilmette, Illinois, September 6, 2001).

————. "Obedience" (lecture, Haifa, Israel, July 26, 1991).

Star of the West.

————. Vol. V, no. 15. Oxford: George Ronald, 1984.

————. Vol. VIII, no. 14. Oxford: George Ronald, 1984.

————. Vol. XII, no. 14. Oxford: George Ronald, 1984.

Taherzadeh, Adib.

————. *Child of the Covenant: A Study Guide to the Will and Testament of 'Abdu'l-Bahá.* Oxford: George Ronald, 2000.

————. *Covenant of Bahá'u'lláh.* Oxford: George Ronald, 1995.

————. *Revelation of Bahá'u'lláh: Adrianople 1863-68.* Vol. 2. Oxford: George Ronald, 1992.

————. *Revelation of Bahá'u'lláh: 'Akká, The Early Years 1868-77.* Vol. 3. Oxford: George Ronald, 1988.

www.bahai.org.

INDEX

'Abdu'l-Bahá
Administrative Order, succeeded
by, 9, 12, 16, 19, 65, 74
authority of, 2, 12, 16, 220, 233
Bahá'u'lláh, disclosure of
'Abdu'l-Bahá's station by,
25-29
Center of the Covenant, 9, 11-12,
16, 18, 20-21, 25-31, 33, 34,
36, 38, 39, 41, 46, 230, 232,
233
Covenant of, 9, 16, 220
Exemplar of Bahá'u'lláh's
Teachings, 18, 29, 31, 33, 34,
38-39, 40, 233-34
infallibility of, 13, 30, 31-33, 38,
75, 120, 227, 234-35, 258,
259
interpretations of, 30-31, 32-33,
138, 185, 227, 259
Interpreter, 11-12, 18, 20, 26-27,
29, 30-31, 34, 36, 38, 70,
135, 181, 195, 196, 230, 232,
233, 235, 271
Kitáb-i-'Ahd, station conferred
on by, 11, 27-29, 30, 32, 33,
37, 38, 41, 181, 230, 232,
271
Kitáb-i-Aqdas, stationed
conferred on by, 26-27, 29,
30, 32, 37, 181, 230, 232
Most Great Branch/Most Mighty
Branch, 28-29, 34, 37, 40,
48-49, 59, 60, 231, 232, 244
Muhammad-'Alí, Mírzá, confirms
Covenant-breaking of, 49-51,
54-56, 63
"Mystery of God," 21, 33, 34, 40
name of, 29, 34
obedience to, 30, 31, 33, 39, 41

'Abdu'l-Bahá (*continued*)
station of, 3, 25-27, 29-31, 33-35,
39-40, 46, 70, 232, 235
Tablet of the Branch, 25-26, 32
titles of, 28-29
Will and Testament of (*see* Will
and Testament of 'Abdu'l-
Bahá)
writings of, 183
Administrative Order
'Abdu'l-Bahá succeeded by, 9,
12, 16, 19, 65, 74
Covenant of Bahá'u'lláh, 1, 9, 12,
13, 16, 17, 18, 65, 182-83,
229
criticism, channels for, 190-93,
200 (*see also* skepticism
toward authority/institutions)
development of, 259
establishment of, 9, 63-64, 74
individual's relation to institutions
of, 187-90, 198, 199, 202-03
institutional elements of, 182-83,
195, 270
origin and nature of, 73, 182,
187-89, 190, 198
protection of Faith, 160
spirit, instrument of, 272
twin institution/pillars of, 65 (*see
also* Guardian/Guardianship;
the Universal House of
Justice)
uniqueness of, 10, 64, 74, 187,
201, 227
Will and Testament of 'Abdu'l-
Bahá, 3-4, 63-64, 73-74
World Order of Bahá'u'lláh,
relation to, 12, 63, 64
See also World Order of
Bahá'u'lláh

287